Kings of the Saddle

Kings of the Saddle

Ireland's Greatest Jockeys

Brian O'Connor

First published in Great Britain
2009 by Aurum Press Ltd
7 Greenland Street
London NW1 0ND
www.aurumpress.co.uk

A catalogue record for this book is available from the British Library.

ISBN 978 1 84513 444 0

1 3 5 7 9 10 8 6 4 2
2009 2011 2013 2012 2010

Typeset in Minion by SX Composing DTP, Rayleigh, Essex
Printed by MPG Books, Bodmin, Cornwall

CONTENTS

To my parents, Dolly and Sean

ACKNOWLEDGEMENTS

Thanks are due to lots of people, but most of all to Niamh and the lights of our eyes, Pete and Johnny. To everyone at Aurum, especially Graham and Dan; and thanks to Chris for tolerating all the 'racing-isms'. Cheers to those who helped organise interviews, plus Jonathan Williams who secured the gig in the first place. And to those geeks, nerds and social misfits who invented the Internet – thus allowing access to years of assorted information – one can only say, God Bless You All!

INTRODUCTION

It's a fundamental racing truth that every grandstand jockey has at some stage cursed one of the real deals out on the track as blind and untrust-worthy, with a talent for losing races they really should have won. And of course every grandstand jockey would do a much better job given an opportunity and the required skill and determination, as well as an ability to stop consuming umpteen thousand calories a day more than they should.

Yet jockeys as a breed remain among the most fondly admired and respected characters, not just in racing, but throughout the whole of sport. That remains just as much the case now as it ever was, despite some regrettably frequent headlines in recent years recording the misdeeds of a small few. Certainly there is no comparative level of Irish domination at the top of any other major international sport as there is among these modern kings of the saddle.

Irish-born jockeys predominate both at home and in Britain, but have a reputation for excellence worldwide. That reputation has been carved out over many generations and the dozen riders featured here have added to it with various degrees of distinction.

The courage of those riding in National Hunt racing is legendary. Certainly the physical and psychological fortitude required to perform, while knowing that about one in every ten rides is going to end with a fall, makes other, much better-rewarded, sports stars appear even more pitifully shallow. While the threat of injury may be less, the mental acuity of jockeys making split-second decisions in the high-pressure world of international flat racing is prized around the globe.

Why Ireland has produced so many top-class jockeys over the years is a question with an answer rooted in the unique place that horses have in the national consciousness. The 'Celtic Tiger' years may have transformed Ireland in many ways but what was remarkable was how quickly many people exhibited their new affluence by getting involved in racehorse ownership for the first time. The clichéd figure of the farmer clinging to hopes of owning a champion may not be as relevant as it was but the dream is still alive, albeit often underneath a fancier suit of clothes.

When it comes to dreams, however, the saddle is always the ultimate place to be in. No child running around the garden imagines they are breeding a great horse, or owning it, or training it. It's the role of jockey that always contains the excitement. That's why, despite the injury threat and the demands of keeping weight in check, there isn't a single racing enthusiast who doesn't envy the men and women riding those thorough-breds they see out on the track or on television. Ultimately it is jockeys who are living the dream.

That doesn't preclude some chores, however, and one of the more boring ones must be the demands of yet another journalist looking for 'just a few minutes of your time'. The jockeys featured in this book greeted just such interview requests with various degrees of enthusiasm, resignation and exasperation. One looked for money. What each of them provided, though, was a singular story that has carried them to the pinnacle of their profession. Any deficit in portraying those stories is of course the responsibility of the author.

A note on the quotations
Indented text paragraphs indicate fresh quotations from the jockey under discussion in a given chapter.

I

MICHAEL KINANE

Every one of the jockeys listed in this book will have their fans and critics. The criteria for such conclusions will invariably be personal. More often than not they revolve around the amount of money generated by betting on the skills of these riders. Those of a more aesthetic nature will argue over questions of style, power and tactical nous, but inevitably it will always be a subjective argument. What can be said with some certainty, though, is that the most important figure here is Michael Joseph Kinane.

His thirty-five-year career includes successes in practically every race worth a damn both in Europe and around the world. Along the way he has come by the sort of respect accorded to very few. Tony McCoy still views Kinane's style in the saddle as something to aim for. When Kieren Fallon was still waiting to ride in a race in the 1980s, his old rival was already a champion. Johnny Murtagh believes he has been a pathfinder in terms of an international career. Frankie Dettori maintains he has never had a tougher opponent. But the real measure of Kinane is that, while he has been carving out this sensational CV, he has also changed the face of the sport. Not many can claim to have altered a profession's perception of itself. But that is what the man they call 'Mickey Joe' has done.

These days the likes of Murtagh and Pat Smullen are esteemed jockeys internationally with a proven record against the best in the world while living in Ireland. So it can seem hard to account for how different it was just one generation ago, back in the 1980s, when being a jockey based in Ireland meant staying in Ireland. It might not have meant knowing your place but there was usually a forelock touch to an overseas rider when it really mattered. There were exceptions, such as when Christy Roche was backed to succeed by trainer David O'Brien and repaid that support with Derby victories at both Chantilly and Epsom. But more often than not, when trainers and owners sent horses abroad or wanted a jockey for the big races at home, they turned to a Piggott or an Eddery.

There were any number of reasons for that at the time. Economically the country was a basket case and limited opportunities resulted in most youngsters heading to the UK anyway. There was also televisual evidence that suggested racing in Britain was far more glamorous and exciting. However, more than twenty years later, and on the back of a period of unprecedented economic prosperity, such attitudes appear to tie in with a terrible lack of national confidence that only seems more pronounced now to those who have experienced both sides of the social coin. Kinane himself remembers it as a culture, a belief that anything from abroad had to be better than the home product. It wasn't just in racing. Ireland in the 1980s was a country still uncertain of itself and its future. Education was about to change attitudes forever in the wider community. But racing's own tightly conservative community was never easily going to alter a mindset that had been cultivated for decades. Now Irish-based jockeys can look their colleagues from America and around Europe square in the eye as equals. Kinane's role in that is of paramount importance.

Staring at the racing world and fancying his chances, though, has always been second nature to Kinane, even in the early days of his career when the likes of Piggott and Steve Cauthen were being parachuted ahead of him. Anyone who has ever been at the receiving end of Kinane's famously glowering expression when he is annoyed about something knows its intimidatory power. There is a hardness there that leaves no doubt as to the resolution behind it, which in turn has allowed the owner to conquer the racing world. When he was a young apprentice, there were very real concerns that weight would force him to follow the National Hunt path that had carried his father to Champion Hurdle success. The steel required to overcome that was an early sign of how, when the thirteen-time champion jockey sets his mind to something, he can be ruthless in attaining it. Never the most ebullient of men in public, and possessed of the stature required for his job, there is nevertheless little doubt that he can be the dominant presence in any room he walks into.

But Kinane's famously intense bushy eye-browed concentration on display at the races is certainly not the full picture. Away from racing there is no more articulate jockey. The old adage about not suffering fools gladly does apply, but it is applied more in self-preservation mode than the usual code for gratuitously ignorant behaviour. There's a wit there, too, that is a long way from the more ribald comedy of some of his colleagues. It's just that Kinane believes in reserving it for those he knows and has at least some regard for. But his friends have come to expect a minimum of chuckles at the races. Because the racetrack is work, where Kinane brings his formidable powers of concentration to bear: any fun stuff can wait for later.

The same has applied to the question of retirement, which has trailed this singularly ambitious man for a number of seasons. Kinane is fifty in 2009 and, compared to the zenith of his career, there have been a few seasons of late in which he has experienced a noticeable lack of major success. Having been top of the pile for so long and ridden for the biggest names in the industry, there had been a presumption that he wouldn't emulate the likes of Piggott and Eddery and ride well into his fifties. That only reveals a lack of understanding of what drives this fittest of athletes.

Kinane admits that in the summer of 2008 he believed he would be considering his future at the end of the year. But then he started riding an unusually precocious crop of two-year-olds at John Oxx's yard. One colt in particular, Sea The Stars, began exhibiting the sort of potential to compare with anything his jockey had ever experienced. It was enough to postpone any idea of throwing in the towel. During 2009 Sea The Stars delivered on all that potential with such wonderful aplomb that Kinane has laughed about the horse adding years to him. It has been the same for the last twenty years: a good horse on the horizon is enough to stoke up any competitive fires that might have been waning. Kinane remains resolutely his own man, and the idea of having anyone else make up his mind for him would offend his personality.

Trusting his own instincts is ingrained, but it is possibly no coincidence that a young Kinane emerged at the same time as Lester Piggott was at his peak. At a vintage period of jockeyship, Piggott was an acknowledged master who determinedly did things his way. In the late 1970s old Stone Face was still No.1 at Vincent O'Brien's Ballydoyle academy and when he left in 1981 it was Pat Eddery who took over. Throughout the 1980s, Eddery, and briefly the top American Cash Asmussen, were the sort of exotic visitors that the local riders had to contend with. Kinane for one examined his rivals, admired their talents, but still saw nothing to suggest he couldn't compete against them. That he emerged to become a successor to these, and other, legendary names only emphasises the value of such self-belief.

They were exceptional riders: P. Eddery, Lester, Willie [Carson] and Cauthen. It may be a little harsh to say it but I would say the top end at that time was better than it is today. Overall, the standard, especially in Ireland, is very good. But we are talking about exceptional riders back then. In my book Lester remains the greatest. He had everything, always in control of what he was doing. And he could be intimidating, a bit of a bully.

It's hard to imagine even Piggott could have intimidated his young rival during Kinane's meteoric rise to the top in Ireland. Not every graduate of the Liam Browne apprentice academy on the Curragh might have made it as a jockey but it was a rare one indeed that didn't know how to stand up for himself. Browne's most famous pupil learned quickly, even if it meant giving up a normal learning-by-your-mistakes adolescence. It was a double-edged sword: learning the right things but the hard way. 'It's hard to ask a fellah of fifteen to behave as an adult,' Kinane remembers. 'Coming to terms with that is difficult but that was what was required.' Browne also provided rides, enough of them in 1978 to provide an apprentice title. Four years later came an intoxicating taste of the high life as Dara Monarch, ridden by Kinane, followed up an Irish 2,000 Guineas victory with success in the St James's Palace Stakes at Royal Ascot. If that provided evidence of a big race temperament, then one man paid particular attention, someone Kinane still insists moulded him into the jockey he is.

In hindsight it seems almost inevitable that the best young jockey in the country in 1984 should team up with the most powerful trainer. But while hindsight is wonderful, it can also be deceiving. Having ridden for both Browne and for Michael Kauntze, Kinane felt his career was on the verge of stalling. He was worried because in any sport, standing still is almost always a precursor to slipping into reverse. Dermot Weld for his part had to take something of a leap of faith. Admiring the young rider was one thing: ignoring general racecourse gossip about a bad temper and occasional over-impetuousness out on the track was another. There were widespread rumours of Kinane having an attitude problem and many predicted the new partnership would not last a season. Those whispers proved to be very wrong, although at the start there was evidence behind the scenes of sparks that could have fuelled the rumours.

Weld generally still likes his horses ridden a certain way, just off the pace and brought with one winning run. It's not as easy as it sounds to do that on a consistent basis and Kinane initially found these tactical arrangements difficult. So with no Sunday racing in Ireland then, the traditional day of rest turned into a tutorial on how Weld, the champion trainer and former champion amateur jockey, wanted his horses ridden. The pupil was hauled in to the Rosewell House stables and made to study endless re-runs of races on the video recorder. 'And we went on doing that Sunday after Sunday until he fucking got it right,' Weld later recalled. Kinane still refers to the room where these video sessions took place as the 'torture chamber' and frequently the two men lost their cool with each other. But it worked where it mattered, out on the racecourse. By the end of his first season at Rosewell, Kinane was champion jockey, with eighty-eight winners.

DK is a marvellous man who moulded me as a jockey. We still get on great. He has been instrumental in the success I have enjoyed. But he isn't easy sometimes. He's a very dominant man, very strong, very intelligent: you have to be strong to be able to stand up to him. When things went wrong there were times you'd come back in and he'd be great. But then there were other times when you wouldn't expect it and he'd be very tough. I suppose a hurt pocket can make a man's perspective change!

Not everything in the garden was rosy, however. Dominance at home was not being matched by opportunity away. Weld's champion sprinter Committed won the Group 1 sprint at York under the Australian Brent Thompson. When she landed the Prix de l'Abbaye at Longchamp a couple of months later, it was with Cauthen on board. In 1985, Kinane rode Theatrical to an impressive success in the Derrinstown Derby Trial but it was Piggott who rode the colt at Epsom. It was the old story of being good enough for Ireland but not anywhere else. However, the new champion was not prepared to settle for that role. With the number of sessions in the Weld torture chamber decreasing, Kinane decided to put his Sunday schooling to use. Soon Dublin airport had a regular customer.

I took the view of 'have saddle-will go'. I became a very regular traveller to Italy because I knew if I wanted to break out of Ireland and sell my wares, I would have to travel. It wasn't like it is now with everything televised. You had to get out there. Irish racing was viewed as the poor relation then and I wanted to develop and not be seen as just an Irish jockey. I was hungry, I had a young family and I wanted to better myself. There's no doubt I sacrificed a lot of my personal life with my wife and kids. I missed out on a lot. But I would say they will tell you that they gained a lot out of it as well. There's no doubt if you are going to make a career for yourself in sport, a certain amount of selfishness is required. It has to become second nature to just go and do it. But the link with Italy paid off with Carroll House.

As well as Italy, big races had also come Kinane's way in India and in the mid-1980s Group 1 victories for Weld arrived in the shape of a second Prix de l'Abbaye for Committed, another Irish 2,000 Guineas on Flash Of Steel and a 1,000 Guineas victory on Trusted Partner. But for the prestigious races in Britain and France Kinane remained a bit player. Weld was convinced of his jockey's talent on the big stage but the idea of looking to Ireland for a rider in a major race remained frustratingly alien to Europe's elite trainers. All that changed in 1989, however, in the Irish Champion Stakes at the now defunct Phoenix Park racecourse.

Carroll House's regular rider Walter Swinburn was committed to riding in England and trainer Michael Jarvis felt the Irish champion was an option.

> Because I was such a regular in Italy riding for anyone who'd pay me, it wasn't so hard for Michael Jarvis to sell the idea of me riding Carroll House to [Antonio] Balzarini who owned the horse. But it was still unusual for an Irish jockey to be booked for a race like the Champion Stakes. That was a real shop window, a great opportunity. Because the ground was too firm for Carroll House, he hung like a bastard and it was only brute force that got him there.

That didn't stop Swinburn having first refusal on Carroll House for the Prix de l'Arc de Triomphe on the first Sunday in October. However, when he was claimed to ride Alisya, the Jarvis team turned again to Ireland. Twenty-four hours earlier The Caretaker had landed the lucrative Cartier Million under Kinane at the Phoenix Park. But in terms of international significance, it paled next to the Arc. On very different ground conditions to the Champion Stakes, Carroll House thrived, 'a piece of cake' as his rider now remembers. It wasn't quite that. Carroll House won impressively but not before getting close to the runner up, Behera. A prolonged stewards' enquiry stretched nerves to breaking point in the winner's enclosure and Kinane needed to use Cash Asmussen as an interpreter in order to get his point across. Only when an official reminded him to go and get his rider's prize did the Irish jockey know he had held on to Europe's most coveted all-aged race.

This victory soon had an impact. Pat Eddery's commitments to Prince Khaled Abdullah meant he was unavailable to ride Tirol for Richard Hannon in the following year's 2,000 Guineas at Newmarket. Hannon's solution was to look to Ireland and the emerging big-race talent that had proved himself in the previous autumn's Arc. Eddery made no effort to disguise his view that Tirol was the best hope of defeating the French favourite Machiavellian, and Kinane pounced on the chance, winning his first English classic.

A couple of months later Henry Cecil, who had been impressed by the Irish champion's riding of Alydaress in the 1989 Irish Oaks, offered the ride on his supposed second string Belmez in the 1990 King George at Ascot. Cauthen's choice of Old Vic over his three-year-old stable companion returned to haunt him as Belmez got the better of a sustained battle by a neck. But by then Kinane's international exploits had gone well beyond Ireland and Britain.

Dermot Weld's vision of the world racing scene had always been expansive. But even by those standards his decision to run Go And Go in the 1990 Belmont Stakes was audacious. No non-North American-trained horse had ever won a leg of the US Triple Crown. Bold Arrangement had come close for Clive Brittain in the Kentucky Derby four years previously, but Weld figured the mile and a half of the Belmont Stakes in New York would be an ideal opportunity for a European horse. The distance is beyond the norm in America and it comes at the end of an intense five-week Triple Crown campaign. Weld also had the knowledge that the Moyglare Stud-owned colt had proven form on dirt as a two-year-old. It all came together gloriously. The Kentucky Derby winner Unbridled, running without the drug Lasix, could only struggle home third as Go And Go powered eight lengths clear of the field. A horse that at best was a Group 2 standard at home had trounced the USA's best. It wouldn't be long before the other side of the world found out how dangerous Messrs Weld and Kinane could be when travelling.

Kinane is rarely sentimental about the horses he rides – 'You have to love what you do and you have to love the animal. But you also have to separate yourself and walk away' – but Vintage Crop, the chestnut gelding that broke the mould for international racing, remains a favourite. Mostly it's his courage. And when he was asked for everything, he always delivered. Sometimes the asking had to be forceful, but there was never any shirking. In that he was very unusual. Most horses can be pushed only so far, and only so many times. Vintage Crop was a horse to take you to the end of the world, and in 1993 it felt like he did.

It's hard to put into context now how new the attempt was for a northern hemisphere-trained horse to win the Melbourne Cup. Internationalisation has made the race an accepted target for stayers around the world these days. But at the start of the 1990s there was an exotic flavour to attempts to lure the best of Europe to Australia's flagship race. Previous efforts by Weld to attempt such an audacious raid had floundered in a mire of official red tape and travel restrictions. By 1993 those problems had been sorted out. More importantly, the trainer knew he had a unique horse capable of overcoming the demands of travelling to the other side of the world. There was also the not inconsiderable bonus of suspecting that Vintage Crop had about 7 lb in hand of the handicapper after an Irish St Leger victory.

The English-trained Gold Cup winner Drum Taps also made the trip south and the two Europeans were trained in quarantine at Sandown racecourse outside Melbourne. It takes a trip to Australia to understand fully the hold the Melbourne Cup has on the public imagination there. There is blanket media coverage for weeks beforehand that no single sporting event on this side of the world can rival. The actual modestly sized Cup at the centre of the spectacle is the most coveted trophy in Australian sport. The odd rogue Kiwi might be allowed to take it across the Tasman Sea, but in 1993, this European attempt was positively Homeric. So much so that the locals largely viewed the visitors as curios; fascinating in an exotic kind of way but not real contenders. Many local horses run three days before the Cup. It's the tried and trusted method down under. Any other way looked like poncey Euro-shaping. To the Aussie way of doing things, a six-week gap between races was ludicrous. But the Aussies were about to have their eyes opened.

Vintage Crop didn't sail through the 1993 Cup like some handicap good thing. The initial sprint from the gates left him initially flat-footed and Kinane had to push him to get a decent position. Then the field slowed right back going down the back straight and the change of tempo was unusual for a European stayer. When Kinane got the leaders in his sights, a sod of muck from the rain-sodden turf hit the horse in the face. But that was when that famous courage kicked in. Vintage Crop suddenly surged into the open, overhauled the leaders and passed the post clear. The general reaction was so stunned, the race commentator's first words were famously off-beam: 'And the Cup is going to England!'

A great horse has to have attitude, who'll want to go to the pain barrier for you. Vintage Crop was one of the handful I've ridden who was willing to do that. I remember riding Theatrical in Germany one day, when he was beaten by Acatenango. He was so tired he could barely walk back afterwards. Vintage Crop was the same. The third year he ran in the Melbourne Cup (1995) he finished legless in third. He went out on a limb for us. Mind you I got heavily criticised for that ride, which pissed me off. Vintage Crop had seventeen stitches in an elbow and really shouldn't have even run, and it was all because of carelessness on their part out on the training track. Dermot told me to stay on the outside and not have him knocked about. I had a poke during the race to see if I could get in a bit but I couldn't. And the Aussies don't like horses being ridden on the outside. It's their way. And their way is the only way. They castigate their own so they loved having a go at an outsider. The Aussies are great. They tell you straight what they think. But they turn on you quick. They probably just didn't like us taking the Cup off them the first year.

Yet perhaps an even more satisfying victory had come five months before Vintage Crop changed the face of world racing at Flemington. Commander In Chief was the Henry Cecil second string for the Epsom Derby behind the odds-on Tenby, but an impressive piece of work by the supposed No. 2 before the race convinced his new jockey that this was a major chance. So it proved, as Tenby dropped away quickly and Commander In Chief swept clear for an easy win. By now the title of 'super-sub' was hanging firmly around Kinane's neck.

In 1993 he rode Group 1 winners in Ireland, Britain, Australia, Germany and Hong Kong. At the start of the year he had also stunned most of the racing world by turning down the job as Sheikh Mohammed's retained rider. Steve Cauthen's decision to retire produced a vacancy that any other jockey in the world would have snapped up. But Kinane has always followed the beat of his own drum. Taking the job would have meant breaking his link with Weld. It would also have cut into the time he spent in Hong Kong during the winter. Already an iconic figure to Hong Kong's feverish betting public, Kinane has always enjoyed riding there and it has been good to him. But, most importantly of all, he didn't fancy moving his wife and young family to live in Newmarket.

> Having to live in England was a huge factor. The lads over there are run ragged for little or no gain. The quality of life is very different. I suppose I could have been champion jockey many times if I'd gone, maybe got the Godolphin job (the Maktoum-family-owned racing stable) but would that have made me happier than I am now? I certainly can't regret anything because my career has been so good to me. And I ended up riding for them anyway.

An agreement with the Maktoum family at the start of 1994 in fact allowed Kinane the best of both worlds: living in Ireland but travelling around Europe to ride in the top races. It was a remarkable transformation since Carroll House had struggled past the post in the Champion Stakes in 1989, and the pay off was almost immediate. Kings Theatre was agonisingly overhauled in the last strides of the Epsom Derby by Erhaab but carried Sheikh Mohammed's maroon and white colours to victory in the King George. The same silks won out in the Coronation Stakes with Kissing Cousin, while there was a St James's Palace Stakes success on Grand Lodge that contained every element of the Kinane magic.

Always tactically astute, Kinane's naked will to win practically lifted Grand Lodge over the line. The only negative was a whip ban but, once again, when it mattered the Irish 'super-sub' got the job done. There was a glimpse of the future, too, when Cezanne continued what would turn out to be a remarkable record in the Irish Champion Stakes – Kinane has won the race six times in total – by winning at Leopardstown in the new Godolphin colours. Godolphin's increasing influence was to become more obvious as the 1990s wore on and a 1996 win in the Ascot Gold Cup on Classic Cliché was another vintage piece of opportunism. Frankie Dettori might have been Godolphin's jockey but, when he wasn't available, Dermot Weld got used to releasing his jockey. And it wasn't just the Maktoum family that was clamouring for the Irish champion.

Michael Stoute engaged Kinane for the vastly improved older horse Pilsudski in 1997 and only an exceptional Arc winner in Peintre Celebre prevented a marvellous autumnal clean sweep. Another Irish Champion Stakes was followed by victory in the English equivalent before an ambitious trip to Tokyo for the Japan Cup. 'That was one of the great days,' Kinane remembers. 'He [Pilsudski] died a death for me. It was a pleasure to ride that horse. He had lovely balance and you could really get behind him. A lovely horse to ride. But if Tokyo was a wonderful climax to another successful year, there had been a glimpse of the future just a month earlier in October. Second Empire landed the Grand Criterium at Longchamp to add to an already impressive list of classic contenders in a rather famous training establishment in Co. Tipperary.

The phoenix-like rise of the Ballydoyle stable, backed by the power of Coolmore, in the 1990s carried with it great romance on the back of the Vincent O'Brien legend, as well as a more concrete investment calculated to blow away almost any opposition in European racing. John Magnier's determination to continue the model of moulding future Coolmore stallions from his own racing centre meant that no stone was left unturned in finding the best. Michael Tabor's investment added to the financial clout. Aidan O'Brien was later described by Magnier as 'Ireland's worst kept secret' but the installation of the training protégé into the most pressurised job in racing was still a gamble. A counter-balance, though, was the selection of jockey, something that almost everyone regarded as inevitable. Christy Roche rode for O'Brien in Ireland but in 1997 the decision was taken to have Kinane on board Ballydoyle's overseas runners. The pay off was instant, with Second Empire, as well as Saratoga Springs in the *Racing Post* Trophy. It only proved to be a taste of what was to come.

Kinane said of the Coolmore operation:

They had the standard of horse that everyone wanted to ride. It was obvious with the investment in horseflesh there. And as much as I had a fantastic job with Dermot, and the opportunities to travel as well, it was just a natural progression. At the time Walter Haefner [owner of Moyglare Stud], who was always a great supporter of mine, asked: 'Michael, is it money?' and I said, 'No, it's just the standard of horse.'

It proved to be a correct decision. Any fears that O'Brien, whose career up to then had been mainly in the National Hunt sphere, might crumble under the weight of expectation quickly disappeared. This wasn't going to be a repeat of Michael Dickinson at Manton when a hugely talented jumps champion failed to cut it on the flat. It didn't take long for evidence of a substantive talent to emerge. King Of Kings, an exuberantly talented if less than straightforward son of Sadlers Wells, won the 2,000 Guineas in style. A month later he failed to make an impact in the Derby but the trio of Ballydoyle horses that ran behind High-Rise emphasised the rapid growth of a new racing superpower. Over the next five years came spectacular confirmation during a period of unprecedented dominance. A dazzling array of equine talent was produced by Coolmore, and Kinane was the perfect jockey to exploit the potential. It wasn't just Ballydoyle horses either. In fact the irony is that possibly the best of them was trained hundreds of miles away in Chantilly.

The legend has grown of how Magnier's chief talent scout Demi O'Byrne just happened to spot on television a rangy two year old, Montjeu, winning by a street in France. The impression was enough for the Coolmore syndicate to buy the Sadlers Wells colt but leave him in training with John Hammond. Through the summer of 1999 Montjeu cut a swathe through the classic generation in Europe. An easy French Derby success was followed by an even more impressive victory in the Irish Derby. On board for them both was Cash Asmussen. But for Montjeu's Arc warm up in the Prix Niel, the decision was taken for Kinane to ride. When that yielded another win, Kinane stayed on board the head-strong but brilliantly talented colt for a titanic Arc victory when he overcame trouble in running to overhaul the Japanese star El Condor Pasa. If anything, though, that was only a prelude to the first half of 2000 when Montjeu looked all but unbeatable.

Kinane is full of praise for the colt:

He was probably the most talented horse I've ridden up to this year. At his very best in the Tattersalls and the King George and in the Arc he was a phenomenal athlete. He had loads of temperament, but I've rarely ridden another horse that could do what he did. There were six runners in that Tattersalls, all Group 1 winners, and he treated them like cattle.

The same comment could also apply to the King George where Montjeu never came off the bridle and recorded the sort of swaggering success that conjured up memories of Nijinsky in his pomp. An attempt at another Arc failed as he trailed in fourth to Sinndar and two more failed starts brought an anti-climactic end to a career that at its peak compares to any horse of any generation.

But the year 2000 also saw Kinane enjoy four Group 1 victories on a very different sort of colt. If Montjeu swaggered, then Giants Causeway stared the opposition in the eye and dared them to pass. In the St James's Palace, the Eclipse, the Sussex, the Juddmonte and the Irish Champion Stakes he challenged the best milers and ten furlong horses in Europe to a fight and came off best every time. But one final slug-out in the Breeders' Cup Classic came up agonisingly, and controversially, short.

Kinane had already come in for some criticism earlier that day at Churchill Downs when settling Montjeu at the rear of a slow pace in the Turf. But Montjeu was by then only a shadow of himself. Giants Causeway, in contrast, was on top form for his first glimpse of dirt. Despite the alien conditions he was in position A to challenge the leader Tiznow when Kinane's whip briefly became entangled in the reins. With just a neck in it at the line, opinions were divided as to the importance of the incident. Many still believe the two horses could have gone around the track again and Tiznow would still be in front. Kinane himself believed his mistake didn't affect the result. O'Brien disagreed. 'Obviously the horse would have won if he hadn't lost the reins. There's no doubt about that. Anyone will tell you that,' he still insisted days afterwards. It was a reminder that, behind the mild manner, O'Brien was able to stubbornly fight his corner. No one has ever mistaken Kinane for a pushover either. Two strong personalities were never going to see eye to eye on everything, as became clear later.

But before that came any number of glorious days. In 2001 O'Brien saddled twenty-three Group 1 winners, including the English-Irish Derby double with Galileo. Victory at the Curragh filled an annoying gap in

Kinane's own classic CV. A High Court injunction against a two-day Turf Club suspension was necessary for him to keep the ride on Galileo in the King George but then Coolmore's stallion requirements propelled O'Brien to turn Galileo into something he wasn't. A classic mile and a half horse, he just came up short against Fantastic Light in a titanic Irish Champion Stakes clash and then fizzled out in the Breeders' Cup Classic. Time has shown that Galileo's stallion credentials needed no such deviation.

> Galileo was imperious on Epsom Derby day. From the time we left the gates he was going to win, which very seldom happens. He was beautifully balanced and he is undoubtedly one of the best Derby winners ever I would say. The thing was he would have loved a little dig in the ground and he never got it that year. We came out the wrong side of a tactical battle at Leopardstown in the Champion Stakes but only because he cracked in the last hundred yards on the very fast ground.

Later that year Kinane broke his Breeders' Cup duck in the Juvenile with Johannesburg, and in 2002 success just kept on coming. He picked the wrong horse in the Derby, with High Chaparral getting the better of Hawk Wing but Rock Of Gibraltar dominated the milers and brought off a seven-race winning streak in Group 1s that secured a place in his jockey's affections.

> Rock was the best fun I've had on a horse. It was push button stuff. He loved racing. He'd be bucking and kicking going to the start but then he wouldn't pull in the race. All I had to do was pull out and go.
> I half knew my fate on Hawk Wing in the Derby the day before. I rode in the Oaks and I couldn't believe how soft the ground was. Hawk Wing was a fantastic horse but he didn't quite stay, whereas High Chaparral was so tough. If only one of them had run, he'd have won by twelve or thirteen lengths and everyone would have been saying he was one of the greatest Derby winners ever. And the other one could have been home in his box. High Chaparral winning his second Breeders' Cup is one of the Aidan's

greatest training feats, to get him back to that sort of pitch. I still can't believe it was a dead heat – but I suppose half is better than none.

That Breeders' Cup triumph for High Chaparral at Santa Anita in 2003 was the last major triumph for Kinane as the Ballydoyle No.1. It proved once more his supreme professionalism. By then the relationship between Kinane and O'Brien had dissolved. Throughout the season, racing's rumour mill had fizzed with gossip about how the trainer was looking for a new jockey. Sceptics initially dismissed it out of hand but beneath the surface there was real friction. O'Brien wanted someone new. Kinane has mostly kept his counsel on the split but insists this was no summary sacking. The rider had been prepared to jump ship for some time. In fact, he believes the news that he was going to ride as stable jockey to John Oxx on the Curragh caught Ballydoyle on the hop.

The relationship broke down. In any partnership, dialogue is the key. Once that relationship breaks down, it's inevitable that things will break up. But I was going and they didn't think I was as far down the line with John as I was. It was time to go. They might have made their minds up but I had my mind made up too. There was no point in prolonging it and staying around in a job that I wasn't enjoying any more anyway. The last year was particularly difficult. It's very difficult, day to day, when you're riding horses, and you don't know what is improving between races; you're not hands on but still trying to make decisions. It's good between Aidan and myself now. We had our moments like anybody else. But I don't dislike Aidan. I don't dislike anybody in the whole operation. I had too many good times for that.

The relief felt at getting out of Ballydoyle's pressure-cooker atmosphere was obvious in 2004 when the new Oxx-Kinane team hit Group 1 winning form with Azamour. Placed in both the English and Irish 2,000 Guineas, the Aga Khan-owned colt landed the St James's Palace Stakes at Royal Ascot before handing Kinane a sixth win in the Irish Champion Stakes. Afterwards the winning jockey was invariably asked to compare Azamour with some of his previous winners. This was usually the cue, during his time at Ballydoyle, to reach for the sort of superlatives that read well on a stallion brochure. With no such expectations this time, the response was a wry: 'I don't do politics any more!'

Azamour continued his Group 1 form into a four-year career, scoring in the Prince Of Wales at York and the King George over a mile and a half which was relocated to Newbury owing to Ascot's reconstruction. 'He was very timely,' remembers Kinane of Azamour. 'A great horse to ride immediately after what had happened at Ballydoyle. And I had him for two years.' But the link with O'Brien was far from severed. The stability that Kinane had provided must have looked even more desirable to the Coolmore powers after Jamie Spencer lasted just one season and the baggage Kieren Fallon brought to the job caught up with him. When the British Horseracing Authority banned Fallon from riding in the UK, and American organisations reciprocated it, a yawning gap opened up in overseas riding arrangements: Ballydoyle came a-calling again.

The highlight was undoubtedly George Washington's scintillating victory in the Queen Elizabeth II Stakes that set up another hopeful tilt at the Breeders' Cup Classic. It looked hopeful, considering sons of Danehill have rarely acted on dirt, and sure enough 'Gorgeous George' struggled behind Invasor. Tragically, though, that wasn't to be the end of his relationship with the Classic. A failed stallion career saw him return to racing action and on the rain-soaked slop of Monmouth Park in New Jersey in 2007, this most enigmatic of horses tried again to beat the best of America. He was beaten before the straight and then sustained a fatal leg injury.

Kinane notes that George Washington was courageous to the end. 'It was an awful thing. He saved me because he kept himself on one leg until we pulled up. I don't know how he stood up. It was terrible, but he somehow looked after me.'

However, increasingly through 2007 O'Brien was turning to Johnny Murtagh to ride abroad, a move that heralded his replacement of Fallon for 2008. That impacted on some opportunities for Kinane but the link with Oxx paid off in spades in 2009. The relationship between the two men is rooted in a mutual respect. 'John's a lovely man, a pleasure to work with. Like anyone who has thirty or forty staff and 150 horses to look after, he can throw the odd wobbly. But when John gives one of those occasional curses, it's meaningful!' laughs his stable jockey.

In turn, Oxx bows to no one in his appreciation of Kinane – who is one of many top jockeys to have ridden for the trainer. In the past, Oxx has employed the likes of Pat Eddery, Cash Asmussen, the Australian Ron Quinton, as well as having moulded the career of Johnny Murtagh. There appears to be a meeting of minds in the current link which explains how their partnership continues to thrive.

'He is Ireland's greatest jockey,' explains Oxx, simply. 'Historically that's a fact. He has done it all. He's a most professional man. It would be hard to find anyone more dedicated, or determined, or consistent. That's important. He is never too up or down, never any huge mood swings, just totally professional.'

Attempting to place Kinane's impact in context, Oxx continues: 'Years ago the jockey situation reflected the strength of racing in England and in Ireland. Between the wars, and immediately afterwards, the presumption was England was the place to go and a lot of young Irish jockeys went there. What happened then was that things changed on the training side. Vincent [O'Brien] and Paddy Prendergast emerged and had a lot of success. But it took a lot longer for the way Irish jockeys were viewed to change. The strength of racing in England meant the jockeys there were assumed to be the best and if someone like Lester was available, then every trainer here wanted him. The result was that Irish jockeys took a lot longer to get established. It was Mick who really led the way. He did it all, and led the way for someone like Johnny Murtagh, who is one of the top guys now. But it's not just him. In Ireland we have the best crop of jockeys riding in Europe. And Mick has been the example to them all.'

Due in no small part to a relative lack of major success for a number of years up to 2009, there have been the usual whispers from the grandstand jockey brigade that Kinane, at fifty, may no longer be the rider he was. It's an accusation that illustrates racing's terribly fickle nature, and it doesn't cut any ice with the man employing him. In contrast, Oxx has noticed a subtle change of style.

'Mick used to have a reputation of being a bit hard with the whip and I'm sure there are punters out there who would love him to be flogging horses to death,' Oxx believes. 'But he knows what he has got under him now more than at any other time in his career. His style is a bit quieter now than it was. He knows not to be too hard on a horse. He would be the first to admit that he's not as young as he was, and maybe not as strong, but his judgement and his fitness are still very good. You certainly won't find anyone more professional or motivated. He's definitely got a bit more in him.'

That point was rammed home with a vengeance when Sea The Stars cut an imperious swathe through the 2009 classics. The hugely impressive half brother to Galileo became the first horse to complete the Guineas-Derby double in twenty years. Hugely talented he may be, but at both Newmarket and Epsom there was a sureness of touch from the man on board that contributed to an overall impression of raw racing class. Kinane's admiration for Sea The Stars is boundless.

> He is right up there with the best I've ridden, the all-round package. He has the physique, the talent but also the temperament. I've been very involved with this horse on a daily basis and that's been lovely. It's what I like. In a way he has kick-started things again. The reality is that it is very hard to get on horses like Sea The Stars and it doesn't matter if you're young or old.

A generation ago, racing found out how dangerous it is to under-estimate Michael Kinane. Only the most blinkered can have failed to learn the lesson by now. It is the sport's good fortune that Kinane continues to emphasise this with his victories.

Classic Wins

1982
Irish 2,000 Guineas   Dara Monarch

1985
Premio Parioli   Again Tomorrow

1986
Irish 2,000 Guineas   Flash Of Steel

1988
Irish 1,000 Guineas   Trusted Partner
Premio Parioli   Gay Burslem

1989
Irish Oaks   Alydaress

1990
Belmont Stakes   Go And Go
English 2,000 Guineas   Tirol

1992
Derby Italiano   In A Tiff

1993
Epsom Derby   Commander In Chief
Irish St Leger   Vintage Crop

1994
Irish St Leger   Vintage Crop

1995
Derby Italiano   Luso

1996
Irish Oaks   Dance Design

1997

English 2,000 Guineas   Entrepreneur

1998

English 2,000 Guineas   King Of Kings
English Oaks   Shahtoush

2001

Poule d'Essai des Pouliches   Rose Gypsy
Epsom Derby   Galileo
English Oaks   Imagine
Irish Derby   Galileo
English St Leger   Milan

2002

Poule d'Essai des Poulains   Landseer
Irish 2,000 Guineas   Rock Of Gibraltar
Irish Derby   High Chaparral

2003

Irish 1,000 Guineas   Yesterday

2005

Irish 1,000 Guineas   Saoire

2006

Irish St Leger   Kastoria

2009

English 2,000 Guineas   Sea The Stars
English Derby   Sea The Stars

Other Major Winners include

1982

St James's Palace Stakes   Dara Monarch

1985

Prix de l'Abbaye   Committed

1986

Indian Derby   Sir Bruce

1987

Moyglare Stud Stakes   Flutter Away

1988

Indian Derby   Cordon Bleu

1989

Irish Champion Stakes   Carroll House
Prix de l'Arc de Triomphe   Carroll House

1990

King George VI & Queen Elizabeth Stakes   Belmez

1992

Hong Kong Derby   Sound Print
St James's Palace Stakes   Brief Truce

1993

Eclipse Stakes   Opera House
Bayerisches Zuchtrennen   Market Booster
Melbourne Cup   Vintage Crop

1994

St James's Palace Stakes   Grand Lodge
King George VI & Queen Elizabeth Stakes   Kings Theatre
Irish Champion Stakes   Cezanne

1996

Hong Kong Derby   Che Sara Sara

1997

Hong Kong Vase   Luso
Eclipse Stakes   Pilsudski

Irish Champion Stakes	Pilsudski
English Champion Stakes	Pilsudski
Grand Criterium	Second Empire
Racing Post Trophy	Saratoga Springs
Japan Cup	Pilsudski

1998

Sussex Stakes	Among Men

1999

July Cup	Stravinsky
Prix de l'Arc de Triomphe	Montjeu
Grand Criterium	Ciro

2000

Tattersalls Gold Cup	Montjeu
St James's Palace Stakes	Giants Causeway
King George VI & Queen Elizabeth Stakes	Montjeu
Secretariat Stakes	Ciro
Sussex Stakes	Giants Causeway
Juddmonte International	Giants Causeway
Irish Champion Stakes	Giants Causeway
Prix Vermeille	Volvoreta

2001

Dewhurst Stakes	Rock Of Gibraltar
July Cup	Mozart
King George VI & Queen Elizabeth Stakes	Galileo
Moyglare Stud Stakes	Quarter Moon
Breeders' Cup Juvenile	Johannesburg
Prix Jean Luc Lagadere	Rock Of Gibraltar

2002

Hong Kong Cup	Precision
St James's Palace Stakes	Rock Of Gibraltar
Sussex Stakes	Rock Of Gibraltar
Eclipse Stakes	Hawk Wing
Prix du Moulin	Rock Of Gibraltar
Breeders' Cup Turf	High Chaparral
Canadian International	Ballingarry

2003

Irish Champion Stakes	High Chaparral
Moyglare Stud Stakes	Necklace
Breeders' Cup Turf	High Chaparral

2004

St James's Palace Stakes	Azamour
Irish Champion Stakes	Azamour

2005

Juddmonte International	Electrocutionist
King George VI & Queen Elizabeth Stakes	Azamour
Sussex Stakes	Proclamation

2006

Queen Elizabeth II Stakes	George Washington

2007

Coronation Cup	Scorpion

2008

Indian Derby	Hot Stepper

2

PAUL CARBERRY

It is a tricky thing, talent. Having none is a pain, but the other extreme can be a drag too. If you are loaded with the stuff, a whole question of duty comes into the equation: duty to that natural gift, exploiting it to the fullest, being able to look back from dotage and knowing the last drop was squeezed out. That's all very worthy indeed, and an outlook often encouraged by those dutifully chugging along in comfortable mediocrity themselves.

Calvin Coolidge, America's thirtieth president, insisted that the world is full of talented but unsuccessful people and that nothing can take the place of persistence. This from a man who, even compared to some of the dullards who have sat in the White House, set such a standard in boredom that when he died it was famously asked how anyone could tell.

Paul Carberry is not a Cal type of man at all. It's unlikely he goes along with the whole duty thing either – but he might. It's hard to know. Public displays of introspection are not really his thing. Neither is any long-winded analysis of why he is able to make the job he does look almost ridiculously simple sometimes. That's not because of any lack of mental acuity on his part but because he probably knows deep down it is a futile exercise.

Carberry rides horses the way the rest of us breathe. It's that simple. It is little wonder then that even in a sport where opinions breed faster than rabbits, there is one thing on which there is a startling unanimity. Paul Carberry is as phenomenally gifted a rider as has ever put two legs on either side of a horse. Conor O'Dwyer, a double Cheltenham Gold Cup and Champion Hurdle winner, rode until he was nearly forty-two before retiring and never ran into anyone like his former colleague. 'The greatest natural talent I've ever seen,' is his simple verdict. 'There are brilliant riders out there who have worked on their game but from day one Carberry has not had to improve on anything. It was all literally there from day one.' Tony McCoy says the same. Richard Dunwoody inspired a generation of riders during his own illustrious career but cheerfully admits he has never met anyone like Carberry.

And yet the choice of words employed by his admirers carries an edge. Everyone agrees on the skill, but loaded into that unanimity is a prurient inference that it hasn't been fully exploited by its owner: that it has been almost too easy for him. It's a strange and very modern aspect among sports fans that the cultivation of talent must be taken very seriously indeed. Wayward souls might still inspire affection but also regretful shakes of the head. Ability has its responsibilities as well as its privileges and there will always be those Calvinist roundheads who distrust the cavaliers. Carberry is in his mid-thirties now and edging ever closer to retirement. After a career as rich and varied as his, the argument goes, it would be a shame to look back from old age and feel regret.

The good news, though, for those who still relish a maverick spirit is that such a scenario is unlikely. And even if it does happen, the idea of Carberry boring anyone else with regrets is unthinkable. There is a tower of evidence over the last twenty years that boredom is what he dreads most of all. No one can have it every way and there is no doubting the enthusiasm with which he made his choice long ago. 'We're here for a good time – not a long time' is a philosophy that Carberry has fervently followed. Even at thirty-five, he can still raise a whole lot of hell. That he has managed to have that cake and still scoff from the top table of his profession is a wonderful reassurance that sometimes raw talent really can be enough. Sure, there may be more races that he might have won but, as he knows better than anyone in the weighroom, there's more to life than winning races. And it would be a true ingrate who sails through a career in such an apparently carefree manner as Carberry, and then starts bleating on the other side.

There have been times when the man has truly seemed as blessed off the saddle as on it. An appetite for living on the edge hasn't come even close to being sated by the rigours of riding over fences. Instead, there is a catalogue of myths, legends and yarns that have stretched around the world. Even as far away as Australia, Carberry's determination to have a good time can draw attention. A newspaper down under recently reported an incident when the man nicknamed Alice – 'Living Next Door to Alice' by Smokie is his party piece – climbed out the window of a speeding car, crawled across the roof and got back in through another window. The list of exploits is endless and usually involves horses, drink and a penchant for disrobing and hanging off both animate and inanimate objects in the early hours. For others, such behaviour could result in the summoning of either the police or a shrink. But there don't appear to be any dark, self-destructive demons in Carberry. It's just the natural reflex of a man easily bored and seemingly incapable of sitting still.

Everyone agrees there is no malice in what he does. In fact, his resolute pursuit of fun usually means he is more of a danger to himself than anyone else and so the more risqué, off the wall behaviour is viewed indulgently. Even when it does go beyond the pale, the slim figure with the schoolboy haircut and permanently cheeky grin can get away with it, which is no mean tribute to his innate likeability considering what happened in October 2005.

Burning a copy of the *Irish Times* is something that quite a few people must have considered over the years but not at 12,000ft on a packed Aer Lingus flight between Málaga and Dublin. Carberry's playfulness with a friend's paper turned very nasty very quickly. 'One woman had her head in her hands. I think she thought we were all going down,' said another passenger afterwards. Police were waiting at Dublin airport and Carberry was charged with 'threatening, abusive or insulting behaviour' under the Air Navigation and Transport Acts. By now even that famously impudent grin had disappeared.

It looked a lot more serious seven months later when he received a two-month jail sentence and was released on bail of €1,000. The judge said he found Carberry's evidence contrived. Pictures of jockeys scurrying out of court houses have been depressingly frequent in recent years and there were plenty of 'chumpion jockey' headlines churned out. In the end he was spared jail. Instead he was sentenced to community service, which included teaching children in a disadvantaged area of Dublin to ride.

It was an embarrassing incident all round for Carberry and his family. But, after riding his luck on the legal roller-coaster, he went back to riding winners with a fluency that suggested nothing had happened. Within the game there was as little surprise at that as there was that he had got into trouble in the first place. After all, outrageous talent rarely comes neatly wrapped. The weird part, though, is that no one has ever looked neater on the back of a steeplechaser.

Like most great instinctive talents, a lot of that comes down to not getting in the way. If you can't help, then at least don't hinder is a rule of thumb that has sustained Carberry throughout his career. It's obvious almost from the moment he gets on a horse. Perched high on the withers with just a toe in either iron and a long length of rein, there is as little interference with the animal underneath as he can manage. It's a flat race technique brought to the rigours of jumping but with no allowance made for the difference. Not unnaturally for a man who likes to enjoy himself, there is also an implicit understanding that if the horse isn't relishing what he's doing, there isn't going to be much joy at the end for either party. The remorseless push and shove of some of his more industrious colleagues is not a favoured option. At least not until the closing stages when it counts. Then all that unfussy finesse turns into a much more dynamic blend of streamlined power.

If pressed to pinpoint a particular ride of his over the years that he feels was exceptional, Carberry is unlikely to reach a verdict. There is a modesty there anyway which encourages a natural inclination to self-depreciation, plus there's a good chance that he can't remember some of them.

But if ever a major victory summed up the talents of a jockey, it was Aitmatov winning the 2007 Hatton's Grace Hurdle at Fairyhouse. On desperately heavy ground, Aitmatov looked a spent force before the straight as the good mare Sweet Kiln made the best of her way home. From the stands she looked a certain winner, galloping remorselessly through stamina-sapping mud, while it appeared that Aitmatov's jockey had accepted inevitable defeat. Except he hadn't.

Carberry's rivals have always had the difficult job of trying to 'read' what their man has left in reserve. That confident style means it can often look like his mount has a lot more left to offer than it actually has. But on this occasion it appeared that his chance had gone. Instead, Aitmatov looked like he was being nursed home. Far from a certain stayer in the first place, he had been coaxed into a challenging position before his jockey's backside lost altitude – this was a clear signal to many backers that they had done their dough. Not for the first time, however, Carberry had a surprise in store. Far from giving up, the jockey later explained he was allowing the horse to get a breather. It takes some kind of nerve to take a pull in a Grade 1 with the leader getting further ahead, but Carberry has always obeyed his instincts and there was enough coming through the reins in that mysterious language between horse and rider to suggest there was one last kick left. When to play it would be critical.

Only on the approach to the last did there seem any danger to Sweet Kiln. A final tired leap out of the ground suddenly meant that danger became very real. Crucially Aitmatov challenged wide of the mare. Carberry knew better than most how tough she was. Having ridden Sweet Kiln's former stable companions Limestone Lad and Solerina, from Michael Bowe's stables, he realised she would fight back with a target to aim at. Flinging everything at Aitmatov in an irresistible last throw of the dice, he infused the exhausted animal with some of his own will to win. Sure enough, Tom Doyle steered Sweet Kiln across the track to ensure a final eyeball-to-eyeball fight but it was too late. At the line Aitmatov's head was down in front. It was a ride that had everything, patience, brains, guts, inspiration and raw strength when required. Michael Bowe watched it unfold and hasn't bothered with a replay ever since.

'Tom Doyle did nothing wrong at all but I couldn't watch it again,'

Bowe reflects. 'That's Paul though – a law unto himself. I hate being in opposition to him. I know from when he was riding for me how good he is at weighing up what's against him. He's actually a very deep thinker about how he rides a race. I was always very reluctant to give him instructions. I suspect he rehearses races in his mind and he knows exactly what he's going to do. That's not the way people think of him but I noticed you'd be talking to him in the parade ring and his mind would be so focused, what you'd be saying was going in one ear and out the other. There was no point giving instructions.'

Bowe continues: 'He's actually a very canny fellah in many ways but the sort of natural horseman that comes around once in a blue moon. I remember the day Solerina beat Hardy Eustace in the Deloitte Hurdle at Leopardstown, he was particularly brilliant. She was a mare with her own way of doing things and he just played along with her – so natural.'

Even as a child there were suspicions that the little lad with the crooked grin and the bullet head was out of the ordinary. Just after his first birthday, he was blissfully unaware of how his father, steering home L'Escargot to beat Red Rum in the Aintree Grand National, would become such a fundamental influence on his life. It was pretty damn big for Dad, too.

In 1975 Tommy Carberry was at the height of his own remarkable career. A month before L'Escargot put paid to hopes of three-in-a-row around Aintree for Red Rum, Carberry Snr had partnered Ten Up to land the Cheltenham Gold Cup. It was a third success in steeplechasing's blue riband for the jockey (L'Escargot also won in 1970–71) and only a positive dope test on Tied Cottage a month after he scored in 1981 prevented a fourth Gold Cup victory going on the record. Also in 1975 he won the third of four Irish jockeys championships in a row, even if that year's title had to be shared with Frank Berry. Just to round things up nicely, there was an Irish Grand National success on Brown Lad. Such was his dominance, any race Carberry didn't win in Ireland in the 1970s probably wasn't worth winning.

In a golden age for Irish racing it was a time for a top jockey to make hay and that's what Carberry did. He even found time to marry Pamela Moore, daughter of L'Escargot's trainer Dan Moore and sister of leading trainer Arthur Moore. As L'Escargot stood steaming in the famous Aintree winner's enclosure, it was Arthur, standing in for his father, Dan, who planted his trilby between the horse's ears for the photographers and began a big race celebratory tradition that still continues. In television interviews the winning jockey, wearing the famous colours of the ex-American ambassador Raymond Guest, blithely dismissed his own role in the victory but with a glint in his eye that suggested the Liverpool pubs were in for a hammering that night. Was it any wonder then that a video of the famous day would later be played until it unravelled by Carberry Jnr. The impressionable youngster sat at home imagining that the arm of the sitting room sofa was L'Escargot. It must have all seemed impossibly exciting.

At three he was able to ride a pony. From the start, school had a tough time competing with the thrill of being in control of a big animal. When the thrill was multiplied by the discovery of hunting, the scholastic life hadn't a prayer of securing a new convert. In Co. Meath, the Ward Union Hunt is an institution, established in 1854. That's a long history but it's hard to imagine there has ever been a more devoted rider than Tommy Carberry's boy. As a teenager he was already riding a thoroughbred when he went hunting. Pretty soon there was word going beyond south Meath about a youngster who was already labelled mad but was as brave as a lion over ditch, drain or dyke.

With his father retired from riding and established as a trainer, there was a stable full of racehorses to practice a burgeoning talent that was precocious enough to make sixteen-year-old Carberry realise a childhood dream at Aintree in 1990. Joseph Knibb, trained by his father for family friends, was entrusted to the boy wonder in the Foxhunters for amateur riders over one circuit of the famous old track. They made it to the seventh before falling, just three fences before Becher's Brook. Joseph Knibb lost a little confidence when negotiating the mammoth ditch in front of The Chair. His young rider didn't.

The Grand National was the race we dreamt about riding in when we were kids. It was the one we wanted to ride in for real, just to go over those fences. I was disgusted when we came down. Becher's was just three away.

It took six more years for Carberry finally to conquer those famous fences, which must have seemed an interminable length of time. By now the thrill of setting a jumping horse at an obstacle – any obstacle – was a narcotic that demanded every available fix, which made his next move seem all the more quixotic. Tommy Carberry was a great jockey and is a fine trainer, but it's probably just as well for his family that his income has come from horses and not from any foray into the match-making game.

Paul insists it was his Dad's idea to begin an apprenticeship at Jim Bolger's stables in Co. Carlow. Tommy's ability as a rider had also stretched to regular employment on the flat over the years. In 1979 he had tasted Group 1 victory on the Vincent O'Brien-trained, Robert Sangster-owned, Fordham in the Joe McGrath Memorial Stakes, now the Irish Champion Stakes, at Leopardstown. Riding on the flat might have meant paying closer attention to weight but, besides the grind of visiting a sauna every day, the physical demands paled next to the dangers of riding over fences. Financially, the top end of the summer game was a lot more lucrative too. To the father there didn't seem to be a debate. There was no questioning the boy's talent. It was within his grasp to reach the pinnacle of the safer, richer and more glamorous branch of the sport. Breaking into the flat was a logical move. But logic is a pretty grey subject to a teenager with balls to burn and a compulsion always to see the other side by jumping over it on the back of a horse. To the son it was always going to be a temporary diversion. A few days of the Bolger regime only stiffened the youngster's resolve.

Carberry is very definitely not a Bolger type of man. Even now, when the common consent is that he has mellowed somewhat, Bolger remains a strict, authoritarian figure to whom the concept of doubt is as alien as the satisfaction of sparking up a really good smoke. In 1990, however, he made Cal Coolidge look like Keith Richards on a rampage. He was also at that time probably the most powerful trainer on the flat in Ireland. That was some achievement for a man with no background in racing, completely self-taught, who had left a job as an accountant at a car-sale showroom to pursue a dream of emulating his idol Vincent O'Brien. In a decade and a half he had reached the pinnacle of the sport – respected, successful and, for a kid like Carberry, a totally alien character. Maybe Tommy's plan was that Bolger's renowned devotion to the gospels of religion, abstinence and hard work might trim the sails of his hyperactive young fellah. But it didn't work.

> I think he thought he'd put manners on me. I just let him roar away. He thinks he can make and break anybody and he wasn't happy when he couldn't with me. Mind you, I wasn't enjoying it much either. It was hard work but there were stupid things too. Like he made everyone go to mass during Lent – every day. He made us. I didn't mind – it was an hour off work! And I was always learning a good bit from all the other lads that were there.

It would have been surprising if he hadn't. Up to seven other apprentices were riding out at Coolcullen at the same time. Some, like Willie Supple and Seamus Heffernan, became champion apprentices. A certain A.P. McCoy was also there, as was another A.P., an amateur rider by the name of Aidan O'Brien. It was a startling array of talent, but even among so distinguished a group, Carberry stood out. A lot of emotions were prevalent but only one of the apprentices could get so bored that he lined up expensively bred two-year-olds for a cut at jumping some of the fencing around the place. This at a time when Bolger was training horses of the calibre of the Irish Derby and King George winner St Jovite and the Epsom Oaks heroine Jet Ski Lady. Mischief aside, the experience of riding in flat races was a crucial benefit.

> I started feeling comfortable riding short. Obviously I ride long when I'm hunting but I don't feel right riding long at the races. It looks sloppy and I actually feel stronger riding short. Riding on the flat was OK but it was boring at the end. Jumping was what I wanted to do. I knew that all along.

There was also a long-forgotten race during this time that influenced how the young apprentice was going to approach the rest of his career. It may not tally with the figure of popular repute now but a short head decision that went against him at this time provided Carberry with something of a dark night of the soul. It wasn't something he cared for and he resolved never to go down that road again. It was at Punchestown and he knows he should have won.

I spent the whole day kicking myself about it afterwards. Then I couldn't sleep that night. It really got to me. And when I got up the following morning, nothing had changed. I'd still lost the race. I promised myself a race would never bother me like that again. If you get beat, you get beat; there's no point worrying about it after.

Remarkably, Carberry lasted almost three years at the Bolger academy and both lived to tell the tale. At the end no tears were reported on either side – except maybe those of relief. Instead, Carberry went home to Meath to team up with a man whose racing soul was rather more compatible with his own. Noel Meade had a dual-purpose yard near Navan which was perfect. It didn't do any harm either that he was in thrall to what Carberry was able to do on a horse. Unlike Bolger, his own easy, sociable temperament allowed the jockey to feel the leash wasn't on choke all the time. 'He rides with natural instinct. There are times when I'm not sure why he does things on a horse. I'm not sure he knows himself – but invariably it's the right thing' was Meade's view.

In 1993, Carberry became champion apprentice in Ireland but he did it in his own unique way, finishing the year with a total of fifty-four winners divided equally between flat and jumps. There are still those who insist a wonderful flat racing talent was lost when the final decision was made to concentrate on his first love, but Carberry would have it no other way, especially after an unlikely success on the biggest jumping stage of all.

It seems curiously appropriate that it should come in the one flat race at the Cheltenham festival, the bumper, but that's where the 20-1 shot

Rhythm Section won in 1993, ironically beating the Meade-trained hotpot Heist. Meade's quest for a Cheltenham victory was already an established media story by then, but the combination of Heist and champion jockey Charlie Swan looked irresistible. Carberry, in contrast, was almost ignored in the build up, even though he had been booked for Rhythm Section almost two months before. Events conspired to make the nineteen-year-old come out on top over his champion rival. His ride on Heist will never be a comfortable memory for Swan, who was always having to do too much to get into a challenging position. Even still, it briefly looked like he was going to get there only for the unconsidered Rhythm Section to edge him out on the line.

Soon there were many more opportunities over the sticks coming Carberry's way. After turning down an offer to become Kim Bailey's retained rider, Carberry instead joined forces with the leading English owner Sir Robert Ogden and moved to Britain in 1995. Settling in was not a problem. The travelling was.

> Put me in a cattle shed and I'll be happy. But Middleham is in the middle of nowhere so I was coming home a lot. There were plenty of winners but there was plenty of travelling too and some of the midweek racing over there is terrible. You end up riding for peanuts on shit horses.

But the Ogden retainer was lucrative enough for Carberry to stick at it, although the way he remembers it the commitment required to ride work at the different yards at which the owner had horses was immense. That's hardly surprising considering that Ogden's list of trainers ranged from Nicky Richards in Cumbria down as far as Paul Nicholls in Somerset – 'I was expected to get around to all of them. It didn't make sense. When you ride a horse once, you know him well enough.'

Nevertheless there were good wins, including Squire Silk's victory in the 1996 Tote Gold Trophy, and a memorable first success at Aintree that year on Joe White in the John Hughes Trophy, now the Topham. It was only Carberry's fourth experience over the big fences and the 33-1 shot, who had been transferred from his father's yard to Howard Johnson the previous summer, overhauled Graham Bradley's mount Go Universal to win by a head.

But the Ogden link didn't last. After three years Carberry went home. He'd liked Ogden but felt less warm towards his racing manager. Meade had said his job was always waiting for him if he ever decided to return. In spirit he hadn't really left. Any break from the remorseless grind of churning around Britain's motorways saw him catch a plane back to Dublin from where it was a quick dash to the nearest hunt. Most Sundays were spent riding for Meade as well. Home was where the heart, and the fun, lay. Meade pledged to make him champion jockey, increasing economic prosperity in Ireland promised a good living and there was enough craic going on to keep even a twenty-four-year-old jockey with a fondness for a busy social life happy. Two days before the move back was made public, Carberry broke a leg at Wetherby.

'I break easy,' is his own typically succinct reason for why he has spent so much of his career on the sidelines. There have been years when he has spent up to five months out owing to a chronic list of shattered limbs, torn ligaments, chipped vertebrae and any number of broken ribs and collarbones. It's a timely reminder that behind all the exuberance lies a steely determination. Physical pain eventually, if you are lucky, goes away. The real lasting impact can be mental. Sometimes the thought of returning to a profession where it is a question of when, not if, you get hurt must be unnerving. Despite suffering more than most, Carberry has never wavered. 'It's part of the game. You just have to get up and keep going,' he says simply. Mind you, it does help when you've known since childhood that this crazy, brave sport is all you want to do. It helps even more when in return for all the smashes, you get to taste your own personal pinnacle.

Even if Bobbyjo hadn't had talent, the rangy gelding by Bustineto would still have been a favourite in the Carberry stable. There was something about the way he attacked everything: his work, his races, the life of a racehorse in general. All the Carberry kids rode him at home, their mothers too, even though he wasn't exactly easy. He could shy, and exuberance could lead to a quick exit out the side door. But there was nothing mean about it. Bobbyjo just liked showing the world how he felt. On Easter Monday 1998 he left everybody in the Ratoath area and beyond feeling pretty good. In a titanic finish with Papillon, he rallied to win the Irish Grand National and allow his jockey to emulate his trainer father. It was a heart-warming local success. Even as they were cleaning up at Fairyhouse that night, it provoked ideas of maybe the ultimate prize at Aintree a year later.

By now Paul Carberry had tasted more Cheltenham success – including a SunAlliance Chase on Looks Like Trouble – as well as other big race victories at home on stars like Dorans Pride. But it was still the Aintree National that excited him like no other race. His father figured Bobbyjo was ideal for it, and the son figured the old man should know. Twenty-four years had passed since L'Escargot without an Irish winner. There was a symmetry to the idea of the Carberrys bridging that gap. But that kind of neat ending usually happens only in movies. Still, nothing ventured . . .

The preparation was perfect. Bobbyjo detested really soft winter ground, became only half the horse he was when his feet rattled. He didn't come close to full throttle during the first half of the season. But all the signs were still positive – there was only one day in April in mind. Bobby Burke, the London-based publican who had bought the six-month old foal 'over a drink', nourished his own dreams and heard nothing negative from Tommy Carberry to dissuade them. Sure enough, as the ground started to dry up, Bobbyjo's work stepped up a gear. Eager to protect his handicap mark over fences, it was decided to give him a prep over hurdles at Down Royal. Another teenage Carberry, Philip, who was just starting his own riding career, did the steering. After Bobbyjo won at the northern track, it became harder not to start day-dreaming.

By the time the Carberry clan hit Liverpool, Bobbyjo's jockey was convinced he could win. So much so that he even went to bed at 9 p.m. on the Friday night. Such a move was a tip in itself. The annual Grand National trip to the Adelphi Hotel and other watering holes around the city is a dissolute pilgrimage that would normally be enthusiastically followed by Carberry. A disapproving owner famously once spied his jockey on top of a table in a bar at five in the morning, just hours before an important race, and complained to the trainer. The retort was simple. If Carberry wasn't on a table at five in the morning, the trainer said, he would be more worried in case there was something wrong with him. But this was different. Everything was coming together perfectly. The weather was great and the ground good. Bobbyjo might have been a full stone out of the handicap proper but he was in the form of his life. All that was left was negotiating thirty fences and thirty-one opponents. Burke worried about traffic during the race. The National nightmare is jumping well yourself but being brought down by something else. His refreshed and exuberant jockey calmed the atmosphere: 'There'll be fuck all going where I'm going.'

Like no other race, the National suits Carberry's soul. All that innate horsemanship comes into play. The ability to get a horse actually enjoying himself over those fearsome fences is remarkable. Over the years horses have run far above themselves with that lean figure perched precariously but confidently on top of them. At the start, where others stare nervously down the long line of fences towards Becher's, Carberry can barely wait. But this time on Bobbyjo it was crucial to wait. Getting him relaxed and into a rhythm was the first major task and, as he had promised, Carberry made for the inside rail and the least amount of traffic. Everywhere else the shortest way round is coveted, but at Aintree the drops over Becher's and Valentines are steepest on the inside. The more prudent usually angle away from the inside as they approach Becher's. Carberry practically had paint on his boot from scraping the rail.

Only from Becher's second time round did he start to move Bobbyjo into contention but from three out it was obvious the Irish runner was a major player. By then Scotland's Blue Charm and Richard Dunwoody's mount Call It A Day were also laying down their challenges. Remarkably, so was the 200-1 Irish outsider Merry People. John Qeally's horse looked to be going as well as anything until a crashing fall at the second last which Bobbyjo swerved to avoid. By now there was no more waiting required. Carberry switched to the outside, threw his horse at the last and set sail up the long run in. Past the Elbow he pushed for all he was worth until 100 yards from the line it was obvious Bobbyjo was clear. Standing up in the irons and waving his stick at the packed and cheering stands was a physical demonstration that could only hint at Carberry's emotions.

A lifetime had gone into this moment. That it should come to fruition on a horse trained by his father and nourished by the entire family made it a story that could have verged on the syrupy were it not for the abundant, raw and uncomplicated evidence of what it meant. Ireland's National Hunt population rarely do sentiment. But there was enough of it floating around in Liverpool that day to make the raucous celebrations that followed even more resonant. Bobbyjo returned to the famous old covered winner's enclosure and Carberry reached up, grabbed a timber rafter and swung himself off. He landed into an ocean of happy outstretched arms.

> Winning the National was fantastic. There hasn't been a day like it since. That was what I wanted since I was a kid. If there's one thing I would like to do it's to win it again. It's that good a feeling.

Tommy Carberry proclaimed his son to be a much better jockey than he ever was; he got through the interminable post-race interviews and tried to come to terms with having ascended the Aintree peak again. Paul Carberry immediately got to work on righting the previous night's wrong. A squad of pals dropped everything at home and flew to Liverpool. By five the following morning there were sightings of the National-winning rider performing a party piece entitled 'The Full Monty'. It involved gratuitous nudity on a table full of empty glasses. His modesty disappeared in no time and, having not put a foot wrong all day, no one was surprised that not one glass hit the floor. Alice was in wonderland.

It took only ten days for him to come crashing back to earth. Jump jockeys know that injuries are an inevitable part of their job but the closest Carberry has ever come to tragedy began with an innocuous fall while riding work on Meade's gallops. His horse stumbled, throwing him, and another horse travelling behind couldn't avoid the stricken figure. Dragging himself to his feet, he realised it was painful but nothing that couldn't be lived with. Sore ribs don't rate very highly when it comes to injury. That was a Tuesday. By the Saturday the pain was getting worse. Staying at Timmy Hyde's house near Cashel, Carberry was starting to get worried.

> I knew I was in trouble. I felt as weak as piss. Next thing I just collapsed. It was so hard to breathe. When the horse kicked me he drove the rib into my spleen. Only for the ambulance people coming with oxygen I was gone. They were talking about organising an ambulance to take me to Blackrock in Dublin but even though I didn't know what was wrong, I knew I wasn't able for a trip like that. The ambulance took me to Cashel Hospital and they operated on me there. I was told afterwards if I'd been another fifteen minutes, they wouldn't have been able to do anything.

His spleen was removed and it took five months before he was able to resume race-riding. In 2000 another broken leg put him back on the sidelines. That one stubbornly took its time about healing and the suggestion gained currency that Carberry was just too injury-prone. Even at the best moments, the spectre of injury was never far away. The opening race of the 2000 Cheltenham festival, the Supreme Novices Hurdle, featured an embryonic champion in Best Mate, as well as Sausalito Bay – Noel Meade's latest attempt to break his festival duck. This time luck went with him. Jim Culloty was not at his sharpest on Best Mate, and try as he might Sausalito Bay was too tough. Meade got down on his knees on entering the winner's enclosure ahead of his horse. Carberry wasn't too far from joining him.

The jockey had injured his spine in a fall at Navan two weeks before and a haematoma burst on his back halfway up the run in. 'It was as if someone had hit me with a sword,' he remembers. 'I was in so much pain I knew I wouldn't be able to ride for the rest of the week, so this was my only chance of a winner. I just put my head down and pushed through the pain.'

That kind of resilience only bolstered Meade's unwavering support for his jockey through all the injuries. The trainer believed that all Carberry needed was an injury-free run to become a champion. Finally in the 2001–02 season it came and winners simply flowed. By the end there were 113 and Carberry again emulated his father by becoming champion jockey. There were 116 more the following season in another championship-winning campaign. Nor did his commitments to Meade prevent him associating with some of the top horses seen on Irish racecourses in the last decade.

A win in the Hennessy at Leopardstown on board Florida Pearl in 2000 preceded an agonising defeat to his old friend Looks Like Trouble in the Gold Cup that year. Steeplechasing's Blue Riband also eluded him on Beef Or Salmon, but Michael Hourigan's popular horse did provide another Hennessy in 2006 and a pair of Lexus Chase wins (2004 and 2005), the first of which saw Carberry's exuberance get him into trouble again. With an ailing Best Mate struggling behind him, Beef Or Salmon bounded clear for a popular home victory. Whether it was the Anglo-Irish element, or attempts by Best Mate's more myopic supporters to compare him to the peerless Arkle, Carberry milked the situation by turning round to beckon the English horse to catch him. It might have been only fun but it smacked of rubbing the vanquished's noses in it. The terrible irony was that Carberry was the man on board Best Mate when the triple Gold Cup-winner died in action at Exeter less than a year later.

However, the horse that has generated the most headlines and the most flak is very definitely a Meade inmate. There are plenty who would suggest Harchibald should be an inmate of another type of institution, such is his reputation as a thief. Others, most notably the trainer himself, vehemently defend this most enigmatic of equine athletes as being too generous for his own good. As with most differences of opinion, the truth probably lies somewhere in the boring middle. Harchibald does race generously and he possesses a hurdling technique to die for. And maybe he does race so generously that there's nothing left when whips start cracking. But when it comes down to a scrap, he can make Frankie Howerd look like Conan the Barbarian.

Harchibald has won multiple Grade 1 prizes but dominating his CV will always be his failure in the 2005 Champion Hurdle. Stuck between two supreme battlers in Hardy Eustace and Brave Inca, the good and the bad of this maddening horse were played out in the space of 100 yards in front of a rapt audience of millions. Champion Hurdles are not supposed to be won on the bridle but that's what seemed to be happening as a motionless Carberry delivered Harchibald between his two rivals after the last flight. Halfway up the run in he still hadn't moved. On the face of it there could be only one winner. All it needed was for the horse to get an extra inch of rein and he would win with his head in his chest. But appearances are sometimes deceptive and never more so than with Harchibald.

Those familiar with his form knew Carberry was hanging on to very little and probably nothing. Conor O'Dwyer certainly suspected it. He drove Hardy Eustace for all he was worth. A hundred yards from the line, Carberry could delay the inevitable no longer. He asked Harchibald for one final lunge and got precisely nothing in response. Hardy Eustace went past the line a neck in front. The response to the ultra-popular winner was ecstatic. For the runner up there was only a torrent of bile and invective.

Even for someone with Carberry's laid-back approach to life, the level of abuse was unsettling. It started with cat-calls on the long walk back in front of the stands and continued with shouts in the parade ring. On television, criticism mounted. It sounded like the twittering of little birds compared to the empty chatroom bluster of those hiding behind online anonymity. Even those prepared to put by-lines on their view cranked it up a notch. Harchibald and Carberry were described as a perfect combination – a pair of strutting peacocks. At the end of the day, when his sister Nina won the Fred Winter Hurdle on Dabiroun, the immediate gag was that the wrong Carberry had been on Harchibald.

At the eye of this unnecessary storm, Carberry's response was full of courage: 'I should have waited longer!'

For this wonderfully instinctive talent, everything is 'feel' when it comes to riding a horse. As Meade appreciates more than anyone, an explanation for what Carberry does out on the track might not always be forthcoming. But a lot of jockeys can talk a good game. With Carberry the only language that really counts is the mysterious one that fizzes down the reins. No linguist has ever made the translation look easier or more natural.

Not so long ago, the BBC's Grand National coverage was enlivened when they sat down a group of top jockeys to help preview the big race. They included Carberry's old pal from those apprentice days, Tony McCoy, plus his great rivals in Ireland, Ruby Walsh and Barry Geraghty. At one stage the question was posed who was the best of them all. All replied: 'Paul Carberry.'

Those who grumble that he could have won so many more races had he taken the game more seriously miss the point. Carberry might indeed not have ridden as many winners as some others but that's to measure his career in cold statistics. That's what roundheads do. It's cold, calculating and ultimately as dull as dishwater. They might be worthy, and they may even be right, but they'll never have style. And as for regrets, any cavalier worth his salt will tell you, who cares about such things? Ultimately, really great talent finds happiness in its execution. Judged on that, there's no doubt that that famously impudent grin isn't fake.

Cheltenham Festival Winners

1993
Champion Bumper   Rhythm Section

1998
William Hill Trophy Chase   Unguided Missile

1999
Royal & SunAlliance Chase   Looks Like Trouble

2000
Supreme Novices Hurdle   Sausalito Bay

2002
William Hill Trophy Chase   Frenchmans Creek

2005
Pertemps Handicap Hurdle Final   Oulart
Grand Annual Chase   Fota Island

2006
SunAlliance Novice Hurdle   Nicanor
Champion Bumper   Hairy Molly

2008
Fred Winter Juvenile Handicap Hurdle   Crack Away Jack

2009
Supreme Novices Hurdle   Go Native

Other Major Winners include

1994
Royal Bond Novice Hurdle   Gambolling Doc

1995
Drinmore Novice Chase   Johnny Setaside

1996
John Hughes Trophy   Joe White
Tote Gold Trophy   Squire Silk

1997
Galway Plate   Stroll Home

1998
Irish Grand National   Bobbyjo
Swordlestown Cup   Direct Route
Maghull Novices Chase   Direct Route
Ericsson Chase   Dorans Pride

1999
James Nicholson Champion Chase   Florida Pearl
Aintree Grand National   Bobbyjo

2000
Hennessy Gold Cup   Florida Pearl

2001
Hatton's Grace Hurdle   Limestone Lad
John Durkan Chase   Florida Pearl

2002
Dr PJ Moriarty Chase   Harbour Pilot
Drinmore Novice Chase   Harbour Pilot

2003
Powers Gold Cup   Thari
Deloitte Novice Hurdle   Solerina

2004
Fighting Fifth Hurdle   Harchibald
Royal Bond Novice Hurdle   Wild Passion
Drinmore Novice Chase   Watson Lake
Christmas Hurdle   Harchibald
Lexus Chase   Beef Or Salmon

2005
Lexus Chase   Beef Or Salmon
Deloitte Novice Hurdle   Mr Nosie
Midlands Grand National   Philson Run
Bula Hurdle   Harchibald
Robin Cook Memorial Cup   Sir Oj

2006
Hennessy Gold Cup   Beef Or Salmon
Barry & Sandra Kelly Hurdle   Aran Concerto

2007

Fighting Fifth Hurdle	Harchibald
Hatton's Grace Hurdle	Aitmatov

2008

Powers Gold Cup	Conna Castle

2009

Deloitte Novices Hurdle	Pandorama

3

KEVIN MANNING

Kevin Manning hates talking about his weight. And his height. Which from a scribbler's point of view is annoying. Because no matter how many races the forty-one-year-old rider wins, they will always have to play second fiddle to the matter of how he sustains a career as a top class flat jockey. Since Manning's CV includes an Epsom Derby and a series of international Group 1 victories from Hong Kong to France and Britain, that only emphasises the Herculean achievement he manages daily in beating the scales. Or should that really be beating himself?

Weight is an issue for every jockey. Only the tiny and the fortunate are able to look at food and tuck in guilt free. Except this isn't guilt us ordinary punters with a surfeit of stretchy pants know only too well. Instead there is the nightmare of having to keep on the right side of that maddeningly unstable needle in the scales or else find another job. It's a world where every ounce up or down counts as victory and defeat. Where each morsel feels like a concession and every drop that passes down a parched throat has a bitter tang. Carbohydrate dreams clash with hollow-stomached reality and even the idea of chewing can make you giddy.

It's little wonder then that among the colourful silks and the thrill of the finish lies a darker reality. By definition it is behind the scenes, and equally definite is a haunting truth that the fight is with oneself, a weight battle that must be fought alone. Little wonder then also that so many jockeys have peered into parts of their souls that most of the rest of us hardly know exist. In these more emotionally incontinent times there is no shortage of people willing to bare their doubts and insecurities to the world. But the process which can end up with individual jockeys hating their already rung-dry bodies remains resolutely private.

It's an agony that has driven many to the edge. Some have gone beyond. Famously, the greatest rider of the Victorian age, Fred Archer, a thirteen-time champion jockey and five-time Derby winner, put his body through hell by wasting. Through the ages, riders have purged their systems with all forms of diuretics, steaming themselves to the verge of passing out or simply sticking fingers down their throats. Archer did all that and more. But when his wife died, depression caught hold of the finest jockey of the nineteenth century and he shot himself. Archer was twenty-nine. More modern but just as well-known names have also admitted to suicidal thoughts. Richard Dunwoody was still a teenager and yet to ride a race when his ambition to become a jockey led him to anorexia. The stories are legion, including one of a famous rider whose route home to Tipperary from the tracks around Dublin involved stopping at any number of burger joints, gorging on fast food before then stopping a few miles further down the road and vomiting the lot back up.

So, the wonder of Kevin Manning is just as much who he is as what he is. In bare physical terms the figures are remarkable. Manning may not be quite 6ft in height but the difference is hardly worth talking about. Whip thin he might be, but he still manages to weigh in at just over 8½ st. That's a good 3 st under his natural body weight. It's a frightening concept for the rest of us and the effort of fighting his body's demands is a daily battle that only his colleagues can truly understand. As a result, there's little point talking about it since it achieves nothing. Manning understands that only too well, but there is also a natural inclination towards keeping such matters to himself. In many others such reticence might veer towards moroseness but it is remarkable how Manning can fight the fight and still remain a fully paid up member of the human race.

That's what almost everyone in racing remarks about him, how approachable he is, how personable he can be, despite a weight regime that would be enough to excuse almost any type of self-obsessed behaviour. There may not be too many public utterances but not because he isn't a quietly articulate man with a nice line in self-depreciation. The only thing grim about Manning is his determination to view victory and defeat through the same emotionally level lens. Tooting a confident pre-race horn is not his style.

'Kevin is very popular because all the other jockeys know how hard he has to work. No one works harder,' believes the former champion jockey Christy Roche, who was Manning's predecessor as stable jockey to Jim Bolger. 'He has an unbelievable frame and when you're out there running and sweating every day, putting yourself through starvation, it is incredibly tough.'

Roche enjoyed a long and hugely successful career that took in Derby victories in France, England and Ireland but retirement came as a blessed relief. He cuts a stockier figure compared to his former colleague but controlling weight, and not revealing how hard it was, took over his life. 'I never let on I had a weight problem, and it was very important people didn't believe I had. I managed to keep it under wraps because if people believe you don't have a problem, they believe you are more healthy and strong and will ride better.'

Every day Roche had to work at the weight so much that by the time he got to the races and stood on the scales, and made whatever weight was required he'd let out a big sigh of relief that his work was done. 'Riding the six or seven horses afterwards was the easy part', he continues. 'I did it the old-fashioned way. It was running and the sauna – sweating all the time. In the end my problem was mental because I was always on a knife edge. Any little thing would trigger me off. And the thing was, there was no end to it. You couldn't end the sweating because if you did you were gone. Only those who can handle the problem that comes with weight will get to the top.'

That's why Manning's victory on New Approach in the 2008 Epsom Derby was greeted so warmly in the jockeys' room, even among those just beaten. In many ways a controversial race owing to the colt's late confirmation as an intended runner, the one resolutely positive outcome came from Manning's inspired ride. Jim Bolger, who is his jockey's father-in-law as well as his employer, described it as one of the great Epsom rides.

On a day when he was accused of a lot of things, the one accusation Bolger didn't have to contend with was of nepotism. Securing a winning run for New Approach, who for the first half of the race did as much as he could to lose it, was an exhibition of nerve and timing that the jockey's colleagues appreciated more than anyone else.

Characteristically Manning's reaction was polite and understated, while at the same time leaving no one in any doubt he would rather the focus was centred elsewhere. But repeated analysis of how he had gambled on securing a passage up the inner of Epsom's notoriously difficult straight only emphasised his skill. There was also the chance to examine Manning's face in slow motion replay as New Approach passed the line. Any exultation had to compete with dry-mouthed evidence of the headstrong colt's earlier energy-sapping desire to run faster than his jockey had wanted. Manning's parched lips demanded moisture. Measuring their demands against those of his job, however, is a task that by now Manning has down to a tee. Which isn't the same thing as saying it is easy.

> I don't have a set routine. I just know what I can and can't have. If there
> is a craving for something now, I just have a small amount of it, whereas
> before I tried so many diets. I also do a lot of walking and there's no
> doubt the weights going up in the last couple of years has made things a
> little easier. But the bottom line is that this is a way of life. You either deal
> with it or you don't. And as you get older you do start to mentally deal with
> it better. It doesn't get easier. You just handle it better. What I've found
> over the years is that it is definitely more of a mental struggle than
> a physical one.

Manning knows his body well enough to know what shape he's in even before getting on the scales. During the winter he never lets his weight get above 9 st. That means having to get off 5 lb when the season starts.

> When I was younger I used to let it get up to 9 st 7 lb during the winter but
> it took willpower to get that off. I don't think I could mentally deal with
> doing that now. I'd find it impossible.

Such a lifestyle would have seemed alien to Manning when he was growing up in Killsallaghan in north Co. Dublin in the early 1970s. Killsallaghan remains – just – a small community on the edge of Ireland's capital city. Back then its claim to fame was as the home of the Dreaper racing yard that housed champion steeplechasers like Flyingbolt, Royal Approach and the greatest of all, Arkle. It was conveniently close to Dublin airport, too, where Kevin's father, Jim Manning, worked as a store supervisor. As a sideline he leased up to 20 acres of land near home in order to grow vegetables for the markets in the city. His son was pressed into service at weekends and on holidays, to help him transport produce and sell it. They left home at 4.30 in the morning in order to be in town for five. It was a different world, busier than home. In the capital, as well as the divide between those from north or south of the River Liffey, there is a subtle but real difference between city dwellers and those from the county. 'Country Dub,' is how Manning laughingly describes himself: no culchie, but no townie either.

It was towards the country that Jim Manning gravitated in his spare time. Most weekends were spent at one of the racetracks around Dublin, the Metropolitan courses as they are called. He didn't have to drag his son along to the likes of Fairyhouse, Navan, Leopardstown or the Phoenix Park. Holidays coincided with festivals down the country like Galway and Listowel.

Kevin Manning was entranced by the atmosphere at the races. His father liked a bet but there was also the social side and always, in the parade ring and out on the track, were the horses. The family never had anything to do with them but the youngster was smitten enough for his parents to have bought him a pony. Some happy years were spent going hunting and experiencing the thrill of competition in show-jumping but it was speed that really grabbed the imagination. It was then that a fateful meeting was arranged.

By the late 1970s, Jim Bolger had already begun the training career that was to make him one of the dominant figures in Irish racing for the next three decades. Based in the Dublin suburb of Clonsilla, he was making an impact but was still not above doing a deal for a pony, and Jim Manning's son wanted an animal to go racing with. However, Bolger insisted he wouldn't sell a pony unless he was confident the youngster could handle it. A Saturday morning trip to Clonsilla opened up a new world. At this time there was still a busy training centre in the Phoenix Park on land that wasn't worth the sort of fortunes it would be a generation later. These were real racehorses and Bolger produced one for twelve-year-old Manning to sit on. He cantered it around and the seed of a professional life was planted. The Mannings left not having seen any pony but with an invitation for the boy to come back the following weekend. He was kept to the old experienced horses to begin with, but after a few months there was no need to remember the pony that in fact never appeared.

In 1982 fire ravaged Bolger's yard and the search for his own premises elsewhere began. The trainer viewed forty-one farms before he settled on Glebe House in Coolcullen on the Carlow-Kilkenny border. In December of that year, his horses moved from Dublin and also making the journey was K.J. Manning, apprentice jockey. Actually riding horses was never a problem, but already his shape was becoming an issue. 'I was tall, so getting organised on a horse was a problem at the start,' he remembers. It didn't take long to resolve itself and Manning rode his first winner on board Keynes at the Curragh in April 1983. The following year he became champion apprentice. Among the winners was an Irish Cambridgeshire success on Chamsky for Paddy Mullins. It was an auspicious start. Declan Gillespie remained Bolger's No.1 but there was plenty left for a hungry teenager.

Hunger, however, can come in different forms and ambition had to mix with its more literal cousin. The weight allowances, which are so important to apprentices, could be a mixed blessing. Expected to make low weights, Manning struggled to keep his still adolescent body under control. He remembers doing 7 st 10 lb for Noora Abu at the Curragh once. If that was tortuous, at least it was for a horse close to his heart. The mare was a prolific winner and ran up a sequence of seven victories in 1987, which included the Listed Ballycorus Stakes.

That year ended with a second apprentice title. Kieren Fallon fin-ished runner up. By now Bolger was a top trainer, with classics and international Group 1 victories under his belt. It was an intoxicating time at Coolcullen and one that exerted huge appeal for a young rider whose emotional pull had always been towards the flat rather than over jumps. Weight, however, had become such an issue that he spent a winter riding over hurdles. There were about forty rides and they were enough for him to know that the winter was not to his taste. Even now the memory of getting his weight back under control is enough to make any craving take second place.

'It was very, very difficult for him. He's a big guy and he had to work very hard. But he is a very single-minded man and he gets on with things, leads a really disciplined lifestyle and never moans,' his fellow apprentice Willie Supple remembered later. Another Bolger apprentice, Tony McCoy, has described Manning as the most dedicated jockey he has ever known, which is some compliment considering the source.

It started to pay off, however. In 1988 there was an unexpected bonus when Bolger decided to run Project Manager in the Epsom Derby and put up his twenty-one-year-old jockey. They finished ninth but prophetically Bolger welcomed him back with the words: 'That was your reconnaissance!' However, it was Christy Roche who was No.1 at Coolcullen during a glory period when Jet Ski Lady won the 1991 Epsom Oaks and St Jovite won the 1992 Irish Derby by a dozen lengths. If they were heady times for everyone else, there had to be an element of frustration for Manning, who nevertheless ended up staying at Bolger's, competing for rides with other talented young jockeys such as Seamus Heffernan and Ted Durcan. In 1993 Roche decided to leave and Bolger turned to his new son-in-law. After his marriage to Una, there were inevitable whispers of nepotism behind Manning's back but those in the know have never placed any credence in them.

'Just because Kevin is his son-in-law wouldn't mean a lot to Jim,' believes Roche. 'The way I see it, Jim Bolger sees Kevin Manning as his stable jockey first and foremost.' Bolger himself has declared bluntly: 'He's simply a top jockey. He knows it and I know it.'

And once the trainer knows something, it stays known. The earth's plates have been known to budge quicker than the opinions of a man whose combative style can provoke both admiration and dislike in equal measure. An owner and close friend, Harry Dobson, once described him as the only man he has ever met who has never had a moment of self-doubt. He also said Bolger's one weakness is that he is absolutely certain he is correct. That might not make him a candidate for the diplomatic corps but it does instil confidence in whomever he chooses to ride for him. Roche says: 'It may be a shock to many people but with all the trainers I rode for, Jim is probably the most under-standing of them all. Whatever else you say about him – he always backs his jockey.' It's a view his successor agrees with. But there also seems to be little evidence that the job of working with Bolger every day is one that encourages cosy familiarity. Throw in the family link and it is understandable that Manning also dislikes answering questions about his boss. Normally the 'firm but fair' line is issued and the matter is left at that. However, the relationship is interesting enough for the prickly questions to keep on coming.

> Business and the personal side of things are kept separate. There are days when he could drop in to see the kids, have a cup of tea, and racing is never discussed – ever. But if we're in the yard or at the races it's a different ball game. It's not difficult. We've had this working relationship for a long time, long before I got married. There might not be a lot of joking while we're working but there's a lot of trust. He trusts my judgement. In the parade ring before a race he might ask, 'What will you do here?' but that's basically it when it comes to tactics. It's left to me. If a plan doesn't come off, I hold my hands up, we'll discuss things, and he'll take it on board. I think a lot of people have the wrong idea of Jim, that he's very tough and hard to work for. It's actually simple. He wants things done 110 per cent right and to the best of your ability. Once you do that, he's fine. If you don't, then he will find someone else.

The new partnership immediately clicked, with a plentiful supply of winners mixed in with some quality. In 1994 the flying two-year-old filly Eva Luna delivered Manning a first Group 1 victory in the Phoenix Stakes at Leopardstown. Zavaletta and Perfect Imposter were other good winners that year. Desert Style was a Tetrarch and Phoenix Sprint victor in 1995, while Idris was a prolific Group race winner in 1996. However, there was nothing to equal the achievements of St Jovite & Co from earlier in the decade. Much of that had to do with the re-emergence of Ballydoyle as an international force. In the wake of Vincent O'Brien's retirement, Bolger was dominant: however, the rapidly increasing threat of his former pupil Aidan O'Brien threatened to sideline Coolcullen in the races that matter. Economically the Bolger-Manning team were trying to compete with the most powerful operation in the world. Occasionally, though, there were reminders to the general public of what could be done with worthwhile ammunition.

Margarula began 2002 running in handicaps and getting beaten. Any ideas of classic glory seemed fanciful. A venture into Group company in the Pretty Polly Stakes yielded an honourable fourth placing but nothing to make her 33-1 odds for the Irish Oaks seem generous. O'Brien's Epsom runner up Quarter Moon was a hot favourite for the Oaks and early in the straight she looked to take control of the race. However, Margarula, carrying the colours of Bolger's wife, Jackie, emerged from the pack. Appreciating every inch of the mile and a half she upset the odds to provide the Curragh with an unlikely family success. 'Even though she was 33-1, it was no big surprise to us,' remembers Manning. 'The way she had worked after the Pretty Polly we couldn't see her out of the first three. It was a big step up but fillies can do that.'

A couple of years later another filly started to improve dramatically but Alexander Goldrun was no one-run wonder. Manning was to win ten races on the delicate-looking but iron-hearted bay, including five Group 1s. Longchamp's Prix de l'Opera was the first and was followed by a perfect conclusion to 2004 when emerging best in a thrilling finish to the Hong Kong Cup. 'We were full of confidence going out there,' Manning remembers. 'She had a huge chance after winning the Opera. But her work over there started to get more and more spectacular so she became a filly with an outstanding chance that everyone was expecting to win.' That only proved Manning's ability to get the job done when it really counts. But individual glory is far from a priority compared to what he sees as a relatively minor input into a complicated team process.

I might only appear in the yard in April each season and everyone else has been on the move since January. Three months of work will have gone in to the horses and the trainer knows at that stage what he has. It's only then that I'm legged up to give an opinion. It's the lads doing the groundwork that put so much in. In the spring, I ride out most mornings which is important, especially for getting to know the two-year-olds. It all comes down to feel in the end and that's very hard to explain. But you know when you've ridden a good one. Then it's my job to give Jim an opinion on what ground the horse might like or his best trip or what kind of ability he has. After a while you get the feel for a horse so much, you know if there's something even slightly off with him. It's a series of little things like that which count.

All Manning needed to bring out his best were more opportunities at the top level. Alexander Goldrun did her bit, winning both the Pretty Polly and the Nassau in 2005, and only failing by a nose in an epic Goodwood finish with Ouija Board to bring off a Nassau double in 2006. Overall, however, such dramatics were viewed by many as something of a glorious swansong for Bolger. With Ballydoyle getting ever more dominant, the trainer simply lacked the financial muscle to compete consistently at the top level. But it was Ballydoyle that also helped towards a remarkable change of fortune.

As well as training, Bolger has been a prominent bloodstock breeder over the years. Characteristically, that branch of the sport has also seen plenty of evidence of his ability to stick to an opinion. In terms of stallion choices, the results were not always successful. Bolger heavily backed the Coolmore stallion Last Tycoon, a top sprinter-miler as a racer, and got his fingers burned. The retirement of the 2001 dual-Derby and King George winner Galileo saw him take the plunge on another Coolmore new boy. This time he got it right with a vengeance. As a son of Sadlers Wells out of the Arc winner Urban Sea, Bolger believed Galileo was a 'no-brainer' choice to be a star stallion. But it is easy to forget now that Galileo wasn't an immediately attractive prospect to breeders. His best form was at a mile and a half as a three-year-old which was hardly an ideal commercial proposition. Nevertheless, he started at Coolmore at a fee of €50,000. Bolger thought it a bargain and ploughed his money in. That unfamiliarity with the concept of doubt began to pay off as soon as Galileo's offspring started cantering at home. One in particular always stood out.

The lads in the yard were talking about Teofilo before I ever sat on him. From Day One the vibes were good. He always had the makings of a proper horse. I sat on him in early May (2006) and the feel he gave me was fantastic. You can ride a dozen two year olds in a morning but you will always know the good one, even if they're backward. It's that feel thing again. He had what you want in every horse – ability, temperament, scope, appearance, everything.

Teofilo began his career with a maiden win at the Curragh, followed up in the Group 3 Tyros Stakes at Leopardstown and then returned to HQ to land both the Group 2 Futurity and the Group 1 National Stakes. In the latter, he met the already proven Holy Roman Emperor, the best of Aidan O'Brien's two-year-old team, and beat him comfortably. Bolger declared Teofilo, named after the triple Olympic boxing champion Teofilo Stevenson, the best he had ever trained and nominated Newmarket's Dewhurst Stakes as the final start of his juvenile career. In between, Holy Roman Emperor scooted up in a Group 1 at Longchamp and that was enough to guarantee a re-match at Newmarket. At the end of an epic struggle, in which Teofilo was headed by his Ballydoyle rival inside the final furlong, Manning got his horse back up in the final strides to edge the verdict.

It was enough for the handsome colt to be made clear winter favourite for both the 2007 Newmarket Guineas and Epsom Derby. Bolger even dared to start talking about a possible Triple Crown, taking in the St Leger as well. Sure the best was yet to come, Manning started thinking about classic races that up to then had seemed out of reach.

In the following spring nothing happened to change his mind. Teofilo thrived and so did his jockey's dreams. But on the eve of the Guineas, disaster struck. Teofilo suffered muscle problems which meant Newmarket was off the agenda. A few weeks later the same conclusion had to be drawn about Epsom. Through the summer it still wasn't possible to get Teofilo back to race fitness. The decision was taken to retire him to Sheikh Mohammed's Darley stallion operation, unbeaten but with his vast racing potential also untapped. The vibes Manning got from him in the spring left him in no doubt Teofilo was the real article.

He had everything going for him but especially temperament. I remember in the parade ring before the National Stakes, one of his bandages came loose and we had to stop at the gates out to the racecourse. He must have stood there for two minutes while it was sorted out and he never batted an eyelid. For a horse tuned up to race and all set to go, that was amazing. I had no doubts he would win the Derby for me. So when he got his injury I said to myself my chance was gone. And then the other fellah arrived.

The other fellah was New Approach, another son of Galileo that Bolger purchased for €430,000 as a yearling. Out of the mare Park Express, whom Bolger trained to win the 1986 Irish Champion Stakes, New Approach was a completely different type of animal from Teofilo. Instead of a malleable temperament, the big chestnut possessed a mind of his own. Whether it came to walking under an archway at the Curragh or needing to be ponied to the start by a stable companion, New Approach did things on his own terms. But beneath the quirks lay an engine that had Bolger making comparisons to one of the great American champions of the twentieth century, Secretariat. He also resolved to take New Approach down the same juvenile route he had sent Teofilo. The result was the same, an unbeaten five-race two-year-old career that crowned a new European champion. Manning could again anticipate classic success. But by now he'd had more than a taste of it already.

Finsceal Beo, a contemporary of Teofilo, had been the top European juvenile filly of 2006 with wins in the Prix Marcel Boussac and the Rockfel

Stakes. Unlike the colt, the classic spring of 2007 turned out to be bountiful for her. The rangy chestnut's name roughly translates as 'living legend' and after scampering home in the Newmarket 1,000 Guineas it seemed entirely appropriate. Then Bolger outlined a plan that would make her unique. The triple crown of Guineas races in England, France and Ireland had never been completed. But the timing allowed at least the possibility of Finsceal Beo bringing it off. A furlong from home at Longchamp and the second leg looked in the bag as she hit the front. But her famous finishing kick didn't seem quite as effective on the soft turf and Darjina remorselessly bridged the gap to put her nose in front on the line. 'French soft is different ground to our soft. It rides that bit deeper and when I pulled her out she couldn't put the race away as quickly as she normally would,' Manning remembers ruefully. Sure enough, at the end of a remarkable month, Finsceal Beo returned to the Curragh and won the Irish Guineas in a tight finish.

New Approach's potential was enough for Sheikh Mohammed to buy into the horse and he would race in the green colours of the Sheikh's wife, Princess Haya. His classic impact began even before a race was run. Never one to dilute his views for any audience, Bolger baldly told a mainly British press gathering at his stables that the Epsom Derby didn't figure among his priorities for the upcoming season. The two weeks between the Irish 2,000 Guineas and Epsom was just too reckoned and so New Approach would target the Irish Guineas and the Irish Derby, with his first run being in the Newmarket Guineas. He also argued that an Epsom success did little for a horse's future stud value. Not unsurprisingly the reaction to this in the UK was less than ecstatic. The feeling was that a race already on the ropes had just been dealt another body blow. But no one could be in any doubt about Bolger's thinking.

New Approach got just edged out of the Newmarket Guineas by Henrythenavigator in a display that normally would have screamed potential Derby winner. Bolger, however, again ruled out Epsom. Very fast ground prevailed at the Curragh for the Irish Guineas and again Henrythenavigator emerged best. New Approach, it seemed, would have to wait for the Irish Derby to gain that elusive classic. However, his name remained among the Epsom entries, because of what Bolger insisted was a clerical error, and the weekend before the Derby it emerged that the Irish horse would indeed run at Epsom after all. Bolger was accused of treating punters with contempt after repeatedly going out of his way to insist that Epsom was not on New Approach's agenda. His response to the subsequent furore was to feel sorry for those unable to cope with a little change.

To say the least it became a public relations disaster, but Manning's instinctive distrust of the limelight came to his aid. Happy to stay out of the immediate problem, it helped him focus on what was bound to be a tricky ride. New Approach's style in both Guineas was to race from the front. That would be a big ask over a mile and a half. Asking him to settle, though, would risk a fight that might ruin his chance. Behind it all the Irish jockey also knew that losing risked accusations of how Godolphin's Frankie Dettori might have done better. A condition of sale, however, had been that Manning retained the ride instead of Godolphin's No.1.

New Approach was what he was. There's no secret he was a hard horse to manoeuvre and he gave me a terrible hard time in the Derby, pulling and fighting me. When he did spit it out after seven furlongs, I was amazed at the amount of horse under me. Going down to Tattenham Corner, it was unbelievable how he was travelling. I knew I had everything in front of me covered. Frankie was in front of me on Rio De La Plata and while I knew he was a doubtful stayer, I also knew he had the ability to take me to two out. Even though he'd pulled early on, I knew from six out he'd get home all right. It was wonderful passing the line. The Derby is like the English National. It's the race every kid dreams of when they start riding. It's something to dream about but you never think you'll get on a horse good enough.

Immediately afterwards, the pre-race controversy refused to go away but there was unanimity concerning the brilliance of the winning ride. Manning didn't linger long, leaving quickly in order to get to Paris for the following day's French Derby. Christy Roche remembers ringing him in the taxi. 'I told him that whatever other races he might win, the Epsom Derby will be the one he remembers. I'm not saying it is better than the French Derby or the Irish Derby but there is something about the thing,' he recounts. It wasn't long before there were more Group 1 terms of reference for that theory to be tested.

Lush Lashes, a daughter of who else but Galileo, had failed to act around Epsom's gradients when starting favourite for the Oaks. It didn't take long for her to prove the quality that allowed her to win one million euro for her only two-year-old start in the Goffs Million.

Being dropped back to a mile for the Coronation Stakes at Royal Ascot was a big ask but the summer of 2008 was a true purple patch for the Manning-Bolger team. That point was emphasised at the start of the day when the jockey rode his first ever winner at the Royal meeting with Cuis Ghaire's impressive success in the Albany Stakes. The odds-on favourite briefly appeared to be in trouble before outpowering Penny's Gift. It was a perfect confidence-booster ahead of the Coronation and Lush Lashes didn't let the side down, leading well over a furlong out to prove much too good for Infallible and Carribean Sunset. Typically, Manning happily surrendered any post-race limelight to Bolger. His responses to any 'how do you feel?' enquiries immediately after a race are usually perfunctory. Away from intrusive microphones a different picture emerges, of a quietly confident man who is simply uninterested in the media hype that inevitably accompanies success at the top level.

> I don't feel any need for that kind of attention. I know I'm fortunate to be riding these Group 1 horses and it's a great feeling when they win. But they haven't changed my life or my lifestyle. Whatever race I win, I still come home to my wife and kids and that's the important part. Reading about myself is simply not something I like. Too much of it can make people think there are nothing but ups in this game and that can make the downs seem worse.

An immediate down came when New Approach was ruled out of the Irish Derby through injury. Unlike Teofilo, this wasn't career-threatening and the headstrong chestnut returned to action in the Juddmonte International – run at Newmarket when York became waterlogged. New Approach again pulled far too hard in the early stages and had to settle for third behind Duke Of Marmalade. But the race helped put him right for the Irish Champion Stakes. A heavy odds-on favourite, the Derby winner duly won, but only by half a length from the demonstrably inferior Traffic Guard. Many were left unimpressed but Manning was confident there was plenty left in the tank. New Approach duly proved the point in style a month later when running away with the English Champion Stakes at Newmarket. On the same day Intense Focus secured another Dewhurst success when emerging best in a desperate finish. Even Manning allowed himself a smile of satisfaction at a Group 1 double.

It brought to an end a season that yielded, in all, seven of those vital Group 1 victories for the Bolger-Manning team. Lush Lashes contributed three of them and proved her remarkable versatility into the bargain. Before the mile Matron Stakes at Leopardstown, she landed the Yorkshire Oaks at a mile and a half and to most eyes was a desperately unlucky loser in the Nassau over ten furlongs. Manning looked to be in Position A following the eventual winner, Halfway To Heaven, but ended up a classic unlucky Goodwood loser. Repeatedly denied a run, Lush Lashes still put in one desperate lunge and just failed to succeed. Her jockey returned to the sound of critics sharpening their pencils but Bolger's famous loyalty to his jockeys came to the fore. Dismissing what would have been a coveted Group 1 victory as 'one of those things that happen' is the kind of support that many other jockeys have failed to get over the years.

It's a not inconsiderable plus for a man whose dedication to the job of passing the winning post in front shows no sign of weakening. The same comment can apply to the strength of will needed simply to get into a position to do so. The pay off in recent years has been a collection of major international victories that Manning feels are a more than adequate compensation. But no one can argue they haven't been earned the hard way.

Classic Wins

2002
Irish Oaks   Margarula

2007
English 1,000 Guineas   Finsceal Beo
Irish 1,000 Guineas   Finsceal Beo

2008
Epsom Derby   New Approach

Other Major Winners include

1994
Phoenix Stakes   Eva Luna

2004
Prix de l'Opera   Alexander Goldrun
Hong Kong Cup   Alexander Goldrun

2005
Pretty Polly Stakes   Alexander Goldrun
Nassau Stakes   Alexander Goldrun

2006
Pretty Polly Stakes   Alexander Goldrun
National Stakes   Teofilo
Dewhurst Stakes   Teofilo
Prix Marcel Bousac   Finsceal Beo

2007
Phoenix Stakes   Saoirse Abu
Moyglare Stud Stakes   Saoirse Abu
National Stakes   New Approach
Dewhurst Stakes   New Approach
Goffs Fillies Million   Lush Lashes

2008

Coronation Stakes	Lush Lashes
Yorkshire Oaks	Lush Lashes
Matron Stakes	Lush Lashes
Irish Champion Stakes	New Approach
English Champion Stakes	New Approach
Dewhurst Stakes	Intense Focus

4

BARRY GERAGHTY

There is a 'C' word that has trailed Barry Geraghty throughout his career – confidence. The man is full of the stuff. Not in any brash way like Cristiano Ronaldo, but it's there all the same. Unlike the self-confidence of Portugal's most famous footballer, Geraghty's is more subtle, clothed in an easy manner and tempered by the demands of a career that punishes presumption the way Ronaldo goes to town on a second division defence. The 'C' word that first popped into your head has been tossed at him too no doubt, but that's a hazard that briefly escapes only those who attempt the futile exercise of being all things to all men. Since he is in possession of a fully defined personality that manages to give every impression of not caring a hoot what anyone thinks of him, Geraghty treats those occasional brickbats with weary indulgence. That's another 'C' word that sticks to him. Whether it's with a careless shrug or a full-watt grin, he usually manages to 'charm' his way out of any confrontation. It's maddening really.

Most of us know at least one of these infuriating beasts who manage to make life look ridiculously simple. By right Geraghty should be very easy to hate. Hugely successful, he has managed to win almost every major National Hunt race in these islands and is still only thirty. That he has done it while exuding a casual attitude that makes other men grind their teeth with jealousy is made even more unbearable by the fact that much of racing's female population tend to get very girly indeed around him. Articulate, funny and possessed of a cheery optimism that everything will work out fine, there is a lot here to resent, all of which makes his trick of remaining a likeable character all the more disconcerting.

Oscar Wilde wrote that people can be divided into either the charming or the tedious. There is certainly little doubt which side Geraghty falls on. That disinclination to take either himself or his profession too seriously may be a long way from the full picture but it does make for an attractive attitude. 'Pressure is for tyres,' was his famous counter-thrust to some rather po-faced eve-of-Cheltenham interrogation. Little wonder then that his personality has reached beyond racing's borders too.

In 2003 he picked up RTE's sports personality of the year award after a vintage season that included becoming just the third jockey up to then to ride five winners at a Cheltenham festival, a feat topped up just weeks later with a memorable victory on Monty's Pass in the Aintree Grand National. It is one of those prizes that generate more publicity than its actual value merits, but racing still wrapped it tightly to its bosom. Pitted against Geraghty were household names like rugby player Keith Wood, soccer's Damien Duff and the Gaelic Games legend D.J. Carey. Yet the jockey won out. It's a common misconception outside Ireland that racing holds a much more prominent place in the sporting affections of general society than it actually does. In fact this was a rare foray into the sporting mainstream by a racing figure in possession of a fully functioning and distinguishable personality. Geraghty for his part did his duty and said all the right things, while at the same time leaving no one worrying that he might have his head turned. After all, that would not have been cool.

Our first 'C' word, though, is still the most relevant. Only the more bovine are without conceit of some sort and no one has ever got to the summit of a sport without a healthy measure of confidence in their own abilities. In racing terms, though, it's rarely as influential on performance as Geraghty can manage. More than one of his colleagues has pointed out over the years how he rides every horse as if it is a good horse. That may not fit with the reality of the more moderate performers underneath him, but there have been times when very average horses have been inspired by that mysterious transmission of belief down the reins. On the really good ones, the impact can be remarkable. There have been plenty of those, with the Gold Cup and dual-King George winner Kicking King accompanied by star names such as Iris's Gift, Macs Joy, Punjabi and, best of all, Moscow Flyer. A jockey's impact on a top horse is impossible to put in percentage terms but one thing is certain: Moscow Flyer & Co. never received any negative vibes when it counted. The bigger the occasion, the better Geraghty likes it.

> That's me as a person, and me as a rider. I approach most things like that. I'm a great lad for talking my own chances up – for myself as much as anyone else. I rarely see the negative in things. It's the same away from racing. Sometimes I have to get reined back a bit. But at the same time I don't go into the doldrums if things don't work out. You see some fellahs after they've been beaten in races and they're absolutely gutted. We all get our disappointments but if it happens, it happens. There's not a lot anyone can do once it's over. It's the same with everything in life. There's no point hopping your head off a wall over it.

Such perspective on the business of passing a red lollipop in front of everyone else can be misinterpreted sometimes. A reluctance to indulge in stony-faced introspection led to accusations that Geraghty doesn't take things seriously enough: that his laid-back manner and interest in subjects beyond the racing game meant he didn't care. Usually that comes from the more witless, who mistake dourness for substance. In reality, Geraghty's lightness of touch both in and out of the saddle is a major reason why he gets it right more than most. That perspective is a positive boon when the pressure is at its height around Cheltenham, Punchestown or Liverpool. It's no coincidence that he usually gets it right when it really counts on the big stage.

The top English trainer Nicky Henderson would have taken such a temperament into account when searching for a new jockey to replace the just-retired Mick Fitzgerald in 2008. A lot of potential candidates actually lived in Lambourn, where he's based, or at least in the country. But Henderson played his hunch and contacted the jockey based in Co. Meath. It has worked out perfectly for both parties. Geraghty continues to live in Ireland but has got very familiar with nearby Dublin airport as he crosses the Irish Sea at least once a week during the winter. The pay-off for Henderson came with interest at Cheltenham 2009 as his new jockey engineered a 22-1 scoop of the Champion Hurdle on Punjabi. Back in third was the Henderson-trained favourite Binocular but although it was a desperately close finish, with Celestial Halo between the pair, it was Geraghty who somehow, yet again, found those vital few inches that matter.

Sure enough, completing the clean-sweep of Cheltenham's champion-ship races produced a shrug and a grin from Geraghty which, try as he might, couldn't quite disguise the sense of accomplishment.

Big races have always been part of his life though. In 1927, Laurence Geraghty bred the mighty Golden Miller, winner of five consecutive Cheltenham Gold Cups and who remains the only horse ever to win the Gold Cup and the Grand National in the same year. Decades later, his grandson grew up on the family property in Drumree with the legend of the great horse a permanent fixture of his childhood. The box where the history-maker was foaled was called the Golden Miller stable. It wasn't any kind of shrine: just what it was known as. Sheep were kept in there sometimes, then horses when his father took out a trainer's licence and opened a riding school. With three boys and three girls around the place, mucking in and mucking out was not a problem. Ross Geraghty, an older brother, also became a professional jockey and had his greatest moment in 2002 when The Bunny Boiler won the Irish Grand National. And always there was the Golden Miller story to remind them of where they came from.

There were books about him around the place and watching Gold Cups and Grand Nationals on television was more interesting because of him. I remember the year Garrison Savannah won the Gold Cup (1991) and tried for the Grand National a few weeks later. It didn't bother me particularly but we watched the race at my granny's and she'd have cut the legs off Garrison Savannah halfway up the run in. She was dead happy when Seagram went past him.

At fourteen, an already waning interest in school was pushed further into the background when Geraghty started pony racing. By now his father, known as 'Tucker', couldn't help but notice how the boy was a natural on a horse. There was a poise that no manual or coach could teach. It was just there. So 'Tucker' got in touch with his old friend Noel Meade, who provided a first racecourse ride in the autumn of 1996. A couple of months later, a first winner came when Stagalier won the EBF mares maiden hurdle at Down Royal. By now, Meade too was coming to the conclusion that his pal's young fellah was a bit different. The trainer loved all that dash and bravado in a race but burgeoning success wasn't exactly increasing the emerging jockey's shyness. 'A cocky little bastard' was Meade's exasperated verdict on one occasion and that variant on the confidence theme stuck for a while. With some it might have been a serious negative to overcome. Geraghty, however, was so good that his rougher edges were smoothed without any reduction of momentum.

A first significant success came with Miss Orchestra's Midlands Grand National at Uttoxeter in 1998; the winner was trained by Jessica Harrington. The victory cemented a link that was soon to pay off much more spectacularly. A claiming title quickly followed and almost immediately a chance at the real thing in the 1999–2000 season. Geraghty was supposed to go on a jockeys' tour of Australia that summer but, just before it, Meade's stable jockey, Paul Carberry, had a bad spleen injury that put him on the sidelines.

> Noel put me up on a lot of his and I pulled out of the tour. It was terrible for Paul but it was a good opportunity for me. I'd had a few winners already and was in a good position so I thought I'd kick on and make the most of it until Paul came back. It's the same in anything. If you want to get to the top of your job, you've got to get your arse in gear, and I deliberately set my sights on becoming champion jockey.

Once again, evidence came to the fore of how formidable an opponent the quick-witted new kid on the block could be. Establishing an early lead in the table, he made the most of that momentum to top the table with eighty winners. As always, winners provoked even more winners and Geraghty made the most of them.

> This is a job where it's important to be fashionable, have the owners asking for you instead of you asking owners, and the championship was important. A lot of lads say they're not interested in it until about a month before the end when they up the ante. But that ante is there all the time. The likes of Ruby Walsh and Davy Russell aren't driving around the country riding average horses just for fun. That's what I was doing that season. It's probably where Noel came up with his 'cocky little bastard' thing. I wouldn't have seen any reason why I shouldn't be champion jockey. I didn't feel out of my depth in any way.

His self-assurance wasn't misplaced. At twenty, he was Ireland's champion jockey. Numerically the code was cracked, but true top-flight jockeys are judged on top-class rides. Geraghty couldn't have known for sure, but one of the championship contributors was a horse that would change his life.

Moscow Flyer didn't always have star quality. In four bumper starts the best he could manage was a pair of third places. But he proved a very different proposition over obstacles. A first Grade 1 prize fell to him and his young jockey in December 1999 in the Royal Bond Hurdle at Fairyhouse. On the same day Geraghty also landed the Drinmore on Alexander Banquet but it was Moscow who would go on to have a long relationship with stardom. What's ironic now is that for many race fans the athletic bay with the white splodge between his eyes filled the role of villain during his second season over hurdles. He became one of the few horses to claim the scalp of Istabraq when taking advantage of the triple Champion Hurdle-winner's last flight fall in the December Festival Hurdle at Leopardstown. A few weeks later a re-match fizzled out at the second last of the AIG Irish Champion Hurdle when it was Moscow Flyer's turn to fall; that year's foot and mouth outbreak finished any chance of a decider when Cheltenham was called off. But the more astute had seen enough. Istabraq's jockey Charlie Swan wasn't exactly heartbroken when Jessica Harrington declared that Moscow was to go novice chasing. Geraghty reckoned that three Grade 1 wins over hurdles had been just a warm up.

Every fellah needs a good horse in their career and he was mine. Even when I was riding him, I knew he would leave a void when he finished up but it ended up being some void. He really was a horse in a million. I remember going down to the start at Leopardstown one Christmas and Carberry shouting over that I was 'some poxy fucker', steering this horse round for a sixty or seventy grand race. I couldn't really argue with him. Every time he ran in Ireland he was money on and when he went to England he still ended up winning.

He was actually easier to ride on the big days. Especially in the races in England there would always be pace. Once there was pace, he settled and we could concentrate on beating Azertyuiop or whoever it was. It was different in those races at home when he'd be up against small fields on heavy ground and everyone expected us to win easy. He was always taking a pull in them because it was so easy for him. He'd end up pulling and dragging, looking at fellahs standing at the wings, messing around and not concentrating. That's why sometimes those races were more of a challenge. Moscow Flyer had too much time to think and that's when he'd end up forgetting to jump.

It was actually only when he won at Aintree much later that I was able to come back to Jessie and say he was becoming a nice ride. That was the one day he found himself against not great horses and still he settled and did things properly, not pulling my arms out. Up to then he was a nightmare in the lesser races – but a good nightmare!

For much of his career over fences it really did seem like the only danger to Moscow Flyer was himself. The portents were there from the start when making his chasing debut at Fairyhouse in October 2001. For a Grade 1 hurdler it should have been a cakewalk, especially for a horse so obviously capable of jumping brilliantly. But almost as if it was too easy, he took his eye off the job and crashed out five fences from home. As he watched the horse get up and gallop away, Geraghty was torn between frustration and gratitude that everything was OK. The Moscow Flyer love affair was never going to be straightforward and a spooky pattern started to develop.

Three quick wins got the novice wagon back on track but his Cheltenham prep was ruined by a fall five out at Leopardstown. At the festival itself, though, there were no hitches, and the horse pulled four lengths clear of Seebald to provide his jockey with a first success around the famous course. A hugely exciting novice career ended with a win at Punchestown. Already he was favourite for the 2003 Queen Mother Champion Chase.

A winning return the following season was followed by a disaster at Sandown in the Tingle Creek Chase when a loose horse ended Moscow Flyer's race in the early stages. By some freakish coincidence this habit of failing to complete every fourth race would continue through the height of his career. When he stood up, he won. But the timing of when he didn't was uncanny. At least the Tingle Creek got it out of the way that season and, sure enough, the following March Ireland's outstanding two-miler was crowned the Champion Chase winner at Cheltenham with a seven-length defeat of Native Upmanship. Equally surely, after three outstanding wins, he then unseated his jockey at Punchestown.

If Geraghty was sore about that indignity, the pain must have battled with surprise at such an anti-climactic finale to the finest period of his riding career. Moscow had been the Cheltenham centrepiece, but four other winners had made it a festival like no other. Youlneverwalkalone for J.P. McManus in the William Hill Trophy was accompanied by Inching Closer in the Pertemps Hurdle, Spectroscope in the Triumph and Spirit Leader in the County. The festival was still a three-day affair then, and, as he left that Thursday night, even Noel Meade might have forgiven him for being just a little bit cocky.

It was one of those runs where things kept happening. Spirit Leader I thought had too much weight. It was the last race of the meeting, so I dropped her in and doddled round, you know, doing my bit but still fairly content with my lot. Four wins was something else. And up she comes. That's what I mean about how things kept happening.

The sensation lasted to Aintree where a Grade 1 victory on the rangy grey novice hurdler Iris's Gift proved only a warm up to the main act. Monty's Pass was trained in Co. Cork by the point to point stalwart Jimmy Mangan, and had proved his ability to cope with the monster Grand National fences when runner up in the Topham the previous year; the world's most famous chase had been his target ever since. Confidence in the horse grew even more with the ground drying out. Mangan was as hopeful as anyone steeped in the vagaries of the Munster point to point scene could be, and Geraghty wasn't talking down his chances either. Both, however, were in the ha'penny place compared to Mike Futter. The guiding light of the Dee Racing Syndicate that owned Monty's Pass was an Englishman living in the North of Ireland who made his money from running bingo halls. Having steadily backed the horse from 40-1 down to his SP of 16-1, Futter stood to win over three quarters of a million sterling if Monty's Pass and Geraghty got it right. Even with the tapes about to go up, he still couldn't see anything upsetting his gamble. And he was right.

> I fancied my horse out of the way that year and he gave me a brilliant ride. I really was as confident as you can be in the National. He was always cruising and we just kicked on from the second last. I suppose it was nice to do it because of the whole Golden Miller thing but I didn't really look at it that way. I wasn't trying to match anything. It's just that everyone wants to win the National. That's the race you look at as a kid and then head out tearing around on the ponies pretending you're at Aintree. Coming to the Elbow, though, and being able to wave to the stands with a couple of hundred yards to go is a fair feeling.

The view from the summit of your profession when you're just twenty-three is a pretty intoxicating one. Even in a vintage crop of young Irish jockeys, Geraghty stood out. That confidence thing was irrepressible. Naturally articulate and engaging anyway, he was not daunted by the spotlight. There was always a quip to keep everyone happy. Quizzed about his interests outside of racing, he memorably recounted a trip to the fights – 'but you'll never find me taking part in the boxing. I'm a lover, not a fighter!' A ravenous media lapped up the cavalier spirit who was good for a quote and, remarkably for a modern professional sportsman, seemed to be lapping up the attention. There were stories of going on the piste just weeks before Cheltenham – 'but no black runs' – tales of his business interests in pubs and clubs and always that determination to keep the sport in perspective. It was an intoxicating mix and, with the benefit of hinsight, Jessica Harrington's reaction to the RTE award suggested he had been the value bet of the year to win: 'He's young, he's good-looking and he's on top of his sport. And he comes across as a real nice guy. What more could they want?'

What Paul Nicholls had reportedly wanted was to make Geraghty his stable jockey but with prize-money levels increasing rapidly in Ireland, switching to the daily grind in Britain was not attractive. Besides, making the short hop across the Irish Sea on Saturdays and returning home for Sundays promised the best of both worlds. It seemed a charmed existence, an impression deepened when a second championship came his way in the 2003–04 season. But flying so high inevitably invites flak, and Moscow Flyer's jumping frailties cropped up at exactly the wrong time. After three wins in the run up to Cheltenham 2004, a much-anticipated clash with Azertyuiop in the Champion Chase fizzled out at the fourth last when the champion unseated his rider. The following day Iris's Gift landed a momentous victory over Baracouda in the World Hurdle but, after cleaning up the previous year, this festival left a salty taste in the mouth.

Criticism is an occupational hazard for any rider and Geraghty's innate confidence in a race means he can be a target for grandstand jockeys. Sometimes criticism comes from more qualified sources. Michael O'Brien is famously direct with those riding for him and even after partnering Essex to win the 2005 Pierse Hurdle, the trainer left Geraghty in no doubt that he thought he had committed for home far too early. Four months later O'Brien was fuming after Forget The Past was run out of the Powers Gold Cup by Like-A-Butterfly's late rally. It's an argument not confined to one man either. Characteristically, though, it appears to wash off the jockey's back. Since he's the one actually on the horse, it's hardly unreasonable for him to expect to read the ebb and flow of a race better than anyone else. Sitting out the back and pouncing late is all very fine when it works but one mistake can ruin any plan.

And then there is that confidence element: there has been far too much success for anyone to dismiss the impact of Geraghty's belief in the animal underneath him. It might not be a rational, black and white argument but he isn't on board particularly rational beasts. Race-riding has so much to do with that annoyingly vague concept of 'feel' that backing the man at the wheel is usually the best policy. And it's not as if Geraghty can't change tack. Brave Inca may have won the 2006 Champion Hurdle but those waiting tactics employed by Geraghty on the runner up, Macs Joy, were a model. Delivered perfectly from off the pace, the little horse couldn't battle past the winner but he got every chance to try.

No one appreciates that big race temperament more than Tom Taaffe. Possessed of a name synonymous with Gold Cups, Grand Nationals and the greatest chaser of them all, Arkle, this former jockey turned trainer isn't shy of airing his views to riders when he feels they've messed up. So it was no coincidence that it was Geraghty he turned to when the giant frame of a burgeoning talent called Kicking King started to fill him with the feeling he might be in possession of something exceptional.

'Barry has got flak over the years for not holding on to horses long enough but I really believe people have lost the run of themselves about that,' explains Taaffe. 'He's a jockey that goes with the flow of a race and the rhythm of the horse. He's always been like that and I would say it has won him a lot more races than he's lost. Of course, a lot of tactics go into a race beforehand but a lot of the time they are meaningless, whether it's because of horses falling around you, or not being in the position you wanted to be.' Taaffe continues: 'That's when top jockeys take the bull by the horns and use their wits. Barry has always been brilliant at that. You need a guy who is cool on the big days and can rise to the occasion. He mightn't be the man you'd put on a 4-6 shot in a seven-runner maiden hurdle on firm ground at Downpatrick but give him a big race at Cheltenham and it's a different story.'

There's no bigger race at Cheltenham than the Gold Cup and Taaffe's faith in the big race abilities of his jockey were hardly diluted by a string of major wins throughout the 2004–05 season. Moscow Flyer appeared to be at the height of his powers. A memorable Tingle Creek success over Azertyuiop and Well Chief only whetted the appetite for their Cheltenham re-match. At a preview night in Cork just a week before the festival, Geraghty was asked the simple question 'Will he win?' There was no doubting who the 'he' was. Playing the moment and pausing like a dramatic actor, Geraghty said equally simply: 'Doing handstands.' Cue bedlam. Later, in more serious mode, he explained the importance of not anticipating the major occasions too much. 'I deliberately try not to get too excited. You love the buzz, which is incredible, but you can't get emotional about what you're doing. Winning is great but losing is easier if you're not too keyed up about the whole thing.'

But the rising star was undoubtedly Kicking King. Always a chaser in the making, he had enough toe as a callow novice to finish runner up in the 2003 Supreme Hurdle. Three years earlier the subsequent triple Gold Cup-winner Best Mate had filled the same position in the same race. In 2004 Kicking King again had to settle for minor honours in the Arkle over two miles. However, a steady rise to the top of the staying chaser ranks was completed by a spectacular win in the King George VI Chase at Kempton. A howling mistake at the last fence provided the sort of drama that both Taaffe and Geraghty could have done without, but Kicking King was unquestionably a Gold Cup contender. In a country where no race is coveted more, genuine Gold Cup horses are a prized commodity. As if buoyed by the idea of having such a prospect in his pocket, Geraghty went on a rampage, picking up other major pots like the AIG on Macs Joy and the Totesport Trophy on Essex. It seemed nothing could go wrong, which of course is when things usually do.

A fortnight before the Gold Cup, Kicking King scoped badly and Taaffe ruled him out of Cheltenham. It was a devastating blow for a man whose father won the great race three times on Arkle and trained Captain Christy to win in 1974. A week later, however, the horse was showing such vim at home that Taaffe ruled him back in again. To say the least, it was an unorthodox run in to the most coveted prize in National Hunt racing, and Geraghty's instructions ran the range from ride him with confidence to pull him up if he doesn't feel right. Before such decisions had to be made, however, there was the task of steering Moscow Flyer in the Champion Chase.

It was billed as the race of the festival, with the reigning champion Azertyuiop and the fast-improving Well Chief both fancied to reverse Tingle Creek form. A true epic was widely anticipated but Azertyuiop's early fall spoiled that. What marred an eyeball-to-eyeball classic between the remaining two leading players was the utter dominance of Moscow Flyer. Never one to over-exert himself once hitting the front, there was nevertheless a remorselessness to the Irish star that precluded any lingering hopes the Well Chief champ might have had in the straight. As Moscow Flyer went by the post, volume levels soared. The horse's ears were pricked and his jockey's whip waved casually to acknowledge the cheers. It was a display to crown a magnificent career. Not a beat was missed in defeating as good a Champion Chase field as had been assembled in modern times. In fact the only false step was taken in the winner's enclosure as Geraghty attempted a flying dismount that didn't quite have enough Frankie Dettori panache. Stepping off, he promptly skidded on a muddy patch and ended up on his backside. Somehow even that felt right: after all, a Moscow Flyer show wouldn't have been complete without some kind of spill.

Forty-eight hours later there was a surety to the way Kicking King travelled throughout the Gold Cup that made the idea of defeat even more unlikely. The 4-1 favourite knocked any stamina concerns on the head and put in the sort of smooth performance that guaranteed that a less-than-vintage blue riband field were put to the sword in style. At the top of the hill Geraghty was able to take a pull. The Coolmore Stud supremo John Magnier later told Taaffe it was the first time he had seen a jockey do that in a Gold Cup since the trainer's father on board Arkle. At the line there were five lengths in hand of Take A Stand – but that didn't even hint at Kicking King's superiority. Geraghty's celebrations passing the line made Moscow Flyer's look like a dervish on speed: just a single digit held up to denote what number in the winner's enclosure they were heading for.

Not surprisingly Taaffe was the centre of attention. The links with Cheltenham and Arkle and the continuation of the festival link with one of Irish racing's most famous names meant it could hardly be otherwise. There was a wonderful moment when the trainer stepped up to accept his award from Princess Anne and with true egalitarian mischief planted a smacker on the royal cheek. Seconds later his jockey attempted to do the same and was met with a frosty stare. For once, discretion got the better of valour.

It didn't take long, however, for everyone to twig that B.J. Geraghty was now in possession of the two finest steeplechase rides around. It was a remarkable position to be in and one that provoked inevitable questions as to which was the better horse. With different sets of owners to keep happy, such queries could have been difficult, especially when presented with a hypothetical dream where Moscow Flyer and Kicking King clashed over an intermediate two and a half miles. The response was classic Geraghty: 'I don't like to tell the details of my dreams!'

Those dreams were never destined to become reality either. The following season, Kicking King notched another King George triumph, this time around the unfamiliar terrain of Sandown. But it was a hard-fought victory over Monkerhostin and the reason for that quickly became apparent. A tendon injury, caused, Taaffe suspected, by a false piece of ground, finished Kicking King's campaign and meant a couple of years on the sidelines. At the same time, Moscow Flyer was starting to show signs of wear and tear. Races like Navan's Fortria Chase and Leopardstown's Dial-A-Bet Chase used to be routine victories. Now he was beaten in both. After struggling home fifth to Newmill at the 2006 Cheltenham festival, the great horse was retired.

As Geraghty had always suspected, it left a major void. The big race jockey was without his two best big race mounts. And over the years the perception had grown that competing for minor prizes wasn't exactly enthralling him any more. After all, how could a midweek winter meeting at Thurles compete with the likes of Cheltenham and Aintree? Whispers about how motivated Geraghty really was started to get louder: stories about his business interests became wilder until it seemed he was turning into some Rockefeller in silks. There were pubs, clubs, property deals and tales of land purchases that would water the eyes of an eighteenth-century Lord. Why would anyone risk their necks riding over fences with so much going on outside the game? The truth is so simple, it escaped under the radar. Behind all that casual front, Geraghty loves the business of riding racehorses more than he probably likes to admit even to himself.

I suppose it is a negative side of being laid back. Fellahs think I'm complacent. But if there is a perception out there about me, it hasn't come from my riding. Sure, I love riding good horses in good races but I know only too well there are bread and butter days as well.

Certainly his commitment in overcoming serious injury cannot be doubted. Three times he has fractured vertebrae in his back. Another fracture occurred in his neck. A millimetre here or there and the outcome might have been catastrophic but he laughs that off. Thinking too much about such things doesn't achieve anything. It certainly isn't going to change the one inevitability in a jump jockey's life: he will get hurt. Nobody even knew about one of the back injuries until he complained about another problem. It had healed on its own. He can't remember which fall might have caused it.

When they found out all I could think of was 'Christ, this is going to be six or eight weeks in a cast' and all that shite. But the MRI showed it was an old one. That was a relief. Every jockey gets injuries. It's part of the job. I haven't got any aches or pains yet – listen to me, I sound like I'm ninety!

Then there are the bangs that might not be career-threatening but which would leave most lesser mortals in physical and mental turmoil. At the 2008 Easter Grand National meeting at Fairyhouse, a routine-looking fall in a hurdle race turned nasty when a flailing leg caught Geraghty in the face. But for wearing a gum-shield he would have lost most of his teeth. As it was he was immediately despatched to the nearest hospital in Blanchardstown. For company in the back of the ambulance he had the

RTE commentator Tony O'Hehir who had dislocated his shoulder in an accident at the racecourse. It was a very different experience for the journalist, who cuts a rather more portly figure than his fellow patient. As they screeched to a halt at A&E, the doors flew open and the shout went out: 'Two jockeys from Fairyhouse!' Despite his jaw all but hanging off, Geraghty's eyebrow attained Roger Moore levels of altitude. After forty stitches, though, he was back riding the following day.

Being almost 5ft 10in, there is also the daily grind of trying to keep weight under control. 'Weight dictates your life, so I'm on the scales three times a day,' he admitted to one reporter. He says it is not so bad now because his partner Paula is studying nutrition and her input into what he eats has helped stabilise things. Nevertheless it is something that demands constant monitoring. It certainly doesn't encourage the free-wheeling lifestyle of someone who doesn't care, which reflects the competitive heart beating underneath the easy-going surface. Taaffe has had more than a few glimpses of that over the years, including when Finger Onthe Pulse landed a dramatic success at the 2008 Cheltenham festival.

He recalls: 'Barry had been having a quiet enough time of it then and there's no doubt that people change with the various experiences they have. I've always said he is best when he's hungry. The ride he gave Finger Onthe Pulse in the Jewson was exceptional.' But what people couldn't know was that Geraghty wasn't too confident going out that day. 'I met him in the weighroom and he said he doubted if the horse would be able to lie up. I told him if he was thinking like that, he shouldn't be riding the horse, that he would have no problem with the pace. Sure enough, he gave him a brilliant ride. He's a very confident fellah Barry but behind it all he does get upset when things go wrong and he does worry. He wouldn't be human if he didn't. It's not all brazen: there's a good brain there too.'

That sharp mind has served its owner well off the track as well as on it. Taaffe describes Geraghty as 'clever in business' and if the tales of his financial acuity have now reached mythical status, the jockey is clearly no monetary mug. His days as a landlord may be over, having sold his share in the 'Archers' pub in Kells, but he has invested some of those big race rewards in property and also in some land in his native Co. Meath.

> It's amazing how when lads hear you are doing well off the course they think you can't be as committed on it. Yeah, I've bought a bit of property, but lots of people do. This is my pension! I bought a farm of land and something has to be kept on it so I buy a few yearlings and foals. It's nice. On days off I have something to be rooting at on the farm. I don't play much golf or anything like that, so the young horses are a good interest.

It all comes back to the horses. The peripheral stuff never lasts long in competition with them. Geraghty might not wear his devotion to the game on his sleeve but it underpins everything else. There's no other reason why he continues to put his body through the wringer and keeps totting up the miles. Possessed of a personality that would help him in most walks of life, he resolutely keeps chasing that next winner. If it's a big race all the better, especially since the tap appears to be running at full power again because of the Henderson link-up. But the small ones don't appear to have lost their lustre completely either. Ever since he won his first jockeys' championship, the idea of riding a thousand winners has kept the competitive flame burning. It's a target that isn't too far away now and it doesn't look like being any kind of stop sign.

'Touch wood, if I can escape injury, I'd love to be doing this in nine or ten years' time. No question.'

That might not fit with the popular image but life would be very boring if we all lived behind one face. The one Barry Geraghty presents to the world isn't untrue. It's just not the full story. And if it keeps people talking, well, as Wilde pointed out, there's one worse thing than being talked about.

Cheltenham Festival Winners

2002

Irish Independent Arkle Trophy	Moscow Flyer

2003

William Hill Trophy Handicap Chase	Youlneverwalkalone
Pertemps Hurdle Final	Inching Closer
Queen Mother Champion Chase	Moscow Flyer
JCB Triumph Hurdle	Spectroscope
Vincent O'Brien County Hurdle	Spirit Leader

2004

Ladbrokes World Hurdle	Iris's Gift

2005

Queen Mother Champion Chase	Moscow Flyer
Tote Cheltenham Gold Cup	Kicking King

2006

SunAlliance Chase	Star De Mohaison
Coral Cup	Sky's The Limit

2007

Weatherbys Champion Bumper	Cork All Star

2008

Jewson Novices Handicap Chase	Finger Onthe Pulse

2009

Arkle Trophy	Forpadydeplasterer
Champion Hurdle	Punjabi
Triumph Hurdle	Zaynar

Other Major Winners include

1998
Midlands Grand National   Miss Orchestra

1999
Royal Bond Novice Hurdle   Moscow Flyer
Drinmore Novices Chase   Alexander Banquet

2002
Hennessy Gold Cup   Alexander Banquet
Thomas Pink Gold Cup   Cyfor Malta

2003
Tingle Creek Chase   Moscow Flyer

2004
John Durkan Memorial Chase   Kicking King
Tingle Creek Chase   Moscow Flyer
King George VI Chase   Kicking King
December Festival Hurdle   Macs Joy

2005
Pierse Hurdle   Essex
AIG Irish Champion Hurdle   Macs Joy
Totesport Trophy   Essex
Guinness Gold Cup   Kicking King
King George VI Chase   Kicking King

2006
Shell Champion Hurdle   Macs Joy
John Durkan Memorial Chase   In Compliance

2008

Swordlestown Cup	Big Zeb
ACC Bank Champion Hurdle	Punjabi
Long Walk Hurdle	Punchestowns
Fighting Fifth Hurdle	Punjabi

5

KIEREN FALLON

It was David Niven who proclaimed that you always knew where you stood with Errol Flynn: he always, always, let you down. Kieren Fallon's saving grace in the midst of the personal and professional debris that has trailed him for the last decade is that he has let nobody down more than himself. For each Derby-winning high there has been a cocaine-fuelled low. Championships have been followed by court appearances which in turn have dragged the entire sport through a mire of innuendo, stupidity and suspicion.

The result in a lightning-fast, sound-bite media world is that Fallon has turned into journalistic cat-nip, his haunted face adorning tabloid front pages as much as their backs. The presentation might vary – cheat, love-rat, wronged hero – but Fallon is always there, just where he shouldn't be. The latest one-dimensional cartoon of a very un-straightforward man could easily be that of the rehabilitated black sheep, back to race-riding after an eighteen-month ban for a second positive cocaine test. On past form it may be spectacular. The forty-four-year-old has specialised in making a splash for the right reasons after the corresponding negative ripples of his last altercation with authority have finally flattened out. However, an equally persuasive argument can be made that this is precisely when he's most dangerous to himself.

It is all part of the yin-yang thing that has kept racing enthralled and appalled for well over a decade now. No one else can even come close to finding the trouble that Fallon can. And very few in the entire history of race-riding have been better at the job of passing a little red lollipop in front. It's a piece of duality that would have Jung squinting. It has certainly been enough to defeat employers, family, friends and an entire industry which has despaired for this brilliant but desperately flawed individual. To be at the heart of this emotional turmoil must be incredibly exhausting. Noel Gallagher of Oasis used to compare his own dressing room with the five needed for his brother Liam – 'one for each of his personalities!' The evidence suggests Fallon's mental dressing room might require a few walls to be knocked.

In the summer of 2008, as the six-times former champion jockey came to terms with his drugs ban, he gave a revealing interview to the London *Independent.* In it he pointed to the 1978 movie *Midnight Express* as a particular favourite. Playing a clip where the central character, who is in prison for trying to smuggle dope out of Turkey, rails at a judge the line 'what is a crime – what is a punishment? It seems to vary from time to time, place to place' seems to have a particular resonance for him. As does the 'you're all pigs' denouement.

Aside from the fact that the old 'crime today-OK tomorrow' argument is hardly the most encouraging from a man with a history of alcohol and drug problems, it is significant that the victim role is one that Fallon appears to identify with so strongly. After finally putting to bed the paper-thin and woefully ill-judged race-fixing court case begun by the British Horseracing Authority, it was hardly unreasonable for him to have a sense of being hard done by. But such an attitude is interchangeable with so many others. Sometimes the world is presented with a blasé, couldn't give a damn pose. Or a rampant defiance that twenty-four hours later can have plunged the depths of depression before dissolving into desolate regret. With Fallon the parameters rarely stay constant. Through the years it is obvious that what he says at a particular time is often spontaneous and heartfelt – and apt to turn 360 degrees in the space of a sentence.

By turns he can be charming and chilling, inspired and infuriating. The attractive bad boy role he relishes can quickly change into intense vulnerability before reverting back to the rock-hard and inscrutable face

Fallon often chooses to present to the world. It looks a frighteningly intense way to live and it all adds up to the sum of a man who looks desperately ill-at-ease in his own skin.

Comparisons have been made with other Irish sporting stars who came from little, and through talent, but more importantly will, made it to the top. Roy Keane, in particular, has been a popular benchmark. But in terms of personality the two are polar opposites. Keane has a self-confidence that borders on posturing arrogance and which leaves little room for concern about what others think of him. Fallon cares desperately about the opinion of others. During the 2007 race-fixing trial he hid his face as a succession of high-profile trainers filed into the Old Bailey to back him up. Such embarrassment wouldn't have occurred to other troubled Irish sporting heroes. Alex Higgins would probably have resented the intrusion on his feral limelight. In that regard, a comparison to George Best is more appropriate. Soccer's wayward genius might have been maddening, but public affection for him never wavered despite his constant bouts with the bottle. Best was viewed indulgently, as so many talented people with an all too public weakness are. Fallon is skating on the thinnest of racing ice in regard to the betting public's regard for him, which shows only the tortuous path he has taken. But enough still remains for an awful lot of people to want him to pull the frazzled threads of his career together into one final, spectacular bow.

The memories of big race victories on stars like Hurricane Run, George Washington and Ouija Board are still fresh enough to make such an outcome possible. Compulsive personalities, however, are hardly ideal allies for such symmetrically heart-warming finales. For much of his career Fallon's addiction to winning was enough to overcome his horror of boredom. Drink, he confessed, helped him feel comfortable among people who otherwise intimidated him. Then it became oil coursing through the engine of his social life. He has always liked to live life on that figurative edge, convinced of its dark excitement. The company he has kept away from the track, though, has often scraped away any pretence of glamour, leaving instead only addiction's sordid flipside.

In 2007 he tested positive for cocaine in France just two months after his return from a six-month ban for the same offence. When confirmation of that positive test came later that year a lot of influential people within racing threw their hands up in despair. They included the all-powerful Coolmore team who had backed their man through more than a year of controversy. But this was too much for many. That one compulsive individual should waste so many chances when so many innocents in the world get none seemed almost offensive. That the confirmation came just a day after vindication in racing's notorious race-fixing trial just summed up people's weariness with Fallon. No matter how much talent is indulged, eventually it has to stand on its own two feet. The blame game can only be played for so long.

In fairness, Fallon's face at the end of that trial indicated that a similar realisation had hit home. What should have been his finest hour was destroyed by the drug news he knew was about to be released. The dread is written all over him in photographs taken outside the court. Those eyes that can blaze with determination and anger are peering into a future that must look bleak. A few months afterwards he flew to Palm Springs in California and checked into a clinic where he was treated for depression.

Returning to Newmarket, Fallon began riding out for Michael Stoute, declaring his satisfaction with life again and pledging to return to race-riding. Many greeted the news wearily: others with outright scepticism. But if there is one thing certain, it is that if he wants to try to return to the peak of his profession again he will get the chance.

Winning beats anything else in racing and Fallon has proved he has few peers in getting one horse to go faster than another. The hysterical condemnation that resonated through the industry after his second positive drugs test will count for nothing with many owners and trainers desperate to win. It has always been so. That current broadsheet trend to view sporting greatness as a product of personal substance is as off-kilter as it is wearisome. Some television football analysts in particular seem to forget the abundance of evidence which confirms it's possible to be a top player and a shit person at the same time. There are some who would view Fallon in the same way, but it is his misfortune to possess a personality that means he will always be more of a danger to himself than to anyone else. There are plenty who have parasitically fed off an inherently generous nature. However, that nature has also created a hardcore of friends and fans who will hear nothing said against their man and who believe he is much more sinned against than sinning.

Fallon's movie choice tends to back up that view. It's not too surprising he can identify with the role of victim. The farcical race-fixing controversy that dogged him for three years and two months before a judge finally had the grace to bow to the inevitable, would have scarred anyone. So would some of the tabloid dramas that have surrounded his private life. But we are, after all, also talking about a man who has dragged himself from nowhere to the heights of a very wealthy sport. Fighting the legal fight is an expensive business and Fallon's lifestyle can be profligate, but unless he's taking financial advice from Nick Leeson we are talking about a man a long way from the skids. Nevertheless, the victim role is one that he appears to believe, the small man taking on the establishment, a permanent outsider. That chippy determination will fuel any comeback. It certainly fuelled much of Fallon's spectacular rise to fame and notoriety.

Plenty have remarked on the unusual route that rise took. Fallon is from the small village of Crusheen, less than ten miles north of Ennis. In the 1990s Crusheen, or at least one of the hills around Crusheen, gained its own notoriety as the place where the All-Ireland winning Clare hurling teams of 1995 and 1997 were run to the point of collapse by their trainer, Ger Loughnane. These days it is in the commuter belt of the county town, Ennis. Back in the 1960s and 70s Crusheen was very different but hardly the hutted backwater that some portrayals would indicate either. It was a typical rural Irish village where education was regarded as vital. Fallon never sparked academically, though. Instead, a love of the outdoors mixed with a liking for boxing and hurling. Emigration was a fact of life but the Fallon family had some land and were able to keep a couple of Connemara ponies on it. The future champion's father also made a living as a plasterer and a taxi driver. It was an eminently recognisable and normal upbringing for any young person in

Ireland at the time. What really marked Fallon as different, though, was when he left Crusheen and went to Kevin Prendergast's yard at the Curragh. He was just a fortnight shy of his eighteenth birthday and had never sat on a racehorse before.

What is a unique riding style evolved out of a sink or swim school of apprenticeship. Informed of the fundamentals, the new boy was hoisted on to the back of his first thoroughbred and left to find out how to work it. Considering Fallon was three years older than most apprentices when they start, and had none of the pony racing background that many aspiring Irish jockeys possess, his progress was remarkable. Inside a fortnight he was riding work alongside Prendergast's stable jockey Gabriel 'Squibs' Curran. Never shy of hard work, he fitted in with the rest of Prendergast's staff, and in the rough and tumble of weekend nights out in Kildare town a boxing background came in handy.

But it was in the mornings that those watching intently might have spotted something different. Fallon's style in the saddle is self-taught and a product of his own view on how to persuade a thoroughbred to run faster. Other jockeys have tried to emulate the shape he makes on a horse just as many tried to copy Lester Piggott. It's an equally pointless exercise. The secret isn't in the style, or indeed the lack of it. Compared to the likes of Frankie Dettori or Michael Kinane, Fallon can in fact look positively agricultural. Riding longer than his rivals and throwing the reins loosely at his horse, it often seems he has more in common with his National Hunt colleagues than the cream of the flat weighroom. 'Paddy Kiely rides again!' quipped one respected racing pundit during a particularly desperate finish, in reference to the former jump jockey who was never mistaken for Joe Mercer during his own career. During winter breaks in America, Fallon's style of riding would cause merriment on the back stretch where streamlined tidiness in the saddle is everything. He has admitted to envying Dettori's aerodynamic polish. But the lessons learned at Prendergast's mean the chances of any dramatic changes are nil.

Instead, the wonder of Fallon's riding is all in what you don't see. The deliberately long irons allow his legs to exert maximum forward propulsion. Upper-body strength only adds to the cocktail of physical power and natural horsemanship that fizzles down those loose reins. His trademark is a piercing whistle to encourage the animal. His rivals have come to dread the sound, more than any shouting or swearing. Overall, the effect is that reaching for the whip is usually a last resort. Aidan O'Brien has always admired that ability to get the most out of a horse without indulging in any showy flailing. In fact, his former stable jockey reaching for the stick was often the great trainer's cue to walk away. The relationship between horse and rider is complex anyway, but it was while learning by his mistakes on the Curragh that the teenager with the hard fists and soft hands learned to unravel that mysterious language coming from the animal underneath.

In 1987 Fallon had progressed to finish runner up to Kevin Manning in the Irish apprentice championship. But he realised that the potential for stalling in an intensely competitive but relatively small home racing scene was all too real. The racecourse caller Des Scahill arranged for Fallon to travel to Jimmy Fitzgerald's yard in Malton in North Yorkshire. Fallon showed up looking a little heavier than his fellow Irishman had been expecting – 'It's a bloody flat jockey I want, not a bloody jump jockey. I've got plenty of those!' Fitzgerald might have possessed a sulphuric temper but he was also a horseman to his fingertips. The same was true of his new arrival. Together sparks flew in terms of personality but also in winners. In 1988 there were thirty-one for Fallon. They helped the boy from Crusheen settle into life in the UK and also into the different rhythms of racing across the water. But it didn't take long for him to grow too big for Fitzgerald's dual-purpose yard.

Taking the decision to team up with Lynda and Jack Ramsden in 1993 seemed a natural fit. The Ramsdens were no establishment figures. Instead both appeared to relish their role as racing outsiders. He was a former stockbroker and there was enough originality in him and his wife to open a racing stable on the Isle of Man. That didn't last long but back on the mainland things gathered pace. She oversaw the actual horse training while her husband did the planning. To him a horse was a set of form figures, a handicap mark and a pedigree: to her a living creature in a stable. The combination proved irresistible. What both agreed upon was the importance of a stable jockey and Fallon fitted the bill. Jack Ramsden admired the Irishman's horsemanship and his ability to blend into a team. Solo-merchants with a propensity for blabbing were not appreciated. Under Ramsden's guidance Fallon began to perfect the tactical side of the game. Excuses were cheap when the money was down. Jack Ramsden liked a bet and his success rate was being helped by the growing confidence of the new stable jockey. Fallon's profile was also growing, but it was for all the wrong reasons that he first hit the national headlines.

Fallon has a hair-trigger temper that he has always found difficult to control. In 1994, that temper led him to drag Stuart Webster off his horse just after the finish of a race at Beverley. Always handy with his fists, there has been an impulse to act first and talk about it later. What he assumed there would be to talk about after such a moment of lunacy in front of television cameras only he will ever know. A grudge between two jockeys turned into one of those news programme kickers where the audience is invited to giggle at a piece of stupidity. It wasn't so funny to racing's rulers, or indeed to Webster, who later claimed he was assaulted in the weighroom afterwards. That came to nothing but the Jockey Club didn't hesitate to suspend Fallon for six months. His habit of getting into trouble with officialdom had taken a significant extra step forward. The man at the centre of the furore later chose to look at the upside.

'You have to look at the positive in everything,' Fallon says. 'It's the only way to look at it. That looked a low point in my career but it turned into a high point because I went to California.'

At various times during his turbulent career America has proved a welcomingly anonymous sanctuary. When things have got too hot in Europe, Fallon has headed to the US where the local show is the only show. Foreign guys who don't ride like American jockeys are just curiosities among the multi-national back-stretch community. More than a decade later, it was Florida that offered a temporary break from the headlines. In 1994 it was the back stretch at Santa Anita and Hollywood Park that provided the grounding in morning pace work which added

vital subtlety to the power. Fallon returned to ride in Britain a more
confident jockey. But even when his instinct was to shy away from
controversy, he couldn't help getting dragged into it.

Top Cees was an important 1995 winner in the Chester Cup. However,
an article in the following day's *Sporting Life* newspaper alleged that the
Ramsdens, along with Fallon, had deliberately stopped Top Cees from
winning an earlier race at Newmarket in order to lengthen the horse's
odds in the Chester Cup. The consensus was that the subsequent libel
case was Jack Ramsden's idea but Fallon also felt obliged to take action as
a gesture of support. The trial took eighteen days, at the end of which the
jockey was awarded £70,000 in damages. Fallon's reaction was relief at it
all being over, except he suspected the fall-out would linger for a long
time.

'I'm used to the English press pursuing me – it all stems from the Top
Cees libel case and ever since they've been trying to crucify me,' he later
told a local newspaper in Co. Clare. 'I would have won a championship
[2004] only that the Jockey Club suspended me a lot of time when I
shouldn't have been suspended. They did their best to beat me. They
don't like an Irish jockey being champion every year.'

Such simplistic arguments hadn't prevented Pat Eddery dominating
the championship for years but that victim role has become a comfortable fit. However, by the end of the Top Cees trial, Fallon was heading
towards being champion jockey for the second time. He had finished
1997 with 202 winners, among them two classics and a plethora of other
Group 1 prizes. Along the way there had been a major dust-up with
Henry Cecil over the Eclipse Stakes defeat of his superstar filly, Bosra
Sham, but the boy who hadn't even ridden a racehorse at eighteen
was undeniably at the top of his profession. And he had done it the
hard way.

More than a decade later it is hard to remember just how much of a
shock it was that Cecil should have turned to Fallon when looking for
a new stable jockey. Flat riders based in the north of England remain the
poor relations of their brethren in the south, but back in 1997 Fallon's
meteoric rise to Cecil's elite Warren Place stables in Newmarket was a

leap into the unknown for both parties. Cecil affects an absent-minded English eccentricity that is at polar opposites to the determinedly rough-house Irishman. At the time the BBC's perpendicular-eared racing correspondent Julian Wilson described it as akin to discovering 'that Michael Heseltine has married Amanda de Cadenet.' However, unlike the 1980s' wild-child, Fallon's gift for self-promotion came solely through the depth of his talent in the saddle.

It wasn't all smooth. The vastly superior Reams Of Verse eventually won the 1997 Oaks after an undistinguished ride threatened to snatch defeat from certain victory. And Bosra Sham's Eclipse defeat, when Fallon disastrously attempted an ambitious run up the inside at Sandown, led to a lengthy and highly visible Cecil sulk. But the margins between victory and defeat, perceived genius and supposed incompetence, are always thin. What Fallon failed to get away with on Bosra Sham came off spectacularly in the Prix de l'Arc de Triomphe eight years later. Hurricane Run's passage from the back of the Arc field has been repeatedly cited as an example of Fallon at his best. Instead, it can easily be argued that all he got right that day was his luck. After getting shuffled back, his options were effectively nil. Coming round the outside at Longchamp is the preserve of the very few. It even managed to get Nijinsky beaten in 1970. Fallon's decision to chance a run up the rail was a no-brainer. Where he got lucky was in being on an exceptional horse at the peak of his powers. Hurricane Run even overcame having to be switched inside the final furlong before powering clear. But victory meant his rider was credited with every kind of racing virtue imaginable: with Fallon, though, nothing is ever that simple.

A total of 204 winners in 1998 guaranteed a second championship and the following year came a Derby success on Oath. It looked like the unlikely partnership was made in heaven, which is usually when all hell comes piling in on top of him.

The story of Cecil's wife and her relationship with a top jockey widely rumoured to be Fallon was tabloid heaven. Fallon, a married man with children, denied any involvement and still does, but hot on the heels of the story came a split from Cecil for 'personal reasons'. If it seemed like a disaster, then little time was needed to find out how the man at the centre of racing's buzzing rumour mill is always capable of landing on his feet. Michael Stoute had been reported as being interested in hiring Fallon before Cecil beat him to the punch. Now his interest was rekindled. The tabloids might have got their teeth into racing's 'bad boy' but his career hardly missed a beat. Stoute had a comparable-sized string to Cecil and there was enough quality there to make hopes in top-class races perfectly viable. Those hopes were vindicated in style despite a horrific fall at Royal Ascot 2000 which almost finished Fallon's career. Only a monumental effort of will and the skill of his surgeon allowed him to return from an injury to his left shoulder. But it was worth that effort.

Golan added to Kings Best's 2,000 Guineas victory and both North Light and Kris Kin secured Derby successes that only confirmed their jockey's mastery of the tricky Epsom circuit. Stoute described Kris Kin's win as being one of the great Epsom rides. The Barbados-born trainer and his Irish jockey enjoyed a warm relationship. A much more ebullient character than his neighbour Cecil, Stoute appeared to relish Fallon's dangerous edge both in and out of the saddle. It looked like the champion jockey had found a spiritual home at last. But beneath the surface were some fundamental problems.

Eating might not be an expansive option for jockeys but drinking always has been. Alcohol helps them to cope with those constant hunger pangs and it dehydrates. More than one high-profile rider has been seduced by the delusion that boozing is almost medicinal. By his own admission Fallon liked a drink. It helped his confidence in social settings. But by the winter of 2002 he was getting through a bottle of vodka a day. 'I was a wild man. I knew every off-licence within five miles of every racecourse. They were like pit-stops for me,' he said. Eventually he checked into a treatment centre in Cahir, Co. Tipperary seeking help and emerged with his hunger for success renewed. In 2003 he was champion again with a career high of 221 winners in Britain. With Fallon, however, little is straightforward. Conquering alcohol and other personal demons ultimately had to be done by him. But other clouds had gathered that remained steadfastly out of his control.

A BBC *Panorama* programme in October 2002 hung much of its report into 'The Corruption of Racing' on a copy of a Hong Kong Jockey Club file. The thrust of the programme was that racing was institutionally corrupt and that the Jockey Club was inept. Fallon's was the banner name. His response to questioning was mute but the glare he delivered to a reporter spoke volumes. And in the background, resonating through the story, was the continuing growth and importance of internet betting.

The fundamental principle that a punter can also be a layer on the web with no need for a bookmaker has revolutionised the betting world. All it takes is one person online who fancies a horse to find someone else who doesn't and then the trade-off on what price they will do business at can begin. Internet companies such as Betfair or Betdaq provide the forum, charge a small commission and then let business take its course. And as with most revolutions the establishment has taken its time catching up with events. But what was to become the race-fixing scandal had its roots in the most old-fashioned racing concept of all – information.

The inflexions that can be put on a single word in the betting context are many. What may be a casual tip to one person can sound like a plot to someone else. What is undeniable is that if a punter goes online knowing a certain horse isn't going to win, the profits are potentially enormous. Races that might attract a couple of hundred people to the track and a handful of bookmakers are generating millions online. The days of the clichéd cloth-capped bookie perched on a box armed only with a piece of chalk are gone. Nowadays, a laptop is an essential piece of bookmaking equipment. The real turnover is being generated by people sitting at home watching television. In 2003 the Jockey Club signed an agreement with Betfair which gave them unprecedented access to client records and betting patterns. Perception has become all-important and the ride Fallon delivered on Ballinger Ridge in a nondescript race at Lingfield in March 2004 looked awful.

Ballinger Ridge was clear and had the race sewn up when Fallon sat up. It was only in the dying strides that he appeared to realise the threat from Rye and it was too late to prevent Ballinger Ridge getting beaten. Under the memorandum, Betfair had alerted the Jockey Club to suspicious betting patterns as Ballinger Ridge had lengthened in price. Fallon got a twenty-one-day ban from the Lingfield stewards for dropping his hands. But it wasn't long before a tabloid had a story of undercover reporters being told by Fallon that Rye would beat Ballinger Ridge. The result was more headlines that were annoying but could be swatted away. However, when City of London police arrested Fallon and seventeen others investigating alleged race-fixing in September 2004, it got much more serious.

There were many willing to speculate that the controversial Irishman had finally gone too far. Police involvement meant events had escalated to a dangerously different level. More sober race followers were willing to reserve judgement, though. A form-guide to police involvement in racing's dirty linen in the past did not make encouraging reading. But there could be no denying the seriousness with which they now pursued the case. By the time the matter finally made it to court in 2007, there was widespread expectation of a 'smoking gun' piece of evidence that would condemn Fallon and his other accused: either a taped conversation or an incriminating document. But instead of a smoking gun there was only a steaming turd of a case. Which doesn't stop there being residue. 'You are guilty now until proved innocent. What will happen when this case is thrown out?' Fallon predicted. 'It won't make any difference. The mud sticks – my life is already fucked.'

It all comes back to what constitutes information. Every jockey gets asked for tips. It's an occupational hazard. Such gossip is the lifeblood of the racecourse and beyond. During the trial it emerged that the England international footballer Michael Owen was regularly texting Fallon about his mounts. Such communication is commonplace, even if most inquisitors don't have Owen's profile. How to deal with it is up to the individual jockey. Most riders come up with something obvious or vague and keep moving. How to distinguish that from something more sinister is a problem that has defeated both the City of London police and the British Horseracing Authority in such embarrassing fashion. The race-fixing trial might have cost £10 million and the prosecution may have brought

5,000 exhibits as well as 40,000 pages of evidence, but what they lacked was something concrete. There was nothing on tape and nothing on paper. Instead, there was only an unfortunate Australian steward hung out to dry as well as a lot of supposition.

The result should have been sweet for Fallon but there was to be no immediate return to the saddle. Instead, more fallout from his tortuous personal life plunged him back into controversy. The man nicknamed 'The Assassin' had nowhere left to run. Some very private demons were released back into the public domain. Addictive personalities are rarely one-dimensional enough to abuse just a single poison.

So much was obvious to racing's most powerful and successful team right from the start. That John Magnier, Michael Tabor and Aidan O'Brien should have been aware of Fallon's frailties and still turned to him to rekindle the fortunes of Coolmore-Ballydoyle is as significant a tribute to the talent underpinning the problems as Fallon is ever likely to receive. When Jamie Spencer left the yard in the spring of 2005 there were other options for Magnier & Co. Johnny Murtagh had got his act together personally, was riding well and had a history of success with O'Brien. Pat Smullen was a rising-star with championships under his belt. There were some who believed O'Brien's best hope was to suck it up and ask Mick Kinane to come back into the Coolmore tent. But even with all the baggage he brings, Fallon was the man they hired.

A trip to Barbados to meet the syndicate partners helped him make up his mind. A lucrative retainer on the table helped even more. There was also the added bonus of returning to Ireland, away from the full glare of British media and the pressures of the race-fixing controversy. The sole problem appeared to be the inevitable split necessary from Michael Stoute. But the Newmarket trainer is nothing if not a pragmatist. He might have stood up for his wayward jockey in more than one tight spot, but the lure of Ballydoyle has almost invariably proved irresistible down the years. Fallon found himself following in the footsteps of Piggott, Eddery and Kinane, a triumvirate of jockeys who were at the peak of the game when he himself had just darkened Kevin Prendergast's door on the Curragh. Turning it down was never going to be an option.

As with almost all the major jobs he has held over the years, Ballydoyle's new boy hit the ground running. Footstepsinthesand and Virginia Waters provided a Guineas double at Newmarket which only sealed the mutual admiration society between O'Brien and Fallon. Ireland's champion trainer loved the horsemanship that his new jockey brought to the job. Spencer had reportedly resented the idea of riding work most mornings while Kinane had been discouraged from doing so. Fallon, however, relished the chance to ride out as often as possible, getting to know the horses and finding out the lie of the land around the world's most famous training establishment. From his employers' point of view there was the added bonus of being able to keep tabs on their fun-loving jockey.

Fallon himself has acknowledged his ability to get into trouble. 'You know, if I get into a room with fifty people, in ten minutes I will end up talking to the only two bad ones in there,' he once remarked. Racing in Ireland has a much more staccato rhythm to it than in Britain. For much of the spring and autumn there are days when there is no racing at all, and what cards there are can often be divided with National Hunt racing. The result for Fallon was a lot of free-time, never a good idea for a man with a low boredom threshold. There was always the option of riding in Britain for other trainers when he was not required by O'Brien but compared to the quality on offer at Ballydoyle everything else seemed underwhelming. The point was only emphasised with the emergence of a vintage crop of classic horses in 2006. Alexandrova and Dylan Thomas were joined by the most exciting of all, George Washington, who proved to be an exceptional Guineas winner. However, at the height of the summer, everything changed.

Just a day after riding Dylan Thomas to an Irish Derby success, Fallon was charged by police in London with conspiracy to defraud Betfair customers. With the charge came an automatic suspension of his UK riding licence. He appealed it, but before Fallon's ride in the Eclipse Stakes, the BHA panel turned down the appeal. Fallon was banned until the end of the race-fixing trial over a year later. The suspension was not reciprocated in Ireland and France but the impact on the entire Coolmore operation was obvious to everyone, including their jockey. Many of the stallion maker races are in Britain but with Fallon unable to ride, it placed an obvious question-mark over his role. The following day he travelled to Chantilly to ride Ivan Denisovich in the Prix Jean Prat and provided a positive sample for cocaine which led to a six-month ban.

Combined with his suspension from riding in the UK, it looked the end for Fallon and Coolmore. Always intensely conscious of any bad publicity, the intensely private Magnier now found himself embroiled in a barrage of negative stories. But there was also the widespread view in Ireland that the jockey was being victimised by not being allowed ride in the UK: guilty until proven innocent indeed. Coolmore stood by their man. In June 2007 Fallon returned to action at an otherwise mundane midweek meeting at Tipperary. With his by now heightened sense of the theatrical, he made sure his first ride back, The Bogberry, won. Heartfelt gratitude was expressed to Magnier and O'Brien and the centre of attention expressed his confidence that the race-fixing issue would be quickly resolved and that his personal problems were all behind him. It all sounded positive, but behind the scenes were stories of how Fallon was living on the Ballydoyle estate practically in a state of curfew. The doubters didn't have long to have their point proved.

A couple of months later Fallon travelled to Deauville for the Prix Morny. In hindsight the name of the winner he rode, Myboycharlie, sounds like a bad joke. Despite having tested positive just a year earlier, the Irishman clearly hadn't learned his lesson. The sample he provided tested positive for cocaine again. That wasn't confirmed until the following December but when it emerged, the day after the end of racing's trial of the century, it marked the end of any more indulgence from a lot of people. Coolmore finally decided to draw a line in the sand and hired Johnny Murtagh. Fallon looked to have blown the best job in racing as well as the patience of an entire industry.

What the future holds for the man at the hub of such attention is impossible to predict. After so much turbulence, there is a widespread hope that he can maintain some equilibrium in his life. That wonderful natural talent on the back of a horse means fears of a depressing decline, in the manner of George Best, are real enough and well-meaning. But anyone suggesting he could live a better life away from racing is wide of the mark. Fallon has consistently said the only place he feels comfortable is on the back of a horse. It's hard to escape the conclusion that it will be only when he is similarly at ease with himself out of the saddle, that he will able to kick on with his life.

Michael Stoute has continued to use his former jockey. There are signs that others will be willing to tap into Fallon's famous horsemanship as well, none more so than Aidan O'Brien. The Coolmore trainer said: 'The reality is these demons were always there. Kieren might not admit that but until he deals with them they will always be there. You can't mix those things with sport or life.' O'Brien continues: 'He is an extremely gifted sportsman but that has probably been part of his downfall. Because he is so natural, he doesn't have to work as hard as some other jockeys to get it right. He's at an age now where he can't afford another slip up. If he can get it together, he still has another chance of getting the last bit out of his career.'

Fallon in turn would argue that he was such a late-starter that he can get quite a bit more out of the game than that. There are cases of jockeys riding at the top level well into their fifties to back him up. Certainly it seems extremely unlikely that we have been surprised by Kieren Francis Fallon for the last time.

Classic Wins

1997

English 1,000 Guineas	Sleepytime
English Oaks	Reams Of Verse

1999

English 1,000 Guineas	Wince
English Derby	Oath

English Oaks	Ramruma
Irish Oaks	Ramruma

2000
English 2,000 Guineas	Kings Best

2001
English 2,000 Guineas	Golan

2002
Italian Oaks	Guadeloupe

2003
English 1,000 Guineas	Russian Rhythm
English Derby	Kris Kin

2004
English Oaks	Ouija Board
Irish Oaks	Ouija Board
English Derby	North Light

2005
English 1,000 Guineas	Virginia Waters
English 2,000 Guineas	Footstepsinthesand
Irish Derby	Hurricane Run

2006
English 2,000 Guineas	George Washington
French 2,000 Guineas	Aussie Rules
English Oaks	Alexandrova
Irish Derby	Dylan Thomas
Irish Oaks	Alexandrova

2007
Irish St Leger	Yeats

Other Major Winners include

1997
Prince Of Wales's Stakes   Bosra Sham
Sussex Stakes   Ali Royal

1998
St James's Palace Stakes   Dr Fong

1999
Tattersalls Gold Cup   Shiva

2000
Coronation Cup   Daliapour

2001
Eclipse Stakes   Medicean

2002
Coronation Cup   Boreal
King George VI & Queen Elizabeth Stakes   Golan

2003
Ascot Gold Cup   Mr Dinos
Coronation Stakes   Russian Rhythm
Breeders' Cup Filly & Mare Turf   Islington

2004
Breeders' Cup Filly & Mare Turf   Ouija Board
Phoenix Stakes   Damson
Racing Post Trophy   Motivator

2005
Coronation Cup   Yeats
Eclipse Stakes   Oratorio

Arlington Million	Powerscort
Irish Champion Stakes	Oratorio
Prix de l'Arc de Triomphe	Hurricane Run
Hong Kong Vase	Ouija Board

2006

Tattersalls Gold Cup	Hurricane Run
Ascot Gold Cup	Yeats
Irish Champion Stakes	Dylan Thomas

2007

Irish Champion Stakes	Dylan Thomas
Prix de l'Arc de Triomphe	Dylan Thomas

6

NINA CARBERRY

In most areas women who seek equality with men can justifiably be said to lack ambition. But race-riding is different. When it comes to being a jockey most women actually want to look like men. It's to do with perception, or at least it used to be. Identifying a female jockey among her male colleagues during a race used to be a straightforward exercise in spotting the floppiest style and the weakest finish. Lester Piggott once dismissed an entire sex by observing that women's bottoms are the wrong shape, a declaration that still begs the question as to what shape he feels they should be. Such rampant male chauvinism, though, is starting to disappear, more quickly around the rest of the world than in Europe, it has to be said, but nevertheless it is now possible for a woman jockey to stick her head above the sexist parapet and not encounter withering hails of scorn.

Nina Carberry is different, though. The idea that she might be treated any differently from her male colleagues doesn't occur to her. Allowances don't exist in the mind of the twenty-four-year-old rider, except for what her junior rivals might claim. The gender thing simply isn't an issue. Carberry is a jockey, end of story. And the best part of all is that there isn't a race-fan with a pair of working eyes in these islands who doesn't agree with her. Carberry is distinguishable from her male rivals only in the unmistakable style she brings to the toughest sport of all, National Hunt racing. It's why she is a truly unique figure. No woman has ever disappeared better into a crowd of men.

That's no mean feat, for in the last five years there have been few more recognisable faces in Irish racing. The wide, uncomplicated smile when returning to the winner's enclosure has made this slight, blonde figure one of the most popular personalities in the game. There is an infectious enjoyment to what she does which is impossible to ignore. Many people's automatic reaction these days when picking up a race card is to check which horse Carberry is riding in the bumper, the National Hunt flat races that round off most fixtures in Ireland and which attract plenty of robust betting. The cry of 'come on, Nina' is as much a feature of betting shop punters now as 'come on, Lester' was when the old bum bigot was in his pomp – only first names required.

But some habits and some chauvinists die hard. Carberry has ridden in some of National Hunt racing's greatest races and is a four-time winner at the Cheltenham festival. However, she remains technically an amateur jockey, even though it's a curio of racing in Ireland that being an amateur is a full-time job. Her inclusion in any list of Ireland's greatest jockeys is to risk grumblings about tokenism and no doubt some of her professional colleagues might feel sore at being overlooked. More likely, though, is that no one knows better than those riding alongside her how exceptional she is. Enda Bolger, a champion amateur jockey himself and now renowned as the top trainer around the cross-country courses at Cheltenham and Punchestown, is in no doubt, and he has employed the very best talent in the jockeys' room over the years.

'If I had the choice of any rider for a big race, Ruby Walsh would be my first choice of all time. If I couldn't get Ruby, Nina would be my next choice, over everyone else. I truly mean that,' he says. 'This girl is unique. She has a gift for getting horses to run for her. It doesn't matter if it is in a mile flat race, a two-mile hurdle, a three mile chase or the La Touche over banks. She wins them all. I've never seen anyone like her. She'll pop up one day in a hunters chase and the next she's winning a seven-furlong race at Beverley or somewhere. That's a hard thing to do. McCoy can't do that. But she can do anything.'

Bolger continues: 'She's modelled her style on her brother Paul and she's not a whip person but she gets the job done. And when she gets off she's knowledgeable enough to let you know if you're wasting your time with a horse. Everything's there. On top of that, she comes in beaming if she's had a winner. What more could you want?'

It's this versatility that makes Carberry such a stand out in world racing. Possessed of an innate style in the saddle that allows her to blend into any company on the flat, she remains primarily a National Hunt jockey. Bringing that flat race polish to the rough and tumble of riding over fences has proved an irresistible combination. So much so that in racing's opinionated village one of the few occasions for unanimity is in the absolute certainty that no woman has ever been better at the business of negotiating a racehorse over obstacles.

Elsewhere around the globe the impact of women is concentrated almost exclusively on the flat. Famously, in New Zealand fifty per cent of the jockey population is female. They include the controversial figure of the champion rider, Lisa Cropp, who has taken her talents across the Tasman Sea and ridden in the Melbourne Cup. In Canada, Emma Jayne Wilson leads a strong crop of women at the top end of the national table, having become the top rider at Woodbine, the country's principal track. In 2007 she landed Canada's best known race, the Queen's Plate, on the 15-1 shot Mike Fox. Clare Lindop became the first Australian woman to win a Grade 1 on Exalted Time in the 2006 Adelaide Cup and in 2008 landed the Victoria Derby. But towering above them all is Julie Krone. The diminutive American retired in 1999 having won $81 million in prizemoney, including a Belmont Stakes victory, before returning three years later and winning a Breeders' Cup race on Halfbridled.

Such levels of success have not yet occurred for women in Europe's top flat races, although there have been some notable achievements. Catherine Gannon was a champion apprentice in Ireland in 2004 while Hayley Turner has also been an apprentice champion in the UK and secured a century of winners in 2008. But there remains a prejudice against women riders generally that revolves around the question of strength. Tucking into a horse around the uniformly flat tracks in America may be one thing – so the argument goes – but power as well as balance is required around the undulating and varied tracks of Britain and Ireland. And as for the jumping game, well, before Carberry, that was an entirely different matter again. The former top English jockey Steve Smith Eccles once declared: 'Women jockeys are a pain. Jumping's a man's game. They are not built like us. Most of them are as strong as half a disprin.' Such a view sadly remains prevalent among many of racing's more conservative elements, which only ultimately emphasises more the impact Carberry has had on the jump game.

For those who pioneered the lot of women jockeys, she is a powerful symbol of what has been done in a comparatively short time. It was only in 1972 that women were licensed by the Turf Club to ride on Ireland's racecourses. Joanna Morgan bravely led the way by riding successfully on the flat in the late 1970s. Now a successful trainer, Welsh-born Morgan is unstinting in her praise: 'Nina is phenomenal. Like all the Carberrys, she's a natural. Horses run for her, which is the hardest thing of all for any jockey.' Anne Ferris managed to win the 1979 Irish Sweeps Hurdle and four years later landed an Irish Grand National on Bentom Boy. But they were notable exceptions.

Of course Ireland wasn't alone in its prejudice. It was only in 1969 that Diane Crump became the first female jockey to ride in a pari-mutuel race in America. It took ten more years before the first registered female jockey won a race in Australia. Even now, only the most hopelessly dewy-eyed believe that a level playing field exists between the sexes, which makes Carberry's status all the more remarkable. It's no coincidence that Hayley Turner has said: 'I look up to Nina a lot because of how she rides and her guts and determination. What she's done at Cheltenham is an inspiration.'

The woman herself is far too bright a customer not to appreciate the rather special niche she has carved out for herself in racing but she isn't one to stew on it either. Thriving in a primarily male world is a tough load but she carries it lightly. 'I have five brothers. I'm used to boys around me,' she says. But the fact that she and the five boys come from one of the most renowned racing dynasties in Ireland can only have encouraged her sense of ease among the top echelons of the sport.

Tommy Carberry's credentials for being ranked among the best Irish jockeys of all time are impeccable. Gold Cups, Grand Nationals and multiple championships fell to the man who subsequently trained the 1999 Aintree National winner Bobbyjo. That the horse was ridden by his son Paul seemed only right since this is an extended racing family that would stretch the genealogical abilities of even the greatest pedigree expert. Tommy's wife Pamela Carberry's own background is steeped in the sport. Her father, Dan Moore, trained L'Escargot to win two Gold Cups and a Grand National and was one of Ireland's premier National Hunt trainers during the 1960s and 1970s. His son Arthur Moore continues that tradition now. It would be fair to say that Tommy and Pamela's own family have added to the saga.

Of their six children, Thomas, Paul, Philip, Nina and Peter John are all involved with horses to different degrees. Only Mark makes his living away from the game, as a carpenter. All live within less than ten miles of each other in the Ratoath-Ashbourne area of Co. Meath just outside Dublin. It's a tight-knit family that is made even closer by horses. The sole daughter was on a pony as soon as she could stand up and came through the process of learning to ride the same way as her brothers.

My Mum started us all off. There was one pony we learned on called Jack. He'd been a teaser on a stud and when he got too old for that he came to us. He was still some character. You had to be on your toes around him. First chance he'd get, he'd be down to the trees at the bottom of the field trying to get you off. He was a bit mad. But it was good fun too.

Growing up and going to secondary school in Navan, it wasn't just horses that held the future champion's interest. She became a member of the Irish under-16 basketball squad, did a lot of running for the school and was a good enough high-hurdler to come second in the All-Ireland Championships at under-18 level. There was also time to fit in some surfing, swimming, golf and some long-jump medals too. But everything else started to pale in comparison to the thrills of pony racing. With her father busy training and Paul already established as a brilliant riding talent, it was Pamela who put in much of the driving to and from pony meets around the country. It quickly became obvious that her daughter was just a little bit different from the other budding jockeys. So much so that when she arrived at the Curragh on Irish Oaks day in 2001, the girl who was just shy of her seventeenth birthday was already rumoured to be exceptional. For once, the rumour mill was right.

Sabrinsky started a 7-1 shot for the Masterchefs Ladies Derby over the classic mile and a half course. As per usual in such races, the early pace was hot but there was a poise to the way the jockey in the purple and yellow colours patiently made her ground which was impossible to ignore. Sure enough Sabrinsky shot two lengths clear in the straight and a new Carberry had announced herself on the scene. By then another brother, Philip, had also tasted success on the track, including a 1999 victory in the Kerry National on board Lanturn. He quickly encountered problems with injury that briefly stalled his career. But his sister was only getting started.

I was very lucky. Pony racing was a great grounding for learning about pace and my Mum and Dad were always there. If I was doing things wrong, they'd tell me very quickly. My brothers were great too and they did a lot to get me going. Then it was up to me. It opened up a lot after the Curragh. Ger Lyons [trainer] was a big help. He put me on a lot of his bumper horses and let me ride against pros and that lifted me. Because I started so well, I never experienced any problems about me being a girl. Maybe stuff was being said behind my back but never to my face. If you declare someone to ride your horse, you know what you're getting. It shouldn't be a surprise to anyone.

What was a surprise was the ease with which she switched from riding on the flat, to bumpers, to hurdles and also over fences. There were shades of her brother Paul in the way it seemed so effortless sometimes. Sabrinsky's trainer Noel Meade noticed the similarities quicker than most. 'Nina has great hands and great judgement, just like yer man. And she's a bit more stable!' With Meade's help, her tally of winners started to mount up while riding as a genuine amateur. Carberry's breadth of sporting interests encouraged her to start a sports injuries course at Plunkett College on the north side of Dublin but that had to be abandoned in 2005 for the best possible reasons.

On the run up to that year's Cheltenham festival the young amateur's focus was on one horse, Karanja, a talented six-year-old trained by Victor Dartnall who was among the leading contenders for the Weatherbys Champion Bumper. For weeks beforehand, the memory of the horse she had won on so impressively at Newbury in February was enough to encourage hopes that there might be a first female-ridden winner against the professionals at the festival since Gee Armytage in 1987. So a phone call from her agent the weekend before didn't seem especially important. The Co. Wexford trainer Paul Nolan wanted to use Carberry's 5 lb claim for Dabiroun in the new four-year-olds race, the Fred Winter Juvenile Hurdle. A useful horse on the flat for John Oxx, the Aga Khan-bred runner had yet to win over jumps and was among the outsiders. But a festival ride is always a festival ride.

The opening day of the 2005 festival was centred on the Champion Hurdle and although Hardy Eustace won it in a thriller, at least as much focus afterwards was on Paul Carberry's ride on the runner up, Harchibald. Catcalls and boos were the reaction from some of the huge crowd as even Carberry's daring magic wasn't enough to coax Harchibald past Hardy Eustace after looking to be going best of all a hundred yards from the line. It was unfair stuff and hardly a happy time for the Carberry family. But things got a lot better very quickly.

Dabiroun briefly looked like making a name for himself on the flat just a year previously. His debut yielded a maiden victory at the Curragh on heavy ground, which subsequent events made look even more commendable. Oxx then upped him to Stakes level and Dabiroun finished a fine second in the Loughbrown Stakes. The third and final start of what proved to be a short career on the level also produced a runner up placing. But this was behind no less than Yeats in the Group 3 Ballysax Stakes. The future champion stayer finished a long way in front, but Dabiroun managed to put even further space between himself and the only other runner, Lord Admiral, who in turn matured into a Group 3 class miler. Dabiroun, however, was quickly bought and switched codes.

Considering his flat form, Nolan was entitled to be disappointed by the smartly bred new purchase. He worked well at home but three starts over hurdles in Ireland yielded only one second placing. That came behind a future French Triumph Hurdle winner in Strangely Brown, but still Nolan wondered if Dabiroun was one of those frustrating bridle horses that work well but do little when it counts. If there was an upside, it was that three runs entitled him to a handicap mark that might be lenient if a key could be found. Grasping at straws, Nolan wondered if better ground might be that key. But optimism there quickly diluted, too, since the trainer felt the British Horseracing Board handicapper, Phil Smith, had ruined his horse's chance by slapping too high a rating on him.

The circumstances were hardly auspicious then, but Dabiroun chose to lose his maiden tag at precisely the right moment. Nolan's hunch was right. Good ground transformed the little bay. Carberry rode him with enough confidence to drop him to the rear of the field as the expected hectic pace carried them to halfway. Unusually the tempo eased off, normally a dangerous development for those hanging back for a late run but this time it made no difference. Carberry eased her way to track the leaders from three out and waited until the last to put the race to bed. Dabiroun swept up the famous hill eight lengths clear of his rivals with his jockey waving her stick nonchalantly at the packed stands.

Flushed with success, her brother was quickly alongside with a hug and a kiss. He had finished only tenth on Strolling Home. There was even a crack from the crowd that the wrong Carberry had ridden Harchibald. In the gathering gloom a lot of people hung around the enclosure for the day's last winner to return. Visibility wasn't a problem. The winning jockey's smile was a big enough guide for even the blindly preju-diced. There was enough feel-good factor for everyone. Nolan happily apologised to the handicapper and looked admiringly at his first Cheltenham winner: 'He's been a revelation on this ground. He's as good as he works.' In the midst of it all, Dabiroun's 25-1 SP didn't seem to matter much.

It only took twenty-four hours for Carberry to visit the other end of the sport's emotional spectrum. After her triumph the previous day, there was even more focus on the Irish woman who had been entrusted with the job of steering Karanja around what is usually one of the roughest races at the festival. With no obstacles to jump, no room is expected or given around a track that is much tighter and speed-demanding than is usually assumed.

> The first time we jumped off there was a false start, so we all had to come back. We would have been fine but for that. I knew he could be a bit tricky so I really wanted to get him in amongst the others. When we were called back in, I was on my own and the horse whipped around. I fell off him and they were gone. Talk about coming back to reality quick. It was desperate. The connections were very disappointed, and so was I. But what's done is done. There was nothing I could do.

Anyone expecting her to climb into a hole and hide was to be disappointed. Carberrys don't do such things. Instead the prospect of turning professional became a very real possibility. On the back of Dabiroun's victory and the resultant boost to her profile it seemed a good time to take the plunge. College immediately bit the dust. Meade, however, had other ideas and offered her the job as his stable amateur. Since the former champion trainer has an almost constant flow of expensively bought young horses running in bumpers, it is a coveted position. Niall 'Slippers' Madden, soon to win the Grand National on Numbersixvalverde, had been champion amateur for Meade. Carberry discussed things with her family. Paul was certain: take one of the best amateur jobs in the country.

'It's a wonderful position to be in,' she says. 'There are lots of very good horses and I get to pick my rides. If you're a pro, you more or less have to ride everything and your confidence can suffer doing that. But this way I can usually be confident I'm going to end up in the money at least.'

Sure enough, after successfully navigating her way to such a position, she then made the most of the opportunity and became champion amateur in 2005–06 and the following season. Patrick Mullins took the crown for the next couple of years but in 2008 Carberry's season was badly affected by the Meade team enduring a fifty-day run without a winner after Christmas. But along the way, doubters continued to be put in their place.

In 2006 Carberry became just the fourteenth woman to ride in the world's most famous steeplechase, the Aintree Grand National. In Forest Gunner she was on board a horse with a winning record over the fences, and with her family connection to Aintree the Irishwoman became an inevitable focal point for media attention. In fact, during the middle of the decade, the Carberry name was rarely far away from the headlines. In 2007, her brother Philip proved his big-race temperament once again with a 16-1 shock win on Sublimity in the Champion Hurdle. It continued the upward curve in his own career which also saw him win an Irish National on Point Barrow and subsequently open up a lucrative link with the French trainer François Cottin that produced French Gold Cup success on Princesse d'Anjou. Brother and sister are close to each other in age – 'Paul's so much older!' – and have always looked out for each other. So the 2006 comments of the Aintree legend Ginger McCain, the trainer of Red Rum and Amberleigh House, that no woman could win the National can't have gone down too well. As it happens, Forest Gunner got around in ninth. The famously gruff McCain admitted: 'She rides as well as any of the Carberry boys.'

> Ninety-nine per cent of riding well is tactical. If a horse is already under pressure, it's not going to do more for a few more slaps. Some horses are different but then every jockey is different as well. McCoy appears to be stronger in a finish than Timmy Murphy but it's just a different way of doing things. No one would dream of saying Timmy Murphy isn't a top jockey. What matters isn't so much strength as balance and fitness. A lot of the time fitness is mistaken for strength. You have to be fit to push one out from three furlongs out and then get involved in a driving finish.

That's a point taken up by Joanna Morgan. Riding for the legendary Seamus McGrath she once famously edged out Lester Piggott in a photo-finish. 'It's all about fitness, not strength,' she explains. 'No jockey can physically get down and push a horse. It is about balance and fitness, plus that innate quality that all jockeys must have. There are great work-riders who once they get on a racecourse are useless jockeys. They are just unable to get horses to run faster. That's an intrinsic thing that you either have or you don't. It's even more difficult over jumps because then you have to have stamina as well to take all those falls.'

She continues: 'That's where Nina is so good. She's very talented but also so strong. You only have to look at the shoulders on her. I was the same myself when I was riding. My shoulders were broader than my hips. It just builds up.'

Although Meade's extensive string demanded much of her time, Carberry also started to demonstrate a keen eye for form that reinforced her reputation for picking mounts carefully. One such animal was Celestial Wave, a mare trained by the former jockey Adrian Maguire who was starting out on a training career from Co. Cork. Maguire made no secret of his regard for Celestial Wave, and since a good horse is vital in the making of any new trainer, his decision to allow Carberry in charge of his pride and joy was some compliment. Sure enough, they won first time out in a bumper. But Maguire had no problem leaving the partnership intact over hurdles either. How much it meant to the man who ranks highly in the best-jockey-never-to-be-champion category was clear at the Leopardstown Christmas meeting in 2005 when Celestial Wave landed the Listed mares hurdle. Carberry had ridden her from the back to win the bumper: here, the partnership made all the running to win by nine lengths from Brogella. It looked like gravity was the only thing keeping the exultant Maguire from losing contact with the ground. Celestial Wave repeated the dose in another Listed race at Limerick after that.

'Without doubt she is the best girl riding that I've seen,' Maguire says. 'She's strong, bred for the game and has been around horses all her life. She's an exceptional amateur.'

It's at National Hunt racing's major festivals that jockeys' reputations are carved out and, although Cheltenham 2006 was a blank, the following month's Punchestown extravaganza allowed Carberry to display the full range of her abilities. A hugely important Grade 1 victory came in the Champion Bumper as Leading Run edged out the Cheltenham winner Hairy Molly by half a length. Even in the winner's enclosure there were thoughts of what might have been. Leading Run made his debut in 2004 but injury prevented him from racing again until the start of 2006, which meant he was too old to run at Cheltenham. Noel Meade's high opinion of him was justified in style as he maintained a perfect four-from-four record in bumpers.

If that was professionally satisfying, though, the real crowd pleaser came in the unique La Touche race over Punchestown's famous cross country course. Run over four and a quarter miles, La Touche is a bewildering criss-cross maze of stone wall obstacles, colossal banks and any variety of fence. It is a hark back to the sport's hunting and point to point roots. The joke might be that a compass and a map are more important than any piece of tack but it is a supreme test of horsemanship. The undoubted king of Punchestown's banks races is trainer Enda Bolger, who in 2006 was attempting a ninth straight La Touche success. His old hero Risk Of Thunder, the horse famously owned by Sean Connery, had retired with an astonishing seven wins in the race. Most festival racegoers prepared to put their trust in Bolger's magic again and he in turn put his faith in Carberry.

Good Step was no superstar but, coached extensively over Bolger's banks academy in Co. Limerick, he was ready to run for his life. Nevertheless, he remained a stable second string behind the veteran Spotthedifference. That horse's chance disappeared early when he was a victim of the kind of interference that's always a danger in such a race. In contrast, Good Step enjoyed a perfect passage on the fast ground. He raced prominently throughout, secured a dream run up the inner and, at the end of the marathon trip, the big chestnut had a length and a half in hand of his opposition. His owner, J.P. McManus, welcomed the pair back to the winner's enclosure and Bolger sang Carberry's praises. It wouldn't be for the last time.

In 2005, mindful of Punchestown's success with La Touche, and with four days to fill rather than three, Cheltenham's executive decided to run the Sporting Index Chase over their own cross-country course. Purists argued that it was little more than a quixotic filler but there was no doubting the spectacle it provided. Sure enough, Enda Bolger trained the inaugural winner, Spotthedifference, but missed out the following year.

In 2007 he brought 'Spot' back to top the weights and also Heads Onthe Ground, whose 10 st 2 lb weight looked attractive. Punters took the hint and made the McManus-owned lightweight a 5-2 favourite. It takes a leap of the imagination to suggest that over three miles and seven furlongs, and a demanding array of obstacles, there was never a doubt, but try telling that to bookmakers laying the favourite. Carberry was in her element. The challenge was enough to produce all that innate horsemanship and in the last mile, when the race gets serious, Heads Onthe Ground started stalking the leaders. Making a decisive move on the turn up the hill, they shot clear to beat Silver Birch by two and a half lengths. Anyone sniffy enough to park the form at the side got their comeuppance just a few weeks later when Silver Birch landed the Grand National for his young trainer Gordon Elliott and jockey Robbie Power.

It's completely different to riding in an ordinary race. I think they're a lot more exciting but then I'm usually on one of Enda's and he's the top man at it. I actually prefer the Cheltenham course to Punchestown. You have to be able to jump those banks at Punchestown or else you're in trouble. It's very hard to win otherwise. But at Cheltenham there's just one little one so it's not all about how you get on over the banks. The other thing is the pace. Because the races are so long, they go a stride slower and that really has been the making of a horse like Garde Champetre.

A hugely promising young horse when trained by Paul Nicholls, Garde Champetre became the most expensive jumper ever sold at auction in 2004 when purchased for 530,000 guineas by J.P. McManus at Doncaster Sales. It was a huge price tag to justify and Garde Champetre quickly became known as one of the legendary businessmen's more inauspicious gambles.

As a last throw of the dice he was sent to Bolger. That proved to be an inspired decision. The French-bred horse thrived in his new environment.

A visit to Cheltenham in December was frustrating when he failed to finish, but teamed up with Carberry for the first time he dealt Heads Onthe Ground a comprehensive defeat at Punchestown to become a prime contender for Cheltenham 2008. A patient ride from the back again paid huge dividends. Enough of the class which had provoked McManus into parting with all that money remained to allow Garde Champetre to enjoy himself around the Aintree-style fences and brush obstacles as well as the tight turns. So much so that, turning for home, Carberry could allow herself a glance round at her struggling opposition. Unlike Heads Onthe Ground the previous year, Garde Champetre had a massive 12 st 3 lb on his back. But if anything he was even more impressive. The point was only emphasised in 2009 with a repeat festival victory.

> Dabiroun was a turning point in my career because he was my first winner at Cheltenham. But I would be hard pushed to separate him from Garde Champetre. Both were so memorable.

Famously, though, Carberry is no one-trick pony. For those who backed Dolphin Bay in the valuable Murphys Stout Handicap Hurdle at Killarney in 2007 Carberry's efforts are just as likely to stick in the memory. The Co. Kerry track is tight and a big competitive field made it a rough race. In the circumstances, a patient ride from the back was ambitious but Dolphin Bay weaved his way through to hold off the Davy Russell-ridden Jubilant Note by a head. A *Racing Post* analysis of the race described the winning ride as simply 'inspired'. Behind Russell came both David Casey and Ruby Walsh. And the best part of it was the complete absence of anyone pointing out that a woman had won.

Other rides are less demanding but no less special because of that. There is obvious affection for Aran Concerto, which Carberry rode to win on his Naas bumper debut. At the time, Meade welcomed them back to the No.1 spot by memorably describing the horse as potentially the best he had ever trained. A Grade 1-winning novice hurdle career followed but ultimately

Michael Kinane, a career resurgence at fifty.
© *Caroline Norris*

Sea The Stars (Michael Kinane) crowns his classic campaign by winning the 2009 Epsom Derby.
PA Photos

Michael Kinane accepts another Ascot award from the Queen.
© *Caroline Norris*

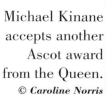

Nina Carberry in typical smiling form. © *Caroline Norris*

One of the world's top female riders canters to the start. © *Caroline Norris*

Boys can be such a pain! Nina Carberry with her jockey brothers - Philip and Paul. © *Caroline Norris*

Pat Smullen, multiple classic winner and champion jockey in Ireland.
© *Caroline Norris*

The top sprinter Benbaun and Pat Smullen win at the Curragh. In 2007 the partnership landed the Group 1 Prix de l'Abbaye at Longchamp.
© *Caroline Norris*

Timmy Murphy wins the world's most famous steeplechase, the 2008 Aintree Grand National, on Comply Or Die.
Getty Images

Timmy Murphy at his happiest, in the winner's enclosure.   © *Caroline Norris*

Jamie Spencer - the baby-faced assassin! © *Caroline Norris*

Tony McCoy, a picture of hollow-cheeked determination. ***Getty Images***

Crowded House (Jamie Spencer) is an impressive winner of the 2008 Racing Post Trophy at Doncaster. ***Getty Images***

Petit Robin (Tony McCoy) clears the water jump at Newbury on route to victory in 2008. ***Getty Images***

Johnny Murtagh,
enjoying his life and
career to the full.
© *Caroline Norris*

Soldier Of
Fortune (Johnny
Murtagh) wins the
2008 Coronation
Cup at Epsom.
Getty Images

Ruby Walsh,
Ireland's champion
jump jockey, looks
like he's helping
the horse even
more than usual!
© *Caroline Norris*

Even Ruby Walsh can't escape
the dangers of riding over fences.
© *Caroline Norris*

Ruby Walsh,
widely regarded
as a complete
National Hunt
rider.
© *Caroline Norris*

that ended in disappointment at Cheltenham. But Carberry admits that riding horses like him is a major pay off of her job.

> The Aintree National has always been special to our family. My earliest memories are of watching that race and wanting to ride horses in it. I'll never forget 1999 when Bobbyjo won. I was just fourteen and naïve. Winning just seemed so easy. Now I look at it and if by some miracle I was ever to win, I'd just retire straight away. It couldn't get better than winning a National. Even getting placed would be enough.

Questions about her eventually turning professional have persisted for years now. Many are convinced it wouldn't be a problem. Others are less sure, not in terms of her talent, but simply because she looks to have the best of both worlds as she stands. 'If you're going out for five or six rides a day and getting slapped off the ground a couple of times a week, that's a real test of mettle,' says Adrian Maguire. 'I think she's doing the right thing staying amateur. She'd be mad to turn pro.' Enda Bolger agrees. 'If she turned professional, she could find herself picking up the second choice rides after the likes of Ruby have had their pick. That's hard work. But she will always be a top amateur. She will have the pick of Noel's horses and she can look after herself as well, not get broken up.'

Carberry herself indicates that her future very probably remains in the amateur ranks but refuses to rule anything out absolutely. Things change is her motto. Her current status, however, gives her the opportunity to return to studying in college at night while also allowing her to indulge her passion for horses. Occasionally there's even time to load up the car and head west to indulge in some surfing. As children, she and Philip were taken for lessons to Bundoran in Co. Donegal by their Uncle Arthur. It's a hobby that has stuck – 'I'm not really good, maybe because I need some warm weather to do it!' Nevertheless, Bundoran and Lahinch in Co. Clare still sometimes have a view of all that famous Carberry balance on a board. Philip has even surfed in Hawaii. It's in rather colder climes, however, that he admits that his sister is in her element.

'I was at Downpatrick once, about to get in the car to leave. It was down the track a bit and the leaders went by me in the bumper. This horse kicked a few lengths clear of Nina and I thought that was that. It was only the next morning I found out she'd won. She's always in the right place at the right time. She was like that as a kid pony racing too – just class,' he says.

Long term, Carberry doesn't see herself training, but horses are set to continue being a major part of her life. Buying and selling them she feels may be worth a shot. 'I don't know if I'll be any good. Only time will tell.' Time has already proved her to be a truly exceptional jockey.

Cheltenham Festival Winners

2005
Fred Winter Juvenile Novices Hurdle   Dabiroun

2007
Sporting Index Cross-Country Chase   Heads Onthe Ground

2008
Sporting Index Cross-Country Chase   Garde Champetre

2009
Sporting Index Cross Country Chase   Garde Champetre

Other Major Winners include

2001
Masterchefs Ladies Derby   Sabrinsky

2005
Bewleys Hotel Dublin Airport Novice Hurdle   Celestial Wave

2006

Dawn Omega Mares Novice Hurdle	Celestial Wave
Paddy Power Champion Bumper	Leading Run
La Touche Cup	Good Step

2007

Murphys Irish Stout Handicap Hurdle	Dolphin Bay

2008

Masterchefs Ladies Derby	Miss Fancy Pants

7

PAT SMULLEN

For more than thirty years Paddy Smullen travelled three miles from his home in Rhode to the biggest estate near the Co. Offaly village. Working as a farm labourer didn't allow many fripperies and there were times he and his wife Mary were stretched to provide for their four sons. But for a man devoted to the outdoors almost as much as his family, the work was satisfying. Most of his life he worked for the Cottons, who owned hundreds of acres. Then some of the land was bought by businessman Sean Buckley. However, for the two years before he died, Paddy Smullen worked forty acres of the old estate that had just been bought by his son Pat.

A more prosperous Ireland has brought a supposed mocha-flavoured sophistication into the last decade but it still requires only the faintest scratch at the surface to reveal a tie between man and land that is as old as the country itself. An unspoken but strictly observed hierarchy of class, money and ownership runs through that same land as surely as any grain of rock and earth. Hundreds of years of snobbery, status and 'tuppence ha'penny pissing on tuppence' still slalom through country people's conversation. Paddy Smullen was highly thought of. But he worked land that wasn't his. That is until he was close to his death. The terrible part is that he had so short a time tending what was now in the family. In Ireland such a turnaround was shot through with meaning. Paddy Smullen knew it better than anyone, and his son felt the pride that a simple scrawl on a deed provided.

Pat Smullen was thirteen before he sat on his first pony. It didn't belong to his parents. Ponies simply didn't feature on his or his brothers' horizons. Other animals did. First chance they got, Sean, Gerard, Pat and Brian would go to where their father worked. Compared to any office or garage, the farm offered real interest. Dealing with agricultural animals became second nature, while at the same time incubating a love of the outdoors. And then Sean did what older brothers do: he opened a chink that his little brother Pat stared through and decided he liked.

Sean discovered a love of horses. After finishing his school exams, he got a job with the Co. Meath-based trainer, and former jockey, Joanna Morgan. Her focus at the time was preparing young horses for Breeze-Up Sales. It was hard work but the teenager from Offaly thrived. In time, Sean Smullen moved to Canada and now is in charge of the hugely powerful farm of Frank Stronach, one of the leading bloodstock figures in North America. He also trains a few horses just outside Toronto.

Sean used to watch racing a bit on telly but after his Leaving Cert [exams] this is what he decided to do. He used to come home weekends and before he could afford a car Dad would drive him back to Joanna's. The rest of us would pile in just for something different to do. Joanna being Joanna spotted the other two boys were big and hardy enough but she also spotted that I might be useful to her. So she threw me up on a pony. It really is true what they say about being bitten by the bug. I knew the second I put my leg over that pony that this is what I wanted to do.

Soon every weekend and holiday there were two Smullen boys staying at the Ballivor yard. The younger one had the same willingness to work and a similarly natural way with animals as his brother. But he was also small, light and appeared to have a talent for riding. It wasn't long before there was a graduation to the big hunters at the yard. Within six months of first sitting on a pony, he was riding out racehorses. The boy had found what he wanted to do most. School had never held much interest. Now it was an active barrier. Both Paddy and Mary Smullen fought hard to keep him studying, but they may as well have been trying to flow water uphill. As well as a knack for riding, their third son had a stubbornness that would stand him in good stead. At fifteen he left school and also began journeying a few miles out of Rhode to where he began an apprenticeship with the local trainer Tom Lacy.

It took a leap of the imagination to picture making a life out of a sport that seemed like something others did on television. There was no family link to racing, no money to open any doors, no safety net of any sort. This was a solo leap into what could have been very cold water. But although a lot of it was alien, at the centre were animals and dealing with them felt as natural as breathing itself.

Being young and innocent is a great thing sometimes. It's actually frightening now to think of it. I had no qualifications and no idea what I would do if it didn't work out. But at that age it didn't enter my head it wouldn't work out. I was lucky too in that fear was never an issue. If you're to be successful in this game, then you can't afford to be afraid, even at an early age. There must have been some level of talent there, too, because I wouldn't have progressed so quickly if there wasn't.

Tom Lacy was a small-time dual-purpose trainer who bred some horses and was willing to give this local youngster a chance. It was fortunate timing to begin an apprenticeship. There were some well-handicapped horses in the yard, including Vicosa, who provided Smullen with a first winner at Dundalk. There were also some home-breds up to running in Stakes races. Smullen rode them all despite still being only a claimer. It was a foundation of which he took full advantage. He ended 1995 as champion apprentice with twenty-six winners. In 1996 Smullen was champion again with twenty-nine. But one of those was hugely significant for the future.

Dermot Weld's hunger for success may be clothed in more urbanity than some of his colleagues but easy fluency can't mask the legendary trainer's appetite. After four decades of operating at the top level around the world, even the most mediocre handicap can still get those competitive juices flowing. So the race named after his father Charlie, the C.L. Weld Park Stakes, at the Curragh in October 1996 was always going to get his full attention. Michael Kinane had the pick of Weld's two runners, Absolute Glee and Token Gesture. He chose Absolute Glee but it was a toss-of-the-coin call. Weld doesn't do such calls when it comes to who rides his horses. Picking an up and coming champion apprentice for Token Gesture was loaded with significance.

'The turning point of my career' is how Smullen describes it now and he rode like it on the day. Token Gesture at 10-1 held off the Christy Roche-ridden Melleray by a head, with Absolute Glee a short head further back in third. It was a titanic struggle for a significant Group 3 prize and the nineteen-year-old kid had more than held his own against the top two senior jockeys in the country. Less than a year later that ability to bridge the yawning chasm between claiming apprentice and fully fledged jockey was advertised even more spectacularly.

By now he was riding extensively for Tommy Stack and also as No.2 to Johnny Murtagh at John Oxx's yard. The quiet youngster who had been playing catch-up was now ahead of the game and feeling comfortable in it. So much so that Stack put him up on Tarascon in the 1997 Moyglare Stud Stakes. Ireland's most important race for juvenile fillies is a Group 1 and always intensely competitive. But once again in a tight finish Smullen won by a head from Heed My Warning. In third was Shahtoush, the following year's Epsom Oaks heroine, who in turn led home three stable companions from the yard of a certain A.P. O'Brien.

That strength in depth was a sign of the future. Kinane was still first jockey to Weld but was riding more and more for the emerging powerhouse at Ballydoyle. It was only a matter of time before the two jobs would become impossible to juggle. In 1999 the inevitable happened. Weld needed a new stable jockey. It was nearly three years since Token Gesture but the link had been maintained. Smullen was only twenty-one but Weld judged him ready. The farm labourer's son had taken only eight years from first riding a pony to securing one of the most coveted jobs in Irish racing. He had also begun a much more personal relationship.

Frances Crowley was a successful jockey herself as well as being a Commerce graduate from University College Dublin. Steeped in racing, she is a daughter of the veteran trainer Joe Crowley and a sister of Aidan O'Brien's wife, Anne Marie. During a winter stay in Dubai in 1998 when she worked for the Dubai Racing Association, Crowley and Smullen became more than just weighing room colleagues. The following year they bought a house in Carlow just behind the college. It was halfway between the Curragh and the Co. Kilkenny village of Piltown, where Frances started training at her father's yard. Ruby Walsh and his future wife Gillian were neighbours. Travelling to work required 6 a.m. starts, a rush home for lunch and then possibly a long drive to an evening meeting some-where, but the relationship prospered. In 2001 the couple were married in Carlow on the first Tuesday after the flat season finished. Their honey-moon was back in Dubai. They have two children, Hannah and Paddy.

> Looking back, I was so lucky. A lot of hard work went into it but there are plenty of people who work hard. At every stage things seemed to happen for me. I have to give one hundred per cent credit to Tom Lacy. He put me up on everything he had, an 8 lb claimer riding in Listed races. And Tommy Stack has always been a guy to give young riders opportunities. He could easily have jocked me off Tarascon and no one would have blamed him. But he didn't.

What Stack, Weld and many others had noticed of course was the raw talent that complemented Smullen's appetite for self-improvement. A bright young man with a maturity beyond his years, Smullen could mix easily with owners out of the saddle while remaining deadly focused on it. There was also no arguing with a natural ability to get horses to run for him. With Weld, however, there has always been only one way to do things – his way.

Fifteen years earlier Kinane had found that out, with his experience of the race-replay 'torture chamber'. Tactics are vital to Weld. He feels they win more races than any physical strength or sheer riding ability. Getting his ideas across to Kinane resulted in some memorable flare ups between the pair. Smullen had heard the 'chamber' stories, too, but tempera-mentally he is a different character from Kinane, not as quick to react. That was to prove useful.

Dermot's a man who doesn't suffer fools lightly. He's a demanding man who expects things to be done right. Some people might say that makes him a difficult trainer to ride for and at the start there were many times when I had to bite my lip. If he feels things have gone wrong and it's my fault, then it isn't pretty. But back then he was probably right anyway ninety per cent of the time. I was only a young fellah and it could easily break you being in such a high profile job. I used to hate being summoned up to the office. It was a tough time. But mentally you have to be strong enough to take it. From Dermot's point of view I think it's a test. He wants you to get things right but at the same time he is testing your character a little bit, to see if you're mentally tough enough. So the only thing is to sit there and take it like a man. After a while, I started to get more confidence in myself and began to make points of my own. And that's what Dermot wants: to make you into a person who will voice an opinion. If you're right he will listen.

The breaking-in period paid off in 2000 when Smullen booted home eighty winners, which was enough to claim a first senior jockeys' championship. But that was the year of the Derby and Arc winner Sinndar, when John Murtagh enjoyed the sort of success internationally that used to be Kinane's preserve. The latter had the power of Ballydoyle behind him which was about to explode into a record-breaking year in 2001 with twenty-three Group 1 victories. What their young rival needed was a star horse to prove his mettle. Such an animal materialised in the elegant shape of Vinnie Roe.

A son of Weld's 1995 Irish Derby runner up Definite Article, Vinnie Roe was named after a nephew of owner Jim Sheridan, the well known film director. A Listed winner as a two-year-old, he was good enough to be placed behind Galileo in a Derby Trial before finishing fourth in the 2001 Italian Derby. He was ridden in Rome by Richard Quinn. In his twenty-eight other career starts, Smullen was on board. But it was when he was stepped up to distances over a mile and a half that Vinnie Roe began to look exceptional. The Irish St Leger was open to older horses like the former English Leger winner Millenary, but Vinnie Roe took the first steps to becoming a Curragh legend when beating that horse by a couple of lengths at 5-1. The following month he went to France and took Longchamp's Leger, the Prix Royal Oak. Smullen had found his Group 1 advertisement – 'I was desperate for a good horse to cement the job, and he was it.'

In 2002 Vinnie followed in the footsteps of Vintage Crop and went to Royal Ascot's Gold Cup over two and a half miles. The marathon distance proved beyond Vintage Crop but for much of the race Vinnie Roe looked set to win, only to lose out in a titanic battle with Royal Rebel. It was disappointing but there was no doubt what his next major target would be, and sure enough a second Irish Leger was secured at odds of 4-7.

Then the Vintage Crop echoes continued as Vinnie Roe was sent to Flemington for the Melbourne Cup. He was accompanied by his stable companion Media Puzzle but Vinnie was the star attraction. The intensity of the media and public focus on the 'race that stops a nation' is always an eye-opener for Cup virgins. Smullen was no different. But hot spring weather turned the ground against Vinnie Roe and it was Media Puzzle who won easily under the local rider Damien Oliver. There was subsequent criticism in the Australian press that Vinnie Roe had raced too wide, a heinous crime down under, although that ignored the reality that Oliver had tracked Smullen almost throughout. Michael Kinane had experienced a similar roasting on board Vintage Crop in the 1990s but the idea that different is not the same as wrong still doesn't seem to have percolated into Australian racing's somewhat blinkered psyche.

It was disappointing, but 2002 still ended on an international high. Weld's opinion of Dress To Thrill had always been highly rated, and in the autumn the Moyglare Stud-owned filly started to show why. Wins in the Matron Stakes at Leopardstown and the Sun Chariot at Newmarket preceded a failed attempt on the Breeders' Cup Mile at Arlington in Chicago. But her season didn't end there. On 1 December, the Irish filly ran in the Grade 1 Matriarch Stakes over nine furlongs at Hollywood Park. In a top class six-runner field, Smullen's direct opponents were among the best that America could muster. All five – Pat Valenzuala,

Victor Espinoza, Jerry Bailey, Laffitt Pincay and Kent Desormeaux – were Kentucky Derby-winning jockeys riding on home turf. Smullen took in the names and characteristically dealt with the challenge quietly and determinedly. Dress To Thrill was brought with a sustained challenge to head Golden Apples and Valenzuala on the line.

> Dress To Thrill had tremendous speed and overall I would say she is the best that I've ridden. She doesn't have the profile of say Grey Swallow or Refuse To Bend or Vinnie Roe because that Matriarch was run in December when everybody here had switched off from the flat and was focusing on the jumps. But it was an incredible achievement. Beating the likes of Jerry Bailey and Pat Valenzuala meant a lot to me. The thing is that when she won the Matron and the Sun Chariot they were Group 2 races but a couple of years later they were upgraded to Group 1. She could have been a triple Group 1 winner which would have been more appropriate for her.

In 2002 Smullen experienced a first Royal Ascot success with Irresistible Jewel's Ribblesdale Stakes victory; there was the promise of even greater glory in 2003. The day after Vinnie Roe's second Leger, Refuse To Bend completed a Group 1 weekend double by landing the National Stakes at the Curragh. Media Puzzle's half-brother possessed a precocity that confounded his pedigree. He was definitely a classic contender and, considering his brother's stamina, the Derby appeared a realistic target. It was a thought to keep the cockles warm through the winter. But in the spring they really started to sizzle.

Refuse To Bend started to work like a potential superstar. Curragh gallop watchers started to purr about the Sadlers Wells colt whose pedigree shouted Derby but whose work suggested Guineas. A narrow but decisive victory in the Leopardstown Trial only encouraged hopes of a trip to Newmarket. In the week leading up to the first classic of the year, minds were made up. Smullen partnered Refuse To Bend in a gallop. The horse worked beautifully. As he pulled up, Pat Shanahan ranged alongside on the work companion. The older man is renowned as a good judge. With an Irish Derby and an Irish Oaks under his belt, Shanahan recognises a good one. His message to Smullen was simple: 'You will win the Guineas on that horse.'

Irish horses dominated the betting for the 2003 Guineas but it was Ballydoyle's representative Hold That Tiger that started a 4-1 favourite. Refuse To Bend was 9-2 and saddled with an outside draw. Nevertheless, hopes were high. As he helped his jockey into the saddle, Weld's message was simple: 'Ride him like the top class international jockey you are.' Once again, Smullen responded to the challenge. Despite the draw, Refuse To Bend was soon in a good position up the straight Rowley Mile as several bad-luck stories unfolded behind him. There were none more so than Zafeen, who would prove his class later in the St James's Palace Stakes. But on the classic day he came up three quarters of a length short as Smullen waved his whip in front.

Immediate reaction was that a potential Triple Crown winner had just got the hardest leg out of the way. Refuse To Bend's dam had been a sprinter herself but she'd produced a Melbourne Cup winner in Media Puzzle. Derby odds tumbled. But it wasn't to be. Those spectacular work-outs at home became less consistent. Whereas there had been confidence going into Newmarket, there was just hope at Epsom. Refuse To Bend travelled well to the straight and then faded to thirteenth behind Kris Kin. He joined the likes of King Of Kings and Entrepreneur as speedy sons of Sadlers Wells who couldn't carry that pace to a mile and a half.

> He was a miler-ten furlong horse and simply didn't stay a mile and a half. We all got misled a bit by his pedigree which suggested stamina wouldn't be an issue. He won the Desmond Stakes afterwards at a mile but he didn't really fire after that. He did well as a four year old, though, when he was sold to Godolphin.

Vinnie Roe proceeded to win a third Irish Leger in 2003, beating the Group 1 performer Gamut, and brought off a remarkable four-timer in 2004, beating Brian Boru by two and a half lengths in a performance that suggested the old boy was if anything getting better with age. The previous year Weld had elected to bypass Australia in favour of an attempt on the Prix de l'Arc de Triomphe. Against top class mile and a half horses, Vinnie Roe fell short. This time he would have to concede weight, but over two miles, and on what turned out to be unseasonably soft ground conditions. Weld's dream of a third Melbourne Cup was on.

In pouring rain, and with mud flying, Flemington more resembled an Irish point to point than one of world racing's most famous events. Trainer and jockey examined the race exhaustively beforehand. Vinnie Roe's top weight limited their options. Above all else, they had to secure the horse a smooth passage. Darting in and out of pockets and using up valuable energy was a privilege reserved for the lightweights and the unfancied. Smullen knew it would leave him open for flak if he didn't win but the conclusion was that in similar conditions in Europe he would race on the outside. It suited the horse, so why change tactics?

In most years it would have worked perfectly. Vinnie Roe raced beautifully and turned into the long straight travelling like a winner. But this was the year of Makybe Diva, one of the best Australian stayers of modern times, who was getting weight from the Irish star. Her jockey, Glen Boss, also gambled on an inside route. He could just as easily have paid the price with interference but instead Makybe Diva secured a dream run, saving lengths in the process. She was too good not to win in those circumstances and, try as Vinnie Roe did, he couldn't reel her in.

The criticism of Smullen afterwards made 2002 sound like the chirping of hoarse sparrows. Australia's racing press has a reputation of being hard on all jockeys, even their own. But this was an opportunity to vent some spleen that was never going to be wasted. It's the nature of the media beast that zeroing in on someone you never meet is a lot easier than someone you may need for a quote tomorrow. Japan's finest rider, Yutaka Take, has experienced that in Europe. French jockeys continue to be looked at suspiciously by British commentators until otherwise proven. The charismatic American Cash Asmussen was routinely pilloried in Ireland during a brief but colourful stint as Vincent O'Brien's stable jockey in the 1980s. Lashing out at local boys requires a degree of spine that can often go AWOL. With Smullen, any pretence at balance or comprehension that there are different ways of doing things was parked at the side of hundreds of laptops in favour of heavy criticism of the Irish bloke.

> Every overseas jockey that goes to Australia should be prepared to get slated. If you're not strong enough to take it, then I would say stay at home. It's just a game out there. From the minute you get off the plane there is abuse. It's the way Australians are. Mick Kinane got it – and he won. I remember walking the track a couple of days before the race. Dermot was being questioned by some journalists and with me right there among them, they asked why he wasn't using an Australian jockey. They regard racing three wide as being off the track but there was no way we had a chance if I'd sent Vinnie Roe down the inside asking him to make three runs during the race. It's a different style of racing in Australia. But you can't go from Europe and adapt completely to that style. It simply wouldn't suit our horses. The main thing was that the trainer was happy with the ride.

The Galway festival, on more welcoming ground, has always been one of the great jewels of Irish racing. Held in late July, it boasts the biggest crowds, the biggest betting and the biggest profile of any racing event in the country, despite the action out on the track often being distinctly ordinary. Ever since winning at Galway as a fifteen-year-old amateur jockey in 1964, Weld has targeted the festival. He has trained over three hundred winners there. Classics and international success may define a professional career but, to the general public in the summer, Weld is simply the King of Ballybrit. That puts extra pressure on his jockey. The ammunition for a good week is always there but with that comes expectation. In 2003, however, it would have needed a shock of seismic proportions for a compact grey colt not to win the juvenile maiden – once he left the stalls.

Grey Swallow's reputation preceded him before the Curragh Derby weekend a month previously. However, the two-year-old got upset in the stalls and had to be withdrawn. Weld's thunderous reaction was a sure sign of the high regard in which he held the colt bred by his mother. Grey

Swallow escaped the ordeal without injury, though, and instead made his debut at Galway. Once out of the stalls he was spectacular, wining by ten lengths without breaking sweat.

> I couldn't believe the way he won. He quickened as if there was no hill. He was quite a hyper horse who got claustrophic in the gate. But once he was out he was very good and it takes a good two-year-old to win first time up at Galway. It's not an easy track and it's not an easy track to ride. There are a lot of undulations and trying to get a horse balanced and in position can be a problem. I look forward to Galway week but, at the same time, when I'm driving out the gate on the last day I'm not unhappy. The boss always wants a good week and he's revved up so I want to get the job done.

Despite running just once more that season in a Group 3, the job of turning Grey Swallow into a two-year-old champion was also done. The Killavullan Stakes yielded an eight-length win which was enough to make him the leading juvenile in Ireland and a top classic prospect. In that light, a fourth to Haafhd in the Newmarket 2,000 Guineas and a third to Bachelor Duke in the Irish equivalent was disappointing. But he was given a try at a mile and a half in the 2004 Irish Derby and he proved a revelation. North Light looked to have secured an Epsom-Curragh double when striking the front in the straight. However, Smullen had conserved Grey Swallow's suspect stamina well enough to be within striking distance and all that juvenile class came to the fore when he out-kicked North Light. There wasn't much in it at the line but there was enough to guarantee a memorable local victory. The normally cool winning rider was uncharacteristically emotional and described how nothing could compete with winning your own Derby.

Grey Swallow failed to win in two more starts that year in the Irish Champion Stakes and the Arc. He was back in 2005, however, and proved his quality a second time at Group 1 level in a vintage renewal of the Tattersalls Gold Cup at the Curragh. Behind him were the Arc winner Bago and the top-class Azamour. That was Grey Swallow's sole success of the season and he looked less than his brilliant best in three starts as a five-year-old. One of them yielded a Grade 2 victory at Hollywood Park and his racing career ended in Australia's Cox Plate before going to stud.

In addition to Grey Swallow's Tattersalls Gold Cup, Smullen also secured a third jockeys' championship in 2005. But within the Smullen-Crowley household the year will be remembered for the achievements of Saoire. Just two years previously, tired of the constant commuting, they bought Clifton Lodge stables at the Curragh. Frances Crowley's pedigree as a trainer included prestige wins over jumps like Moscow Express' 1999 Galway Plate but she had also proved herself adept on the flat. Any doubters got their definitive answer with Saoire. As a two-year-old she finished third in the Moyglare under Smullen, but for the Irish 1,000 Guineas the jockey was claimed by Weld for Utterly Heaven. Into the breach stepped Michael Kinane, just forty minutes before Grey Swallow had won the Tattersalls. As a 10-1 shot, the Crowley runner wasn't an obvious candidate for securing a remarkable family Group 1 double but Smullen knew a possible classic victory was in sight for Kinane. That provoked understandably mixed feelings. But there was no doubt in his mind that his wife had the best available on her side.

Mick is still the man. I've never seen a rider like him. He's the most professional man, so strong and tactically aware. I've ridden all over the world and there's no one better. People have this idea of him, that he's not easy to approach, but I couldn't speak more highly of the man. When I started with Dermot and things weren't always so good, Mick would have a quiet word and just tell me to walk away or bite my lip. I'll always be grateful for that.

Utterly Heaven ran a fine race for a 33-1 shot to finish fourth. But despite coming under pressure quite early in the race, Saoire never stopped finding more. It was a desperately tight finish but at the line Kinane had her nose down when it mattered. As her husband weighed in, Crowley pondered the significance of becoming the first licensed female trainer to win a classic in Ireland. Other women may actually have done the same in the past but the records don't reflect their achievement. This one, though, is set in history. It also completed a superb Group 1 double in less than an hour and husband and wife posed happily for photos. Afterwards came a quiet celebration at home. Anyone hoping for party fireworks were disappointed. Neither of them have the temperaments for exuberant celebrations: a small child and a stable full of horses tend to steer most people away from over-indulgence anyway.

Such days are all the sweeter as the racing game tends to throw up more frustration than glory. Even the most successful jockeys have percentages that contain more losers than winners. Sometimes, though, there are incidents that can only be described as colourful. One of those occurred in August 2005 during the first race of a meeting at Leopardstown. It was an ordinary six-furlong maiden that contained an extraordinary incident. Most people in the stands turned their backs as the horses passed the post but the stewards' cameras picked it up. As the jockeys sat up on horses still going at something like 35 miles an hour, Johnny Murtagh leaned across to Smullen and punched him in the jaw. Remarkably, Smullen barely seemed to flinch and remained on the horse. But it was a spectacular reminder of the white hot competition that takes place daily out on the track. This time it was provoked by an incident at the crown of the bend when Murtagh had to snatch up after an incident with Smullen and the Brazilian jockey Valdir De Souza. The stewards later apportioned no blame to anyone for that. Murtagh, however, did.

> For some time before that me and Johnny had been clashing in races. If things got tight, the two of us were usually there. It happens in the whole argy-bargy of race riding. But it got out of hand and became stupid. I was second jockey to Johnny at Oxx's, so I know him well. I think it all came down to us being too alike as characters. You have to be very aggressive and determined in this business. We want to win very badly and when you are competing on a daily basis things can get out of hand sometimes. We're good friends now and it's all behind us. We've grown up and we actually laugh about it now.

Murtagh wasn't laughing at the time. He got a twenty-one-day ban from the stewards that ruled him out of riding Motivator, the horse on which he had won the Derby, in the Irish Champion Stakes.

Another Irish classic fell to Smullen in 2006 when Nightime thrived in the muddy conditions of the 1,000 Guineas and sluiced up to score in the colours of her owner-breeder Gita Weld. More Group 1 glory fell to him the following year as Benbaun graduated to the top-flight with a game success in the Prix de l'Abbaye at Longchamp. Horse and jockey were cementing a partnership developed through a series of valuable sprint victories at the Curragh.

A fourth jockeys' championship also came Smullen's way, a title he then retained in 2008, and it is something he values perhaps more than some of his colleagues. The pattern among most riders in Ireland is to dismiss any talk of the title until the Listowel festival in September at the earliest. And even then there is a grim determination to underplay the whole thing as almost an after-thought. That is not the Smullen way. 'From day one of the season I give it everything. If I'm good enough and the horses stay healthy, then I have a chance. It's definitely something I pursue. In my opinion, being champion jockey is a great achievement, especially in Ireland right now. The standard is so high here, definitely as good as anywhere else in the world, and maybe better.'

Smullen has repeatedly proven his ability against the best that Ireland has to offer while also winning Group 1 prizes in Britain, France and the USA. Following in the footsteps of Michael Kinane as Dermot Weld's stable jockey means he has been touted by some observers as a potential No.1 rider at Ballydoyle in the future. Aidan O'Brien and Smullen are married to sisters and there have been occasions when the champion trainer has used the jockey's services when he has had a number of runners in a race, particularly in the Epsom Derby. There is no doubting Smullen's big race pedigree. There is a noticeable absence of hard luck stories when it matters most, be it a Group 1 or a handicap hot-pot at Galway. Serious about his profession and yet possessing an unassuming and personable manner, he has repeatedly expressed his desire to improve and to compete regularly at the highest level. Weld for one believes it is only a matter of time before his stable jockey is a major presence at the top international table.

'It is inevitable that other trainers are going to come looking for him and I don't have a problem with that,' admits the trainer. 'The more good horses he rides, the better jockey he becomes. I remember saying years ago that Mick Kinane would be a success in any walk of life because he is intelligent and works hard. The same applies to Pat Smullen. He is an excellent stable jockey who rides work on a regular basis and is interested in the entire operation.'

For an ambitious man, 2008 was a largely frustrating year as a fine crop of three-year-olds at Weld's Rosewell House yard fell agonisingly short of cutting it at the very top level. Famous Name looked a likely winner of the Prix Du Jockey Club at Chantilly but couldn't quite overhaul Vision D'Etat and was beaten a head. Defeat tasted bitter but what added to it was the strong suspicion that only a high draw prevented that margin going the other way. Five days later the strongly fancied Chinese White flopped in the Oaks at Epsom, and although Casual Conquest ran third in the following day's Derby, he was a long way behind New Approach and Tartan Bearer.

What it proved to Smullen, however, is that this is the level he wants to ride at consistently, a desire only strengthened by a maiden Breeders' Cup success when America's greatest equine show rolled into Santa Anita in 2008. The inaugural 'dirt marathon' might have infringed the trades description act since it was run on an all-weather surface rather than dirt and the trip is middle distance in European terms. There was also the strong suspicion of it being staged in order to boost possible flagging European morale in relation to America's richest meeting of the year. But it still provided a valuable pay out and Smullen gave a ruthlessly professional display on Muhannak to outride Frankie Dettori on the hot favourite, Sixties Icon. The latter brought Group 1 form to the LA party while Muhannak's black type CV consisted of a more modest Listed victory at Dundalk. It made no difference to the Irishman, though, who powered the English-trained horse to a head success.

Afterwards he sat on a florally garlanded Muhannak in front of the packed Santa Anita stands and soaked in the moment: a marathon distance from Rhode for sure but bridged all the same by Paddy Smullen's son.

Classic Wins

2001

Irish St Leger	Vinnie Roe
Prix Royal Oak	Vinnie Roe

2002

Irish St Leger	Vinnie Roe

2003

English 2,000 Guineas	Refuse To Bend
Irish St Leger	Vinnie Roe

2004

Irish St Leger	Vinnie Roe
Irish Derby	Grey Swallow

2006

Irish 1,000 Guineas	Nightime

Other Major Winners include

1997

Moyglare Stud Stakes	Tarascon

2002

Ribblesdale Stakes	Irresistible Jewel
National Stakes	Refuse To Bend
Matriarch Stakes	Dress To Thrill

2003

American Derby	Evolving Tactics

2004
American Derby   Simple Exchange

2005
Tattersalls Gold Cup   Grey Swallow

2006
Ballyogan Stakes   Yomalo

2007
Prix de l'Abbaye   Benbaun

2008
Derrinstown Derby Trial   Casual Conquest
Breeders' Cup Marathon   Muhannak

2009
Tattersalls Gold Cup   Casual Conquest

8

TIMMY MURPHY

After Comply Or Die's 2008 Grand National triumph, Timmy Murphy was invited to expound on his own journey to Aintree glory from 'rock bottom'. But he wasn't prepared to play ball. Rock bottom, Murphy suggested, is when you're dead. If that wasn't quite the answer a phalanx of copy-hungry hacks wanted, then tough.

Comply Or Die's owner, and Murphy's employer, David Johnson, sat next to the jockey at the post-race press conference and reminded everyone that the man in silks alongside him had already dealt with such issues in his autobiography. It was Brendan Behan who once suggested there is no bad publicity – except an obituary. But his fellow Irishman wouldn't agree. At the high-point of an already illustrious career, Murphy's past refused to relax its grip on the popular imagination. Even if the centre of attention didn't want to focus on it, there was little point in trying to deflect the media away from a remarkable story that at one stage looked like turning into a career obituary.

In fairness to those scavenging for copy-friendly quotes, ignoring it would have been like turning a blind-eye to a rampant elephant marauding through Liverpool. Less than five years previously, the National-winning rider had emerged from Wormwood Scrubs prison after serving eighty-four days for indecent assault and being drunk on an aeroplane. He had also been briefly, and wrongly, placed on the sex offenders' register. In the midst of such turmoil, Murphy's struggle with alcoholism came to a head. Even his closest allies believed one of the most promising careers in jump racing was finished. The job of sorting himself out would surely override any consideration of restoring his place at the top of the jockeys' table. That he has managed both is a redemptive tale of such scale that it will forever be central to Murphy's story, no matter how much success he has in the future.

Of course, after a while, retelling that story can be wearisome for the central subject. Seeing the lowest depths of your life repeatedly referenced every time your name is mentioned doesn't get easier. But Murphy is media-savvy enough to realise it is inevitable. There is also enough of a remove now to ponder the impact his story may have on someone fighting a similarly desperate battle with the bottle. The way he tells it is completely straightforward, with that artlessly brutal honesty that many recovering alcoholics possess. Since he has looked into a personal abyss, emotions that were firmly locked up before are now open for discussion and dissection. Murphy confesses that he used to be a terrible communicator. Now he can be a wonderfully evocative talker – if he chooses.

That much is obvious from his 2006 autobiography. The success of *Riding the Storm* is primarily due to its subject's resolute honesty. He cuts brutally to the point in terms of his problems with drink, with other people, and most of all with himself. In the process there is no hiding any inadequacies. There are times reading it when it is hard to feel sympathy for a person who can appear to be so moody and difficult. Often grumpy, occasionally whinging and sometimes painfully morose, the book's reflection of the man in the middle is a tribute to Murphy's determination to portray himself warts and all. In this age of pap autobiography, it is all the more effective for that.

That was the whole idea. There's no point doing an autobiography if you're not going to tell the truth. By and large the response has been hugely positive. And it has been useful for me. Looking back wasn't so much painful as therapeutic. A lot of the time you do stuff and you don't even realise you're doing it. But reading it on paper gives things a different perspective.

However, if the personal struggle will always be a subject of fascination, then so also is the talent that underpins Murphy's status as one of jump racing's most stylish virtuosos. If the Tony McCoy way is about an all-out will to win, then Murphy's is the opposite. Like his friend and rival, Murphy's own brand of getting to the winning post has become synonymous with him. When the occasion demands, he can ride races from the front and get stuck into a horse with the best of them but his preferred way is to rely on patience and feel. 'A.P. would get the race won at halfway and then struggle home. I'd rather have the horse doing his best work at the finish. Then, if he wins, touch wood, you've ridden the perfect race and the horse doesn't finish legless,' he once said. It's a policy that leaves him open to criticism from grandstand jockeys. But when it comes off, the results can be spectacular.

Comply Or Die's National triumph alone would have justified Murphy's determination to do it his way. That he managed to pull it off on the world's biggest steeplechase stage also proved, yet again, a big race temperament that even at the height of his personal problems remained undiminished. But what appeared to touch him most deeply was that the nine minutes and sixteen seconds it took to enter jump racing's most exclusive club meant so much to those closest to him. The man who had burned so many bridges through his drinking had justified all those willing to give his talent a second chance.

> Anybody who knows anything about racing knows the National, so it is something you only dream about winning. When you're a kid it's the National that you're always riding in when you're on a pony. But you never expect to win it. It all comes down to experience in the end. I don't know how many times I've been buried in the race. I don't know how many times I've been going well after a circuit, got to the Canal Turn second time still going well, and just starting to think there's a chance of winning, when suddenly bang, you're gone. On Comply Or Die the whole thing was to not think about winning. Going to the last ditch I was very happy but all I kept saying was 'not too soon, not too soon'.

That determination to rein things in goes some way towards explaining his subsequent reluctance to play any media games. Timothy James Murphy is his own man. There are some within racing who might describe him as odd – a loaded dismissal favoured by those unwilling or unable to tolerate anyone with even a slightly different take on the world than their own. 'He was harder to handle before the accident than he is now,' grins Michael Hourigan, the trainer Murphy turned to when he was released from prison and who has been a reassuringly constant presence in his life ever since his teenage years.

Hourigan's description of the aeroplane incident on Virgin Atlantic Flight BS901 from Tokyo to Heathrow on 14 April 2002 as an 'accident' is not one that Murphy himself goes along with. He has no memory of urinating against the plane fuselage or groping a stewardess. What he can remember from the alcohol-soaked haze is waking up at Heathrow and noticing the police cars through the plane window. At the subsequent trial it went against the grain to plead guilty to something he couldn't remember but he has never attempted to excuse or dilute the significance of his actions.

The drinking culture that he encountered on leaving school at sixteen is a familiar one to most people in society, not just in racing. Murphy's account of his spell working at Dermot Weld's yard on the Curragh is typical of most young people let loose on their own with some money in their pocket. The weekend has always been a time to cut loose. Struggling into work on Monday morning is an endurance test but for most people that is only a temporary blip. For those unable to keep some boundaries on their drinking, however, the cycle can quickly start to dominate. Alcohol has always been a bad boss. But until that fateful plane incident Murphy considered his drinking to be no worse than a lot of other people. The sad part is that, on the face of things, he was probably right. But not everyone who spends their weekend in an alcoholic haze has a career in the public eye.

The impact of that flight home from Japan is retold with brutal honesty by Murphy and the overriding sense is one of shame and regret at the pain caused to those closest to home. With time now between him and the worst of it, he has logically come to view the series of events in a positive light.

> I was going down a very dark avenue but I was lucky enough to see some light. It allowed me to cop myself on in time before it was too late. When I went to prison I thought I was fucked and I'd never ride again. But if I hadn't gone there, I wouldn't be here now.

Such an attitude reflects a mental toughness that has allowed him to beat the odds. Statistically, it is much more likely for a recovering alcoholic to drink again within a year of stopping than to stay off it. Murphy still goes to meetings and makes an effort to stay away from some public situations but his success on the track is only a reflection of his greater success away from it. Instead of the desperate restlessness of his early career, there is a greater maturity that is set to be enjoyed by the racing public for a good while yet.

That restlessness has been an undoubted feature throughout the first part of the thirty-five-year-old's life in racing. His father, Jimmy Murphy, was a well-known point to point rider and worked at Lady Clague's Newberry Stud near Kilvullen, Co. Kildare. Horses were a constant part of life and, although Helen Murphy hoped her eldest son might pursue another avenue in his life, there was no contest between school and riding. A bedroom wall covered with pictures of famous horses and jockeys was a constant reminder to her of what the boy wanted to do when becoming a man. The problem was that that stage seemed much too far away.

At fourteen, Murphy secured himself a weekend job riding out on the Curragh for Noel Chance. The future double Gold Cup-winning trainer was based five miles from home but the bike ride was nothing to a young teenager in a hurry. He was in such a rush that a year later he planned to run away to England. His parents woke one morning to find an empty bed and some empty drawers. The police were called and the boy returned home. But it was only delaying the inevitable. At sixteen he left home for good and began working for the legendary Dermot Weld.

Despite being at one of the top yards in Ireland, Murphy was not happy.

Once he stepped outside the routine of the working week and the drinking weekend, there was a realisation that he was going nowhere fast. Weld's wasn't an obvious base for an aspiring amateur jockey. There wasn't even the consolation of riding work on some of the yard's classically bred flat horses. That was very much the duty of stable jockey Michael Kinane, who was turning into one of the world's most in-demand riders. Youth, however, doesn't place much store in such reputations and certainly not a youth in a hurry. The restlessness that drove him into racing in the first place also made every passing day seem a disaster. Not for the last time, Murphy's time-keeping was also becoming an issue. Neither party was heartbroken at a parting of the ways. Next stop for the impatient youngster was another mainly flat yard on the Curragh.

Michael Halford couldn't provide many opportunities but his regime suited Murphy better. Halford's career was only starting, too, so an all-hands-to-the-pumps attitude was a necessity in the yard. That included riding work, which suited the new boy, and there was also more of a focus on National Hunt racing than at Weld's. Rides in bumpers and in point to points started to increase.

His first winner came in a point to point on board Gayloire at Kilkuckridge in May 1993. Murphy was just eighteen. Seven months later a first racecourse victory arrived when The Real Article won at Punchestown. Even then there was a poise to him that marked Murphy out from the scores of his amateur colleagues. But he knew that, too, which made his frustration at things not progressing quicker all the more acute. Not that his frustration manifested itself in tantrums or anything like it.

Halford remembers: 'Timmy used to travel with me to the races sometimes and we could go from the yard to the racecourse without a word being said. I certainly had to instigate any chats we had.' But that's just his way, admits Halford. 'He has never been full of chat and he doesn't feel any need to change. It's his nature. But even then he was a uniquely quiet rider. He had always had a lovely sit on a horse. I gave him his first ride in a bumper at Leopardstown and he instinctively knew where to go in the race which is always a great sign in a young fellah.'

It quickly became obvious that riding out on the Curragh might have provided a wage but it was hardly an ideal base for a young man eager to make an impression in point to points. The decision was taken to leave Kildare and start working for Michael Hourigan at his base outside Patrickswell in Limerick. Used to the more formal stable life of the Curragh, there was an initial culture-shock at the more frenetic atmosphere in Hourigan's. Masses of young point to point horses were housed alongside established track stars like Dorans Pride and there often didn't seem to be enough hours in the day to pile in all the work.

Murphy quickly grew to love it. All he had was the promise of being allowed to school horses. There was no guarantee on rides and he wasn't alone in hoping that Mike Hourigan would do for him what he had done for Adrian Maguire just a few years before. Maguire had had a stratospheric rise from oblivion to stardom on the back of Hourigan's support on the point to point field. Now he was one of the top riders in Britain. The dream of something similar happening must have seemed an awful long way away when ferrying horses to wet and mucky fields through the Munster point to point circuit. But Hourigan knew he had a real talent on his hands again.

'Timmy always had oodles of quality and was a quiet, polished rider,' he remembers. 'Him and Adrian were very different. Adrian was an aggressive rider. Timmy was much quieter on a horse. But he was always able to get the most out of a horse without being forceful like Maguire or Tony McCoy. Having said that, he was more aggressive when he was riding in points than he is now. He definitely used the whip more and that got him into trouble later when he first went to England. He is definitely a better rider for having changed that.'

Even when a disagreement with David Wachman, who was learning his own trade at the time, meant Murphy had to leave the yard, he still kept riding for Hourigan. Rides really began to increase during the 1994–95 season, which ended with him sharing the novice riders' championship and finishing runner up to Tony Martin overall.

A switch to England seemed the next obvious step and the chance presented itself to join Toby Balding, where both Maguire and McCoy first dipped their toe into British racing. Not for the first time Murphy went his own way and joined Kim Bailey instead. It seemed a logical step. Bailey had just won the Champion Hurdle and the Gold Cup. He seemed set to dominate British jump racing for years to come. But in this case logic wasn't set to apply.

Bailey's star would start to wane remarkably quickly, but before that Murphy still managed to alienate the Englishman. Lambourn is a notoriously enclosed community where everybody knows everybody else's business. Soon it became widely known that the new Irish jockey liked to drink and liked to go out. In fairness, the two concepts were pretty much synonymous in Lambourn. There was little else to do when not working. Plenty of other Irish jockeys knew that but were able to blend the riotous social scene with getting up for work in the morning. Not for the first time in his life, obeying an alarm clock's trill proved beyond Murphy too often. Bailey told him he could rub along with jockeys who arrived for work on time.

Returning to Ireland was never an option but the freelance grind is notoriously tough. There might be much more racing in Britain but that means the lower class action is populated by a lot of undependable, quirky and sometimes downright dangerous animals. Scavenging for enough rides to make a living can be dispiriting. But Murphy's innate talent allowed him to stand out. At the 1997 Cheltenham festival he made the most of a 20-1 ride on a Martin Pipe outsider, Terao, to land the Mildmay Of Flete Chase. Teraro was a veteran at eleven, and seemed handicapped to the max, but Murphy's quiet horsemanship seemed to reignite him. One man taking notice was Paul Nicholls, who was starting out on his training career. He offered Murphy the job as his stable jockey. It was another wonderful opportunity for a young jockey in a hurry. It quickly became clear that he might just be in too much of a hurry.

Weekends were still an opportunity to push out the social boat. Sunday racing was only starting and venturing back to Ireland for some of the valuable races run on Sundays didn't seem worthwhile. Murphy set out on Saturday and Sunday nights to get drunk and rarely failed to achieve his aim. Problems also arose on the track. In his first season riding for Nicholls, fifty-two days were spent suspended owing to his misuse of the whip. For someone now famous for his quiet style, it is a curious statistic, but some of those days weren't even picked up in flat-out driving finishes. Many came on horses already hopelessly out of sight of victory but who were ridden by a jockey who was prone to the red mists of frustration. Murphy later explained that he would lose his temper on horses he felt weren't putting everything into winning. Even when out of contention he would resolve to teach the animal who was boss. Psychologists would no doubt have had a fine time dissecting the implications of such an attitude from a man who was short of devoting everything to the task of winning himself.

Suspension meant missing out on See More Business's King George VI Chase victory and worse was to come when riding the same horse in the Gold Cup. Starting favourite, See More Business and Murphy were galloping to the seventh fence when Tony McCoy started to pull up the injured Cyborgo. As he took the horse to the right, he carried Indian Trucker with him, who in turn carried See More Business outside the wing of the fence. The Gold Cup was gone in an instant. That incident alone didn't cause Nicholls to look for another stable jockey at the end of that season but Murphy still believes that a Gold Cup victory would have saved his job. That wasn't going to be the end of their relationship, though.

A major job might have gone but Murphy was able to remain one of the leading jockeys around. Riding for Jim Old and Mark Pitman suited him personally and there were major victories such as Ever Blessed in the 1999 Hennessy at Newbury. There was also a remarkably close call in the 2001 Grand National, when Red Marauder and Murphy on Smarty had the great race to themselves after almost untraceable ground reduced it to a shambles. When Red Marauder hit the final ditch a fierce clout, Murphy believed he had to have come down. He hadn't. Smarty had nothing left over the last two fences and trailed home in second. But compared to McCoy, Richard Johnson and Mick Fitzgerald, it was championship level stuff rather than premiership. Even a 2001 Irish Grand National triumph on David's Lad couldn't disguise that, even though the Fairyhouse success was a model of patient horsemanship and big race timing. And then later in 2001 came the chance for instant promotion. Nicholls came calling again.

Numerically, the 2001–02 season turned into Murphy's best ever. With two weeks left, he was just a couple of winners short of his first ever century. There hadn't been any success at the Cheltenham festival but Murphy had been consistent throughout and had cut down on his suspensions with the whip. With Nicholls beginning to threaten Martin Pipe's dominance at the top of the trainers' championship, it looked like the partnership was on an inexorably upward graph. But then Murphy's drinking problems came to a head on that fateful trip to Japan.

'I was a ticking bomb. My old flat mate said it was only a matter of time before I killed myself or someone else,' he later admitted. As it was, a lot of pride had to die in order for him to live. A one-month sentence for indecent assault and three months for being drunk on a plane, to run concurrently, was the verdict at Isleworth Crown Court in July 2002. He was also wrongly put on the sex offenders' list. The shame Murphy felt as he was led away to prison is outlined in heartbreaking fashion in his book. So is the constant fear he experienced in Wormwood Scrubs, the dread of being beaten up, the horror of what his family were going through outside and the desperation of believing he would never be able to earn a living as a jockey again when he got out. What kept him sane was the support of friends, having Big John from Brixton looking out for him inside, and the realisation that drink was ruining his life.

Before the court case, a four-week stay at the Priory rehab centre had shone a light on places Murphy had never felt comfortable looking at before. He learned to talk to people about his problems and was amazed when they listened. Through them he began to realise that he wasn't in charge of his drinking any more. Initially he felt as if he didn't belong among some other alcoholics, those who had spent their lives abusing themselves and those closest to them. It wasn't like he was park-bench material. But it dawned on Murphy eventually that he was checking in at the same stops those people had visited on their way to addiction. They told him how lucky he was to be only halfway to the bottom and getting this chance to climb out.

Prison allowed him time to digest such lessons. When he emerged, it was with the knowledge that only he could retain those lessons and bring them into practice. Only seven per cent of Priory clients are still not drinking a year later. But Murphy has always believed in things happening for a reason and clung to his new sobriety. 'I haven't had a drink since. It's just part of my life now,' he said in an interview. 'But you still have to be very wary. I still go to meetings. I don't know why. Maybe it's just because it's so good to open your mouth and speak to people who know exactly where you're coming from. Even so this illness means only you can help yourself. I admit it's a choice, not like cancer. But it has something in common with other illnesses. It will kill you.'

Little things meant so much more. He had spent much of his time in prison indoors with little or no exercise. Coming out, he could taste the fresh air. A few days later and there were no problems with him flying again, back to Ireland. Best of all, though, was the prodigal son-like welcome back at Mike Hourigan's. It was as if he had never been away. There were unlimited numbers of horses on which to ease his muscles back into riding again and an absence of prying questions from the trainer and his wife Anne. With exercise and regular good food Murphy started to get back into shape and it didn't take long for him to resolve to return to race-riding again. Many old contacts got in touch to offer rides. There was an absence of judgement that only lifted his confidence. And lurking in Hourigan's yard was a horse that would do more than most to re-establish Murphy at the top of the racing tree.

Beef Or Salmon didn't look to be a potential chasing superstar. His sire, Cajetano, was so nondescript he ended up standing in Sicily. Hourigan paid only peanuts for him as a young horse and his habit with hurdles was to try and kick them out of the way. But Beef Or Salmon had such an engine that his trainer resolved to forget about racing in novice company. Pitched into the deep end in Graded company, the big chest-nut with the ratty tail thrived.

Paul Carberry rode him in his first start at Clonmel and the partnership bolted up. But Carberry wasn't available for the Hilly Way Chase at Cork, so Hourigan turned to Murphy. One impressive success followed another, in the Hilly Way, the Ericsson at Christmas and then the Hennessy Gold Cup. Beef Or Salmon arrived at the 2003 Cheltenham Gold Cup as Ireland's best staying chaser, and Best Mate's biggest rival, but fell at the third fence. It was disappointing but his role in Murphy's rejuvenation was pivotal.

'Beef Or Salmon was important to Timmy but Timmy was important to the horse as well. They suited each other,' Hourigan says about a partnership that raced fifteen times for seven wins, including a handful of Grade 1s. Their mutual importance was summed up when time was eventually called on Beef Or Salmon's career at the 2008 Punchestown festival. Murphy made it his business to be there to ride the horse into an honourable sixth behind Neptune Collonges. The ratty-tailed hero had been instrumental, after all, in increasing his profile to such an extent that the top English owner David Johnson decided to employ Murphy as his retained rider when Tony McCoy left Martin Pipe.

Having Johnson's powerful string on tap has transformed Murphy's career, with Comply Or Die's National victory the obvious highlight. It has meant a close association with first Martin Pipe, and then his son David, which, contrary to some expectations at the beginning, has thrived. Doubts were inevitable, initially, after the impact McCoy had at Pond House and on the best of Johnson's horses. There are no two jockeys more dissimilar. One is about all-action dynamism and will to win, while the other's desire is cloaked in a lot more subtlety. Murphy's way leaves him open to more criticism but his commitment to it is unyielding.

'It's a lot easier to knock a jockey coming from behind than one that kicks too soon,' he once told reporters. 'No one seems to have a go at a jockey that makes too much use of a horse and then falls away. They say he gave it a chance and it just wasn't good enough.' But he believes a jockey is just as guilty of giving a horse a bad ride if he makes too much use of him.

'If you force a horse to go quicker than it wants, then it won't get home. The rider who sits out the back and maybe leaves it a little bit late is the one that gets slated. But he may have ridden a better race because his horse is the one finishing. I'm prepared to take that chance.' It reflects the innate horsemanship at the root of how Murphy sees his job. 'Horses are like humans. They pick up on your character and mood, and if you sit on a horse and you're tense he will know. You'll have to force him to do things. McCoy's more forceful than me. He tells his horses what to do, whereas I prefer to ask them. I only use pressure as a last resort.'

The result is spectacular when it works. Three years after delivering what he felt was an ideal ride on David's Lad in the Irish Grand National, there came a similar experience when the Johnson-owned Celestial Gold triumphed in the 2004 Hennessy. It was classic Murphy, creeping from the rear of the field until the pace-setters came into his sights in the straight. 'When those two horses won, they were special. Everything just flowed. It was like looking down on the race from somewhere else, like watching the video and pressing the button when you wanted,' he said. 'That's what I get a real kick out of, riding the perfect race.' A real kick has also come from his association with the John Queally-trained Al Eile, a three-time winner of the Aintree Hurdle at the Grand National festival.

It is the perfectionist's lot to be annoyed by anything less than perfect, which in turn can make them seem miserable a lot of the time. There remain times when Murphy admits the old red mist comes down but now it is for trivial stuff, like those infuriating traffic jams that always spring up when one is rushing to the races. Overall, he describes himself as blessed. Happily married, the father of a son, Shane, whom he adores, and possessed of one of the best jobs in racing, it's not hard to see why. At thirty-five, the rough and tumble reality of life as a jump jockey means he has had to think about a life after riding. It's a sign of the victory he has achieved away from racing that such an idea is not one to worry about. In his autobiography he idly raises the idea of riding until he is forty. But, as he knows better than most, life changes.

> I'll keep going for another bit but you can put me down if you see me riding at forty. I don't know what I will do when I stop: something to do with horses anyway. I don't know anything else.

It might have taken him some time but Timmy Murphy also now knows himself.

Cheltenham Festival Winners

1997
Mildmay Of Flete Chase   Terao

1999
Vincent O'Brien County Hurdle   Sir Talbot

2004
Mildmay Of Flete Chase   Tikram
Pertemps Final   Creon

2005
Arkle Trophy   Contraband
Vincent O'Brien County Hurdle   Fontanesi

2008
Ryanair Chase   Our Vic

2009
Jewson Novices Handicap Chase   Chapoturgeon

Other Major Winners include

1998
Pillar Property Chase   See More Business

2001
Irish Grand National   David's Lad

2002
Ericsson Chase   Beef Or Salmon

2003
Hennessy Gold Cup   Beef Or Salmon

2004

Paddy Power Gold Cup	Celestial Gold
Hennessy	Celestial Gold

2005

Paddy Power Gold Cup	Our Vic
Aintree Hurdle	Al Eile

2006

Betfair Bowl	Celestial Gold

2007

Aintree Hurdle	Al Eile

2008

Pierse Hurdle	Barker
Aintree Hurdle	Al Eile
Aintree Grand National	Comply Or Die

9

JAMIE SPENCER

The multi-million-dollar extravagance of Breeders' Cup day can seem unreal anyway, but in 2004 it had the added factor of being held at Lone Star Park in Texas. Normally a racing outpost compared to the likes of Santa Anita, Belmont or Churchill Downs, Lone Star got its moment in the limelight – and racing's international circus camped down outside Dallas where people wear Stetsons and mean it. For most of the European visitors it felt like a diverting change of pace before the world's richest day's racing returned to more familiar climes. To one of them, however, Lone Star will always have a resonance. Because after almost a year of struggling to cope with the demands of the biggest job in world racing, it was in sun-drenched Texas, of all places, that life started to feel very dark indeed for Jamie Spencer.

Preparing to ride Powerscourt in the mile and a half Turf race, he desperately hoped this would be the horse to save the meeting – maybe even an entire season. By the stratospheric standards of Coolmore's Ballydoyle operation, 2004 had been a disaster – just three Group 1 races in the bag, whereas only three years earlier there had been twenty-three. Nothing had changed in the interim except the man employed to ride the horses. With Michael Kinane gone, Spencer was brought in to be No.1 rider at the No.1 yard. In the blame-game that inevitably accompanies disappointment, he stood out like a cowboy in a wigwam. Puffy flak that whispered around his ears at the start of the season turned into full-on thousand-bomber-raid stuff by high summer and then got really thick in the autumn. The harder he tried, the more things seemed to get worse. Lone Star promised an end-of-term reprieve from the endless criticism; except it didn't come.

Mona Lisa came second-last in the Juvenile Fillies before Antonius Pius threw away another top prize by hanging like a gate in the final stages of the Mile. Yesterday finished out of the money in the mares race and Scandinavia ran stone last in the Juvenile. By the time Powerscourt made it to the start, Spencer's already wobbly confidence was in smoke and going down. Slowly away from the stalls, the Irish colt with the streaky white blaze quickly recovered a position and travelled easily down the back straight. Possessed of form good enough to win a below-par renewal of the race, Powerscourt looked to be a prime contender. And he was, until his jockey rushed him to the lead with a full half mile to go.

Sometimes the only conclusion to come to is that the mind, for reasons we don't necessarily understand, just decides to go to the shop for a pint of milk. Months of stress cumulated into a fusing brain-fade of spectacular proportions. Tactically, Spencer was guilty of a horrible miscalculation. Playing Powerscourt's speed so early left him completely vulnerable. Sure enough, the inevitable happened. To his credit, Powerscourt stayed in front until inside the final furlong but he was eventually overhauled by both Better Talk Now and Kitten's Joy. As they pulled up, Spencer's pale face was a blank, hiding the turmoil inside and the dread of what was to come. True to form, any criticism from O'Brien was kept private. But his was a singular tact.

'Baffling,' was a common description of Spencer's ride. Powerscourt was 'victimised' according to one report. 'Boneheaded,' chipped in America's sports channel ESPN, and even Kitten's Joy's trainer, Dale Romans, took time out from his own disappointment to opine: 'I don't think the jockey knows how to ride a mile and a half race.' When Americans start telling you how to ride over a mile and a half on turf, then you know things can't be right. Spencer later acknowledged it was a bad ride – and added significantly that it wasn't a good night to have had a bad ride. It was a final straw for everyone.

Less than four months later Spencer left the job every other jockey in the world covets. 'It doesn't matter how rich you are if you go to bed unhappy,' he said. The simple statement resonated with meaning. Ballydoyle looked to have emptied him and left nothing but a hollow, broken shell, every shred of confidence shot to pieces. A few weeks later, he got married to the Channel 4 racing presenter Emma Ramsden and the reception was filled with jokes along the lines of how she had got engaged to a man with the best job in racing and was marrying a man on the dole. They were indulgent gags told with affection but no one could entirely ignore the edge either. At just twenty-four years old, the bride groom looked to many like a busted flush.

So how come ten months later that same shell of a man was able to look his peers in the eye as British champion jockey? It completed a transformation as remarkable as it was unlikely and confirmed the inner steel inside the man who looks like a boy but can ride like a demon. 'I want to be as good as I can, be content with life. I can honestly say I've never felt as good as I do now,' Spencer said towards the end of that first championship in 2005. Another memorable title fell to him in 2007 when he shared it with Seb Sanders after an epic season-long struggle. But while 2005 may not have been as spectacular, it was probably more satisfying. A lot of preconceptions were put to bed, none more so than that the 'stickability' required to be a true champion might be lacking in that slight, blond figure.

Up to then there had been an undeniable impression that things may have been just that bit too easy for a young man whose outrageous talent had propelled him to success so quickly. We are, after all, talking about someone who rode a classic winner in 1998 when only seventeen years old. A year later came an apprentice championship in Ireland. Within a couple of seasons the prodigy had been propelled to Group 1 inter-national success from Singapore to France and Britain and back to Ireland. That was enough to have both racing's superpower organi-sations, Godolphin and Ballydoyle, employing his services on a regular basis. Barely in his twenties, Spencer was hailed as an inevitable successor to the likes of Dettori, Kinane and Fallon. It wasn't difficult to see why. Possessed of huge natural horsemanship, he could make the game of passing the lollipop in front of everyone else look ridiculously easy. Soon the whisper grew that it might be too easy.

The desire to win with a flourish sometimes resulted in accusations of undue flamboyance interfering with the business of actually winning. It could appear as if riding a straightforward race seemed boring to him. Instead of sitting just off the pace, Spencer's habit of dropping horses right out the back would occasionally lead to mishaps. For betting shop punters used to the never-say-die power of a McCoy or a Fallon, Spencer's more cerebral approach could be infuriating.

Soon the perception grabbed hold that the youngster would rather win clever than win at all. Like most generalisations it lacked subtlety, but even Spencer has acknowledged there was at least something to it. 'When I was younger, I wanted to win every race but I'd win narrowly. I was winning on the wire to make an impression,' he said. It only contributed to a picture of a talented youngster who might not be a dilettante but certainly didn't seem to have the cut-throat hunger of some others in the jockeys' room. His exploits in 2005 went a long way to destroying that picture. Resolve has never been a problem for Spencer.

Part of the misunderstanding could have to do with the fact that he doesn't fit into the straightforward 'boy-made-good' stereotype. His parents, Enid and George, provided a comfortable environment growing up near Fethard, Co. Tipperary, close to the yard of the top National Hunt trainer Edward O'Grady. Horses were always part of life and in Irish racing terms the family was spectacularly well connected. John Magnier is Spencer's godfather. George himself trained Winning Fair, the 1963 Champion Hurdle winner, who famously only had one eye. It led to his famous quip: 'If he had two eyes he'd have won the Derby!' But when Jamie Spencer was just twelve, his father died. The impact on the family was devastating in a way that is impossible for anyone to understand unless they've been through a similar tragedy. To a youngster on the verge of adolescence it must have been shattering. But even then there was a focus and determination that helped the young Spencer to cope.

Sent to secondary school in Kilkenny College, natural academic ability fought with a desire to make horses his life. At just thirteen he rang his mother to enquire about a day out at Clonmel races. The school said it would be OK, he argued. It wasn't long after arriving at the track that Enid Spencer found out that her son was in fact meeting the Curragh trainer Liam Browne for an interview. Browne's fame for cultivating the talents of Michael Kinane, Tommy Carmody and many other high-class jockeys made him the perfect choice for a kid obsessed with becoming a rider. That Browne also had a reputation as something of a martinet meant nothing. Given the choice, Browne's latest protégé would have left school immediately. As it was, his initial forays into a racing yard were confined to holidays until he was past his fifteenth birthday. Then the schoolboy became an apprentice jockey, although still looking like a schoolboy, and a primary one at that.

Spencer's appearance has been compared to Tintin and even a young Lester Piggott, before his face turned more sepulchral. Certainly, first impressions of George Spencer's blond-haired, porcelain-faced son were that the racetrack was no place for someone so delicate. Yet again, such impressions proved badly off-kilter.

In May 1996 Huncheon Chance, trained by Ian Ferguson, was a first winner for the cherubic kid whose talent was already well-known to those within the game. So much so that in August of that year the legendary Paddy Mullins didn't hesitate to stick him on Notcomplainingbut in one of the Tralee festival highlights, the Carling Gold Cup, a race won by Vintage Crop just four years before. As the jockeys filed out, the raw apprentice looked incongruous among the likes of Kinane, Murtagh and Manning. But there was nothing diffident where it counted. Backed down to 7-2 favourite, Notcomplainingbut was sent to the lead fully five furlongs out and stayed on stoutly to win. It was around now that Browne let it be known he figured this new boy might be the best he had ever trained. There was a clamour for Spencer's services and he began riding for other high-profile trainers like Tommy Stack, whose son 'Fozzy' was a pal from school. It didn't take long for the link to pay off.

Tarascon started a 12-1 shot for the 1998 Irish 1,000 Guineas on the back of a disappointing effort in the English Guineas. The previous year's Moyglare winner had been Pat Smullen's mount, but circumstances left the ride free at the Curragh. Stack decided to entrust the mount to the apprentice, who wouldn't be eighteen for another few weeks. It proved an inspired choice as Tarascon overhauled Kitza in the closing stages to win by a neck. Frankie Dettori was third on La Nuit Rose while future Oaks winners Winona and Shahtoush were strung out behind. The kid was breathing rarefied air that a lot of veterans could only dream of. The following year, 1999, brought Spencer the apprentice title in Ireland with forty-six winners and suddenly the place seemed too small for a young man in a hurry. Fortunately, he had already found out the lie of the land across the Irish Sea.

At the start of that year, the formidable trio of Stack, Browne and the well-known gambler Barney Curley helped advise their eighteen-year-old protégé that a winter spent in Britain would help his progress and keep his weight in check. Curley would oversee Spencer in the new environment and help secure rides. In January he provided one of his own, Magic Combination, at Kempton, in a conditional hurdle. The jockey had ridden just a handful of times over obstacles before, but his jumping pedigree meant no one could have guessed. Magic Combination won easily by fifteen lengths and Curley left no one in doubt about the regard in which he held Spencer. 'This lad is the best I've seen since Martin Molony,' he declared, referring to the legendary rider of the 1940s and 50s.

Molony was a dual-purpose jockey and Spencer has admitted that he would much rather watch jump racing than the flat variety. He has many jump jockey friends, including Tony McCoy, whom he once lodged with. Later that winter he won again on Magic Combination over hurdles, while also creating quite an impression on the all-weather flat tracks. The constant activity kept weight from his tall, spare frame. For Curley there was no point promoting the young Irishman. Only a blind man, he figured, could not spot the potential.

Co. Fermanagh-born Curley is one of those characters that can be filed under the phrase 'colourful'. His fame is principally due to the Yellow Sam sting of 26 June 1975 at Bellewstown when he stung off-course bookmakers to the tune of £300,000. A crucial element to the plot was that there was only one phone at Bellewstown which Curley filled with a large pal who pretended to be trying to get through to a dying aunt. For the crucial half hour before Yellow Sam's race, no outside contact from increasingly desperate off-course bookmakers was possible as they tried to lay off bets with their on-course brethren. Later, Curley raffled a mansion in Ireland before moving to Britain where he has proved a regular baiter of racing authority. To a young jockey on new ground he proved an invaluable guide, even though their first contact was hardly auspicious. Stack, in playful form, told the apprentice to ask Curley if he fancied anything over the next few days. It's a compliment to Spencer's personality that Curley resisted the temptation to slam the phone down.

If I have a problem or a big decision to make, Barney is someone I would always ask advice from. Not so much racing any more because he doesn't follow it as much. But even something like buying a house – I would always ask him if it was value. His judgement is pretty good. I met Barney originally because he's friendly with Tommy Stack. He insisted I had to come to England, kept saying there weren't enough opportunities in Ireland. I never had any idea of going to England. I wanted to stay at home but he kept pestering me all through that winter. Eventually I just said I'd give it a year and see. He's been brilliant, opened up contacts with so many people, and it's great that we're still very good friends.

In 2000 the second Group 1 victory of Spencer's career came in Ireland as Sequoyah flashed home in the Moyglare Stud Stakes at the Curragh. Mick Kinane's unavailability had Aidan O'Brien looking for a replacement and Spencer made the most of his chance, bringing the well-backed favourite from the rear of the field to win by two and a half lengths. Sequoyah later found fame at stud as the dam of the double-classic winner Henrythenavigator. Such surety on the big occasion also had Spencer in demand from Godolphin, but in 2001 the man who secured his signature as stable jockey was Luca Cumani. The Italian, twice an Epsom Derby winner, had helped mould a young Dettori and the Newmarket-based trainer was keen to sign up the Irishman. The Dettori link was also emphasised when the former Derby-winning jockey-turned-agent Ray Cochrane started to work for Spencer. He found out in unusual fashion about his new client's natural balance when riding his 600cc motorbike between Newbury and Windsor races.

'When I took Dettori, the bike was all over the place. I think he was waving to everyone. But although Jamie had a big bag to carry he curled in behind me and you wouldn't have known he was there. He must have the most wonderful balance,' Cochrane remembered.

That horsemanship was advertised on a world stage and the Cumani-Spencer link got a perfect boost when Endless Hall won the 2001 Singapore International Cup at the Kranji track. 'The first thing I noticed was how horses quietened for him,' said Cumani, and that ability to switch horses off and conserve their energy became a prized commodity. Later in the year, King Charlemagne was another Group 1 winner from Ballydoyle in the Prix Maurice Du Gheest at Deauville, while O'Brien also supplied Ballingarry to land the Criterium de Saint-Cloud towards the end of the season. In between, Gossamer proved herself a prime classic contender by scoring in the Ascot Fillies Mile. In 2002 she delivered on that promise in style by running away with the Irish 1,000 Guineas but before that came the fruition of a childhood dream for Spencer.

Edward O'Grady had watched his old neighbour's meteoric progress without surprise. 'Uniquely gifted' had been his succinct summary of the twenty-one-year-old star. He was also aware that riding a winner at the Cheltenham festival, National Hunt racing's greatest event, remained a major ambition. The Weatherbys Champion Bumper, a flat race for future jumpers, looked the ideal vehicle for some cross-code cooperation.

Pizarro joined another O'Grady hope Back In Front, the mount of Charlie Swan, in a race that is invariably competitive and, with no obstacles, very tight. After just three furlongs the veteran jump jockey Carl Llewellyn shouted across to Spencer: 'I bet you wish you weren't here now!' Pizarro dropped back but slowly crept closer coming down the hill. The major home hope, Rhinestone Cowboy, ironically owned by Magnier, was in prime position but Pizarro attacked the hill with relish. The nature of the race means the runners are inexperienced, and a furlong out Pizarro hung right. Spencer desperately straightened up again with Back In Front on one side of him and Rhinestone Cowboy on the other. With just yards to go, Pizarro drifted sharply right again on to Rhinestone Cowboy but passed the line first. A stewards' enquiry, however, was inevitable. It seemed to take forever but the result was eventually allowed to stand and Spencer left with a flat race flourish – rushing to the airport for a flight to Dubai. Behind him were left some bruised egos. 'He'll be good,' grinned Tony McCoy. 'When he learns to keep one straight!'

The banter was not coincidental. Lurking behind a quietly polite television persona lies a livelier individual. Practical jokes are a speciality of Spencer. The former weighroom veteran Pat Eddery might have been a venerated figure to some younger colleagues but sticky additions to his footwear and ripped subtractions from clothing were a constant hazard when his junior compatriot was around. Phone calls from Spencer, pretending to be a journalist looking for an interview, are not unknown among other unwitting jockeys. But the joker is only part of his make up. A real racing journalist, Chris McGrath, was the man Spencer turned to in 2005 to be his agent, and who performed wonders in securing the ammunition for that all-important championship. McGrath later pointed to a certain detachment in his man, an ability to be comfortable in his own company.

Such self-containment can be useful in the public eye. His 2,000 Guineas ride on Hawk Wing, when stepping in for the suspended Kinane, was heavily criticised but that was a result of the draw more than pilot error, something Spencer realised better than most. Nevertheless, he later admitted he switches off the video of that race when it gets to the two furlong marker. The 2003 Eclipse presented different problems after Spencer's ride on the Godolphin pacemaker Narrative. Also in the race were Falbrav and Nayef, the latter owned by Sheikh Mohammed's brother Sheikh Hamdan. When Narrative started to weaken, Spencer allowed him to drift to the rail and, in the process, cut off Nayef's run. Falbrav got away and secured enough of a lead to hold Nayef at the line. For a man riding as second jockey to Dettori, it was hardly a politic moment. The stewards slapped a five-day suspension on him for improper riding and Godolphin's spokesman Simon Crisford pointedly refused to discuss Spencer's future with the boys in blue. The jockey eventually issued a public act of contrition and apologised to Nayef's connections. Ultimately, though, his future lay with the boys of a deeper shade of blue.

By the end of the 2003 season Michael Kinane knew he would be leaving Ballydoyle. That didn't stop him putting in a rousing finale on High Chaparral in the Breeders' Cup at Santa Anita, a performance that only deepened people's surprise that he was being allowed to leave. But the Kinane-O'Brien relationship had always been more professional than personal. After six years together, the trainer fancied a change of rider. Plenty of candidates were mooted by bookmakers in their ante-post betting. Rumours abounded. Ultimately the choice came down to John Murtagh, Kieren Fallon and Spencer and the last had advertised his case with a St Leger triumph on the tricky Brian Boru that season. O'Brien wanted Spencer, a young jockey it was commonly felt that he could mould. John Magnier, the Coolmore supremo at the heart of the world's most powerful bloodstock empire, was happy, too, to have his godson at the helm on the big days. It looked an ideal scenario for all concerned.

The reasons why it eventually turned into a disaster are many but it certainly didn't help that the cream of the Ballydoyle classic crop of 2004 were less than straightforward. In fact quite a few of them could just as profitably have spent the year on a shrink's couch as on a racecourse. And if they weren't fragile mentally there was also the more usual matter of physical wear and tear. Yeats, as his subsequent career has proven, is nothing if not mentally tough. But it was his frame that was to let him down. O'Brien's description of Yeats as a new Galileo meant he spent the winter as favourite for the Derby and sure enough he successfully followed the tried and trusted route to Epsom through the Ballysax Stakes and the Derrinstown Trial. But just days before the Derby came confirmation of what the rumour mill had fizzed with for some time. Serious injury meant that Yeats was out for the season. That was just the latest in a series of hammer blows to a young jockey almost too eager to stamp his authority on a new job.

At the start of May, One Cool Cat went to the start of the 2,000 Guineas as a 15-8 favourite and it was fully expected he would justify O'Brien's colossal faith in him. The only horse he beat was a pacemaker. Two weeks later Antonius Pius went for the French Guineas at Longchamp and looked to have the classic in the bag inside the final furlong. However, for no apparent reason he jinked sharply right, collided spectacularly with the running rail and dropped back to fifth. Spencer had his whip in his right hand and actually did well to stay on board, so the six-day ban he received looked harsh. It did, however, sum up his start at Ballydoyle. A number of suspensions didn't help and the inherent pressure in having such a job began to rear up. Attention is constant, and the fundamental mistrust Magnier & Co. have towards the media doesn't deflect an iota of the limelight. It also didn't help that Spencer was discouraged from doing interviews. Into the vacuum poured any amount of speculation. By Royal Ascot of that year, Barney Curley felt it necessary to come to the jockey's defence.

'His strike rate for Aidan is sixty per cent and he's already clear in the championship. I don't think that's too usual in the middle of June,' said Curley. 'Mick Kinane isn't a bad jockey and neither's Pat Smullen but I think he is riding them all to sleep. I haven't seen him make any mistakes and I'd be the first to tell him.' On the French Guineas, he continued: 'The ban he got in France was diabolical. I can tell you none of it has given him a minute's worry. He was absolutely brilliant on that horse up until disaster struck and if there was any chance of him feeling pressure he wouldn't have ridden the horse that way.'

The negative, however, was that Spencer's 'sixty per cent' strike rate was coming from races that don't really matter in the Coolmore-Ballydoyle scheme of multi-million-dollar business. Group 1 races are what count and, hugely hampered by the lack of firepower, Spencer was in no position to deliver when it counted. Even a grizzled veteran like Kinane could have been forgiven for blinking in the headlights of such cumulative pressure. For a twenty-three-year-old kid it all quickly became too much.

The job probably came too early in my career but there were a handful of other things, too. Yeats getting injured was unfortunate and, apart from him, the three years weren't up to the usual Ballydoyle standard. There were two year olds like Oratorio who turned out very good the next year. Another season and it could have been all different.

A brief interlude from troubles at home could have come in the Arlington Million where Powerscourt attempted to add to an earlier victory in the Tattersalls Gold Cup. But the Chicago foray made things even worse. Powerscourt came through to win all right but once again a Spencer-ridden horse drifted alarmingly. The top American jockey Kent Desormeaux had his run hampered on Kicken Kris. Powerscourt passed the post first but Desormeaux immediately left his rival in no doubt he would lose the race in an enquiry. 'I thought I was going through the fence,' the American said. 'With all due respect I think he knew I was coming. Tracks are only as safe as their riders.' Interviewed after dismounting, Spencer was asked by ABC television if he thought the stewards would disqualify him. His response was illuminating: 'I'll cry if they do.' Sure enough, Powerscourt was thrown out. If there were tears, then they were nothing compared to a couple of months later in Texas.

For O'Brien it was deeply embarrassing. Spencer had been his pick. Under pressure himself to keep the flow of stallions going to Coolmore, he shied away from firing a second jockey in a year, having already dispensed with Kinane, and instead endeavoured to work with his new rider through the winter. O'Brien wanted him to ride at Ballydoyle through the off-season and get to know the horses more. Both men were under immense stress and in February 2005 it got too much. Spencer issued a brief statement saying he had resigned. Later he elaborated: 'There is more to life than horses. I'd been thinking about leaving for a while and in the end it was 50-50 personal and professional reasons. If you don't go to bed content with life, you are doing the wrong thing.' It's a view he still stands by.

I just wasn't happy at the time. It wasn't so bad that I ever thought of stopping riding – I hope I still have ten to fifteen years left – but there's not much point doing something if you don't enjoy it. The possibility of riding there again is not something I think about. But at the same time they have the best horses in the world at Ballydoyle and every jockey strives to ride the best horses. If the opportunity ever arose again, of course I would have to seriously think about it – especially if I was older and wiser!

The right thing at the time appeared to be a lock, stock and barrel move back to Britain. To a large extent it meant starting from scratch again. He might have been Ireland's champion jockey but new arrangements were in place among the racing community and his reputation had taken quite a pounding. It was now, however, that Spencer showed his mettle. He resolved to ride whatever was offered, anywhere. McGrath began looking for contacts and came up trumps on the all-weather with the Welsh trainer David Evans. His horses weren't blue-blooded world-beaters but they were hardy, fit and well placed for the all-weather. Another supportive trainer proved to be David Loder. Slowly but surely winners started to mount up and that vital intangible called confidence started to flow through the jockey's veins again.

We moved in a weekend, filled the car, and got on the boat. I can still clearly remember sitting in the boat thinking I'm going to have to sink or swim now. And it wasn't just because I was on the boat that I didn't fancy sinking. There was plenty of pressure on me to pull my finger out and work harder than I'd ever done.

After a conviction for cocaine possession nearly put a young Frankie Dettori's career on the skids, the all-weather proved a rehabilitative route towards becoming champion jockey. Now it was proving the same for Spencer. Soon the old nickname of 'Head Waiter', first used for Harry Wragg fifty years before, was being hung around his neck and this time was not accompanied with a condemnatory noose. The horses might not have been up to the standards of Ballydoyle, where Fallon took over and promptly delivered a Newmarket Guineas double with Footstepsinthesand and Virginia Waters. But if his predecessor was cut up with envy about missing out on a much better three-year-old crop in 2005, it was hard to tell. Instead, it looked like a weight had been lifted from those slim shoulders. When he rode again for O'Brien, on Mona Lisa at the re-routed Royal Ascot festival in York, the commitment was carried out with the minimum of fuss. Spencer was a freelance jockey fulfilling a commitment and enjoying his job again.

So much so that by the end of the 2005 season he had notched 180 winners from an amazing 1,180 rides. There was a touch of quality among them, too, with David Junior's emphatic victory in the Champion Stakes at Newmarket. But the most memorable Group 1 triumph had come earlier with Goodricke battling to success in the Haydock Sprint Cup. David Loder's announcement that he was set to quit the training game was a blow to Spencer, who had built up a fine relationship with the tall Englishman. Goodricke represented pay-back for some much-needed support during the cold winter. 'That was an emotional day as it was really good to do it for David. At the end of the day you should want to go through a brick wall for a trainer if your relationship is strong enough,' the jockey remembered later, saying plenty with what remained unsaid.

The sense of satisfaction was almost tangible at a difficult job carried out well and with a perfect result. 'There are some days you are tired and can't wait to get home,' says Spencer. 'You go to Newcastle in the evening and then you have to jump into a car and it is four hours to get home. Those days are tough. There was one day when I went to Haydock, rode a winner, and then went on to Carlisle. I drove home after the last race at 9.30. But I rode four winners and it felt like five minutes driving home as I was on a constant high.' Others saw the jockeys' title as merely Spencer's due. 'He's simply a great horseman,' was trainer James Fanshawe's view. 'We've got a lot of home-bred fillies and one or two can be unruly. I'm always impressed when a jockey can relax a difficult filly and Jamie's really good at that. You've either got good hands or you don't and he certainly has.'

It was an amazing thing to do [win the championship]. I was exhausted at the end but very happy. And I can't describe how good it was to work with Chris McGrath. Sometimes you just gel with people and we never had a cross word. The problem was he was too talented just to be my agent.

Brian Meehan's decision to send David Junior to Dubai for the winter paid off spectacularly the following spring as the chestnut flashed home a brilliant winner of the Duty Free race. Meehan immediately nominated the Prince Of Wales's Stakes as a target, but the horse could manage only fourth to Ouija Board. As a result, the heir to the British throne could present the winning trophy to Lord Derby and not David Sullivan, who has built his fortune on the pornography industry. However, the horse named after Sullivan's son quickly made amends by landing the Eclipse at Sandown.

Another trainer to make extensive use of Spencer's services was Michael Bell, trainer of the 2005 Derby winner Motivator, and also of Red Evie, the progressive filly ridden to Group 1 glory by Spencer in the Matron Stakes at Leopardstown on Irish Champion Stakes day. More top-flight success came on Kevin Ryan's Desert Lord in the Prix de l'Abbaye at Longchamp. However, at the end of the season it was Ryan Moore who topped the championship table, clear of his Irish rival. But 2007 proved very different.

A bad arm injury sustained in March ruined any chance Moore had of retaining his title. Instead it was Seb Sanders who emerged as a major threat. The Englishman isn't a particularly fashionable jockey but hard work has carried him to the top of his trade and, with Moore out of the equation, he figured this could be his year. Slowly but surely he started to accumulate winners. They might not have been at the top level but the championship is a numbers game and securing ammunition at the lesser meetings was not a problem. Spencer, in contrast, was able to manage both quality and quantity. Red Evie's Lockinge Stakes victory was followed by an evocative win on board Excellent Art in the St James's Palace Stakes that illustrated all his jockey's brilliance. That the colt was trained by Aidan O'Brien only added to the resonance.

Kieren Fallon's ban from race-riding in the UK had opened up more opportunities for Spencer with his former employers and this was one he took with both hands. Bringing the doubtful stayer from the back of the field, Spencer plunged Excellent Art into a gap between his stable companions Duke Of Marmalade and Astronomer Royal to lead home a Ballydoyle 1-2-3 by a neck. For the 'Head Waiter' it was a *pièce de résistance* and his exultant celebrations passing the post reflected its significance. A similar reaction wouldn't be repeated until the very end of the season in November and it would come after a much longer struggle.

The last two months of the 2007 British flat season were dominated by the struggle between Spencer and Sanders at the top of the jockeys' table. Any potential advantage for one would quickly disappear as the other rallied. It became an absorbing battle in which the lazy characterisation of Spencer as brittle brilliance and Sanders as rugged durability took hold in some quarters. This proved to be way off the mark. Style might not be Sanders' most obvious characteristic but he proved inspired too often on the championship run-in for it to be coincidence. And Spencer was second to nobody in terms of determination. So much was obvious on one day's daunting schedule where he travelled to London for a BHA disciplinary hearing from his home in Newmarket in the morning, then caught a plane to Edinburgh to ride at the Musselburgh track before returning to the Midlands to ride at Wolverhampton that evening. In intensity, and in the attention it brought to racing, this duel harked back twenty years to when Steve Cauthen and Pat Eddery fought out a similar epic.

Ultimately, after putting in 70,000 miles each in travel and pushing themselves to the limit in terms of diet and athletic performance, the whole season came down to the final day. Sanders went into Doncaster one up (189-188) but Spencer had seven rides to his rival's five. The gap quickly widened to two, though, when Sanders took advantage of a wild swerve by one of his rivals, who threw away victory in an early race. It looked like the Englishman's luck was in just when it counted. That appeared to be even more so when Spencer was beaten on a well fancied runner later in the day. However, the Irishman got one back on Generous

Thought and then Sanders got nosed out of a Listed race when Galeota, ironically ridden by Ryan Moore, beat Borderlesscott. With one race to go, Sanders was finished and couldn't be beaten. Spencer had one more chance to draw level and ensure a first tie in the championship since Steve Donoghue and Charlie Elliott shared it in 1923.

With the pressure off, Sanders exclaimed: 'Jamie is a smashing guy and I don't mind if he wins the last. But for me this is the Holy Grail.' Spencer, in contrast, felt more than a little strain as he prepared to ride Inchnadamph in the staying handicap. No one could have known, however, as he gradually eased the horse through to arrive in the straight tanking over his rivals. It looked a case of just pushing a button to win, and, although Spencer tried to bide his time for as long as possible, he eventually had to say go. The response was reassuringly quick. Inchnadamph powered clear to win and relief broke all over his jockey's face.

'I don't get emotional. But as I pulled up it almost overwhelmed me,' he said afterwards. 'It has been a huge effort which I don't think I could go through again.'

Instead, he drove home resolving to sleep for a week. Typically, however, before the seven days were up he confessed to some boredom. That didn't send him scurrying for the next all-weather fixture but happily his focus has remained resolutely on the future. It has been no chore either, with victories like the 2008 *Racing Post* Trophy winner Crowded House, who looked a spectacular talent with a wide-margin victory at Doncaster.

However, classic glory in 2009 came from another source. Sariska may not have had as high-profile a juvenile career but, brought perfectly to the boil by trainer Michael Bell, she lifted the Epsom Oaks in a thrilling finish. The ride cost Spencer a five-day suspension, but in the big picture such a penalty was irrelevant. Instead, Sariska's jockey relished the moment.

Such an outlook is a good result in itself for the man who endured Lone Star.

Classic Wins

1998
Irish 1,000 Guineas   Tarascon

2002
Irish 1,000 Guineas   Gossamer

2003
English St Leger   Brian Boru

2009
English Oaks   Sariska

Other Major Winners include

2000
Moyglare Stud Stakes   Sequoyah

2001
Singapore International Cup   Endless Hall
Prix Maurice Du Gheest   King Charlemagne
Criterium de Saint-Cloud   Ballingarry

2002
Nunthorpe Stakes   Kyllachy

2004
Tattersalls Gold Cup   Powerscourt
Middle Park Stakes   Ad Valorem
Prix Jean Luc Lagadere   Oratorio

2005

Champion Stakes	David Junior
Haydock Sprint Cup	Goodricke

2006

Dubai Duty Free	David Junior
Eclipse Stakes	David Junior
Matron Stakes	Red Evie
Prix de l'Abbaye	Desert Lord

2007

Lockinge Stakes	Red Evie
St James's Palace Stakes	Excellent Art

2008

Racing Post Trophy	Crowded House

10

TONY McCOY

Over the years, hundreds of acres of newsprint and hours upon hours of air-time have gone into explaining what motivates Tony McCoy. Rarely has a sporting psyche been so robustly probed. Descriptions have criss-crossed the psycho-babble lexicon from 'abrosia' to 'zoism'. Such fascination is hardly surprising. McCoy is a statistical phenomenon. Champion jockey for the last fourteen seasons, he is the winning-most jump jockey of all time, with over three thousand career winners and a record tally of 289 in a single season. That he has managed this despite pushing his body to the limits in terms of injury and deprivation makes him a genuine sporting icon in Britain right now.

It's little wonder then that the cream of the journalistic profession have at some stage or other attempted to explain McCoy. The man himself isn't slow to cooperate. Accessible to a degree unthinkable among Premiership footballers or other top-flight sporting contemporaries, he cuts an impressively lucid, if sometimes scarily intense, figure who invariably makes for good copy. Even though questioning inevitably concentrates on the same things – injury, pain, weight – the responses are delivered with appropriate attention and professionalism. McCoy can to an extent understand the attention, and people's curiosity, but also steps back from it. Maybe that's because he has long since known his own motivation better than anyone else.

In his autobiography, published in 2002, he admits he is 'addicted' to winning. The choice of word is no accident. That feeling of passing the winning post in front is something that other jockeys have described as being like no other: maybe not better than everything else but definitely unique. Little wonder then that every jockey wants to win. But McCoy is different. The evidence of the last fifteen years suggests that he *needs* to win. Just as a sad, wrecked, strung-out figure on a street corner will do anything to score, the task of passing the finishing-post in front of everyone else has a hold over Anthony Peter McCoy, that is every bit as compulsive. It means that no one, not even Lester Piggott, has ever displayed such will to win. Over jumps, no one has ever won more because it seems no one has ever wanted it more.

The downside is that, no matter how much success comes his way, it will never be enough. It's racing's fundamental truth that the most important race is always the next one. Each time he canters to the start means a new fix is required. As roller-coasters go, it's as exhausting emotionally as it is physically. Losing establishes only that his determination to succeed wasn't strong enough. So that need to come out on top becomes even more intense. No matter how many races McCoy wins, it only fuels the addiction.

Such desire can look desperately grim sometimes. There have been times when his very sanity has been questioned. At the 2002 Cheltenham festival a run of defeats had those same adoring journos publicly wondering if that will to win had tipped over into graceless pouting at best, and mental instability at worst. That jaw-jutting, hollow-cheeked figure coiled over a horse can seem to relish his own discomfort, a very Protestant outlook on life for the Catholic boy from Moneyglass in Co. Antrim. McCoy insists he's living the dream he has nurtured since childhood, but it can appear joyless sometimes.

The good part is that those who know him best insist that the popular perception is deceptive. Apparently, the man who has never smoked or taken alcohol or developed a taste for anything more narcotic than beating his rivals is well able to enjoy himself. When suspension or injury allows a trip to the sun, he relaxes that determined mask. Both Mick Fitzgerald and Carl Llewellyn have testified to their pal's ability to see out a long night without the need for a drink. It may mean being pressed into the designated driver role but that has proved no barrier to the deployment of a dry wit. At home, McCoy's hospitality is renowned. Jockeys new to Lambourn or in need of temporary accommodation have been known to stay for months on end rent-free. His fiercest rival, Ruby Walsh, famously stays during his frequent trips to Britain. There are plenty who insist their host is a very different animal from the one the public sees on their television screens or on the racecourse, which is reassuring.

We are talking about a man who has jokingly expressed a liking for pain because of the morphine that's used to deaden it. At least it sounds like some of that famously arid humour. More seriously, there is his gut feeling that he is unbreakable. Bones may break but his spirit never will. McCoy believes he will always be able to get up no matter how hard the fall. In anyone else, such conviction might be dismissed as bravado. But it isn't that long ago since doctors x-raying his broken ribs were stunned to see the calcifying process already well underway. Only then did their patient reveal that the fractures had come five weeks previously. Not for the first time the pain barrier was surmountable.

That he still possesses such iron will at the age of thirty-five and after a career that has secured both fortune and fame points to the essence of the individual. By his own admission, McCoy is not a great natural talent. A forceful style in the saddle is only a reflection of the drive within him. But those who criticise him for a supposed lack of sentimentality towards the horses he rides miss the point that he is even harder on himself. His greatest fear of all isn't injury or pain but not being as good as he should be. If that comes across in a brusquely tough manner sometimes, then it is hardly surprising. McCoy learned early that 'nice' is a more ineffectual word in racing than anywhere else.

He was still a teenager when it really hit home. The story of how McCoy's dreams of becoming a new Lester Piggott on the flat ended at eighteen is now one of the most notorious in racing folklore. Over time, it has been embellished and no doubt grown a leg or two but it still centres on one of McCoy's own legs. Riding a wayward colt called Kly Green at Jim Bolger's yard in Co. Carlow, the young apprentice suddenly found himself charging a wooden rail at the bottom of a gallop. The horse collided with it, sending his rider into the air. Even from a hundred yards away the snap of McCoy's breaking limb was clearly audible. Splintered bone stuck through his jodhpurs. The pain came pretty much immediately. On a cold winter morning, shock also quickly set in but not enough to silence his screams of agony. It was then that Bolger, just arriving on the scene and surveying his stricken jockey, uttered the immortal words: 'Are you sure you've broken it?'

He had. Months of inactivity while it healed was the death knell of any lingering ambitions of a career on the flat. An already lengthening body had its metabolism kick-started. When he had entered hospital, McCoy weighed 7 st 10 lb. When he returned to Bolger he was 9 st 2 lb. Morale-sapping sweating got it down half a stone but that wasn't nearly enough for a teenager trying to make his mark against the likes of Michael Kinane and Christy Roche. It was then that the decision was made to try and make it over jumps, and also when Bolger put the final touches to the myth. Even now the words seem fantastically insensitive. To a youngster they must have been devastating. Little wonder then that McCoy can still remember them clearly: 'You want to be a jump jockey. You're some fool. I heard you crying like a baby with a broken leg and jump jockeys get that every day of the week. You're not hard enough. You're not tough enough to be a jockey.'

Many teenagers would have crumbled at the sneering dismissal. Bolger was a champion trainer, a man who had masterminded the careers of classic horses like St Jovite and Jet Ski Lady. In the strict and disciplined yard at Coolcullen his word was law. McCoy's reaction was different. He had to prove Bolger wrong. If he wasn't hard enough, then he would have to become hard. 'I admire Jim as much as anyone in racing – my time there was the making of me – but he definitely gave me the incentive I needed,' McCoy said later. But it was in Britain that the evidence of his motivation was revealed.

There is a long and honourable tradition of Irishmen emigrating to England and becoming champion jockey. In the post-war years Tim Molony was a multiple champion. In the 1970s, Tommy Stack, Ron Barry and Jonjo O'Neill also made it to the top of the tree. Such successes only emphasised the inextricable racing ties binding two countries separated by hundreds of years of bitterness and distrust. That the two Irish-born champions of the recent era should both come from the North of Ireland and grew up during the height of the troubles only emphasises the intricacies of the modern Anglo-Irish reality.

Richard Dunwoody grew up in mainly Protestant Comber in Co. Down before his father's work in the horse industry took the family to England. McCoy, in contrast, is a product of the nationalist community in Antrim, the predominantly unionist county on the north-east corner of the island. Both men have said the sectarian conflict, which disfigured both communities in the six counties for so long, had little or no impact on their growing up. If there were incidents locally they were observed with a certain detachment, as if this was stuff that should be on the television news, not happening nearby. McCoy still remembers the police station at Toomebridge being attacked with a bomb and the resultant pall of black smoke. Years later, when Toomebridge barracks was attacked, his only thought was that the inevitable road-blocks would take a few hours off school.

It's not surprising that the fighting had such an ephemeral practical impact but it would be fanciful to believe it didn't leave a mark. Living in the North defines everyone to some extent, regardless of politics or religion. The unionist population might bellow their Britishness but they do so against a constant suspicion that the rest of Britain is ready to sell them out. As for nationalists, there's the duality of yearning for unity while feeling themselves somehow different from 'down south'. That separation is something that many in the Republic feel in their bones too. The result is a flinty determination, bred into both communities in the North, that can manifest itself in a defiant stubbornness. In a sporting sense, nobody defines it more than McCoy.

That stubborn trait was there in the nine-year-old who suddenly discovered an interest in riding ponies in 1983. Peader McCoy kept some mares and foals at home but his first choice of pony for his son was not an inspired one. She was all but unrideable. However, the boy kept climbing back on her. Ultimately, the pony won and was sold for something more malleable. It would be a long time before another horse got the better of the jockey, especially none of those at Billy Rock's racing stables eight miles away.

Rock and Peader McCoy had known each other for years when the trainer invited 'Wee Aunthany' to help out at his yard. School had already been fighting a losing battle in maintaining the interest of young McCoy and now it had no chance. Maths and Geography couldn't hope to compete with the lure of riding honest-to-God thoroughbred racehorses. The stubbornness that kept making him get back on that pony – and made getting him to school such an ordeal for his mother, Claire – now had an outlet. There would be no turning back, just as there wasn't when he finally told Bolger – after a three-year apprenticeship and a handful of winners – that he was on his way to the ferry to try his luck across the Irish Sea.

Like hundreds of thousands of Irishmen before him, what Britain offered McCoy was 'a start.' Peader McCoy's small-time breeding operation might subsequently have yielded a 1993 Cheltenham festival winner in Thumbs Up, but he was in no position to offer a leg up to his son's riding career. The dynastic nature of Irish racing meant opportunities for someone not steeped in a family tradition for racing were going to be limited. Not having ever ridden over fences was hardly going to help either. What did, was his association with Toby Balding.

The Grand National and Champion Hurdle-winning trainer had just overseen the meteoric start to Adrian Maguire's career in the UK in the early 1990s. But Maguire had lots of point to point experience when he made the move. McCoy, his successor as Balding's conditional jockey, might have had polish from his flat days, but in the blood and guts world of steeplechasing that counted for little. It said something for the new boy's determination, though, that one of his first winners in Britain came in a selling chase at Newton Abbot. 'It was awful to watch,' Balding recalls. 'The horse nearly lost him at every fence but he still won. He just never stopped digging away.' What McCoy now had was the chance to learn on the job. With three or four meetings a day, he could advertise that talent for willing his way to victory. By the end of the 1994–95 season he had made such an impression that he finished the campaign as champion conditional jockey with a new record of seventy-three winners. The new arrival had arrived and he wasted no time battering down any door to the big-time.

A happy coincidence meant that the 1995–96 season began in June rather than the traditional August. Summer racing allowed McCoy get a head-start on his better known rivals. While Dunwoody and Maguire went on holidays, the young pretender kept pounding the motorways in pursuit of winners. Trainers began queuing up for the services of this thin, intensely focused Irishman, including the likes of Paul Nicholls and a certain Martin Pipe. McCoy's ace in the hole, however, was someone rarely seen at a racecourse, Dave Roberts.

Agents are a comparatively modern phenomenon in racing, and over jumps Roberts is the unquestioned master of the job. With a well-thumbed form-book in front of him and a phone permanently clamped to his ear, Roberts had plotted Maguire's lightning-fast route to the top. Now he was about to do the same for the new conditional champion. It meant ceaseless travelling but McCoy's hunger didn't make that a problem. In fact, as his fitness levels improved, and his confidence in riding over fences also increased, the steady flow of winners only made him more determined.

By the time of the 1996 Cheltenham festival he was clear in the jockeys table and Kibreet provided him with a maiden festival success in the Grand Annual Chase. A few weeks later a hugely important first Grade 1 prize fell into his lap with Viking Flagship's victory in the Melling Chase at Aintree. By the end of his first season as a full professional, McCoy had ridden 175 winners, forty-three more than his nearest rival, David Bridgewater. He was champion jockey, the youngest since Josh Gifford in 1962, and it was just over three years since he had lain at the bottom of Jim Bolger's gallops with his leg in pieces. It was an astounding achievement. And now Bridgewater was about to make things even better.

In September 1996 Bridgewater quit the job of No.1 rider to Martin

Pipe, just thirteen months after replacing Dunwoody. Pipe was champion trainer and his rider was invariably odds-on to win the jockeys' championship every year, but he was clearly not straightforward to work for. Losing two stable jockeys in such a short space of time proved that. But in McCoy he had raw material that could be honed – at least to an extent. The younger man has never been slow to fight his corner if he feels there is a need. What they shared, however, was an insatiable desire to win and a sense of always having to fight the odds.

Pipe, as a son of a bookmaker, knew the gamble he'd taken when starting as a trainer in 1973. It was two years before he saddled a winner and he came to the job with no background in racing. As a result, he brought an attitude uncontaminated by convention. By perfecting the 'interval' method of training, where the focus is more on speed than slow stamina work, Pipe notched up hundreds of winners. These included animals of the quality of Granville Again, who won the Champion Hurdle, and the Grand National hero Minnehoma.

A downside of his innovative approach to the job were persistent whispers from other, envious, trainers about doping. The reality was more mundane: the art of training jumpers had been turned on its head. Pipe got his horses fit and ready to run often and hard. The others simply couldn't keep up. If ever a jockey was made to suit such a style it was McCoy. There was no formal arrangement between the two men but winners flowed. At the end of the 1996–97 season, the jockeys' championship had been retained with 190 winners. But this was also the season that McCoy proved his ability to do it on the big stage when it counts most.

As always, the biggest stage of all is Cheltenham. If McCoy was the new boy at the top table, then Make A Stand was very much the interloper among the leading fancies for the 1997 Champion Hurdle. The diminutive chestnut had risen spectacularly through the ratings to land the Tote Gold Trophy at Newbury in February. As a novice, the Supreme and the SunAlliance looked to be easy pickings. But Pipe decided on the championship itself, despite the presence of the title-holder Collier Bay and the well fancied Large Action. Neither could land a blow as Make A Stand made all the running to win in course-record time.

Just two days later, the most coveted festival double of all was landed. Mr Mulligan's form could be in and out but in the Gold Cup he was on very much a 'go' day. Again ridden positively, Noel Chance's washy chestnut jumped his opposition into the ground to come home a clear winner. Only three other jockeys have ever managed the Champion Hurdle-Gold Cup double – Norman Williamson, Fred Winter and Aubrey Brabazon. Just three years after riding his first ever winner over jumps, McCoy was among the elite.

Backed by the power of Pipe's Somerset-based yard, he began a period of dominance unprecedented in the jumping game. The jockeys' championship fell to McCoy almost as a matter of course. Ending the 1997–98 season with 253 winners, he added three more titles with tallies of 186, 245 and 191 respectively. But even by those standards, 2001–02 was remarkable.

In 1947 the legendary flat rider Gordon Richards set a new record total for a racing season in Britain with 269 winners. It appeared an unbreakable tally, especially for a jump jockey. Since it is a matter of when, not if, a jump jockey gets injured, the idea that one could outscore an icon of the summer game seemed outlandish. Yes, there were a lot more races since the post-war period but the task still seemed enormous. Yet on 2 April the incredible happened. McCoy began a nondescript day at Warwick two behind the record. He ended it in front on his own. After two earlier winners, it was Valfonic who earned his own place in the record books by becoming number 270 of the season. The Aintree National meeting began just a couple of days later but Warwick seemed an appropriate setting. After all, it was at such humble tracks that the majority of the record numbers had come in. A month afterwards the season finished with McCoy on the 289 winner mark. His immediate thoughts were that 300 in a season was not impossible.

Such reluctance to dwell on past achievements and instead choosing to concentrate on the future is a defining characteristic of most top sportspeople. What makes McCoy's different is the terrible self-sacrifices that are now part of an almost daily routine. Injuries are part and parcel of the game for all jump jockeys but some are blessed with the sort of frame that makes weight less of an issue. McCoy is not one of them. At 5ft 10in, he isn't the tallest in the jockeys' room. Ruby Walsh is much the same height. But McCoy has the wide shouldered frame of someone designed to carry a lot more than the 10 st he strives to keep his body at. He prides himself on never carrying overweight. But maintaining that record requires a fight that can make those out on the racetrack seem easy. Battling yourself is always the toughest scrap of all. In his autobiography there is an evocative description of the daily struggle with his weight.

'The thought of that steaming bath every morning that I ride hangs over me like a black cloud. I look in the mirror and know that four pounds has got to be shifted from somewhere, yet no matter how hard I pinch myself I can't see a fold of flesh to see where it will come from,' he says.

On some occasions, he admits, he has almost buckled: 'Sometimes I stand outside the bathroom door and can't put my hand on the handle. When I'm in, facing the bath, I stand there looking at it thinking I don't want to get in there. Once or twice when it's really bad I've put my head in my hands and wept because I don't want to do it.'

He continues: 'I know that for the average person a lovely warm bath is a luxury but for me it's torture. You test the temperature with your hand and the heat stings but you know you've got to lower the most tender parts of your body into it or it's a waste of time. Once you're in, the scalding hot tap maintains the temperature. The pain is mental and physical. My sympathy with lobsters is real.'

The pace of that pursuit of winners, however, never slackens. After securing a record-breaking season, 2002–03 ended with 256 more victories. Pipe's ability to churn out large numbers of winners remained undimmed, but there was no denying a shortage of top-class talent. Well Chief's Arkle Trophy triumph at the 2004 Cheltenham festival was a notable exception but there was no getting away from the increasing power of Paul Nicholls' stable. With Ruby Walsh as his No.1 jockey, Nicholls started to exert a stranglehold on the major prizes in Britain.

There was also the increased power of Irish-trained horses at Cheltenham and Aintree. In 2004, after eight years together, came the announcement that many thought they would never hear: McCoy was leaving the Pipe winner-machine.

There were suggestions that some of the trainer's main owners were unhappy with the jockey's aggressive style, but McCoy jumped rather than being pushed. The carrot that lured him would have been enough to make any jockey spring-heeled. J.P. McManus, the billionaire business-man and champion owner, had pursued his fellow Irishman for some years and now secured him as his retained rider. At the time, Jonjo O'Neill was establishing Jackdaws Castle near Cheltenham, David Nicholson's former yard, as a state of the art training base where many of McManus's best horses would be based. McCoy would be the final piece of the jigsaw. The retainer was reportedly worth a million pounds a year to the jockey. Compared to the Pipe arrangement, it was an offer impossible to refuse. Pipe believed the percentages from the guaranteed stream of winners from Pond House was enough of a financial induce-ment. This was in a different league, though.

There was inevitable speculation that McCoy's acceptance of the McManus offer would signal a slow-down in his pursuit of the jockeys' championship. It was judged a sign that his desire for the day-in day-out drudge of the midweek circuit was waning. Commitments in Ireland might take him away more often than before, but the jockey was determined to retain the title. Other speculation that his nearest rival, Richard Johnson, would take over at Pipe's proved unfounded. Instead it was Timmy Murphy who became the retained rider for Pipe's principal owner, David Johnson. A couple of years later Martin Pipe retired and handed over the reins to his son, David. What remained constant, though, was the name at the top of the table at the end of the 2004–05 season – A.P. McCoy with another double century of winners.

There was no questioning his desire, but if he had been expecting a bonanza in the big races aboard McManus's huge string, McCoy was to be disappointed. The star staying hurdler Baracouda ultimately came up short at Cheltenham. There was the consolation of delivering a vintage

never-say-die effort on board Like-A-Butterfly in the Powers Gold Cup
at Fairyhouse but, with the Nicholls-Walsh team getting ever more
successful, McCoy admitted to more than a little envy. As the ultimate
winner he would expect nothing else of himself. The shining light that
provided him with a defining victory at this time, however, didn't carry
the McManus colours.

In a golden period for Irish-trained hurdlers, Brave Inca stood out as
much for his character as his ability. There was enough of the latter to
secure a 2004 Cheltenham triumph in the Supreme Novices Hurdle when
Barry Cash guided him to a narrow defeat of the subsequent Gold Cup
hero War Of Attrition. The following year Brave Inca was the third horse
of the trio, which also included Hardy Eustace and Harchibald, that
flashed past the Champion Hurdle finish line. Cash retained the faith of
trainer Colm Murphy throughout Brave Inca's climb to the top, but
when the partnership subsequently fell at the ninth flight in the Aintree
Hurdle, Cash's days were numbered. For his last start of the 2004–05
season, in the Champion Hurdle at Punchestown, Brave Inca teamed up
with McCoy for the first time.

It seemed a perfect marriage. Brave Inca's ability to keep finding more for
pressure made him appear an ideal fit for the man many believe is the best
ever at dredging out untapped reserves. Sure enough, that Punchestown
race turned into a desperate struggle as McCoy forced Brave Inca back in
front on the line to beat both Harchibald and Macs Joy. But what really
impressed Murphy was the subtlety contained within the iron fist.

'I could only hope they'd click but what amazed me was how quickly
A.P. sized the horse up,' the trainer says. 'The only thing we said to him
going out was "this horse is not slow". It was his first time riding him but
he kept on winding the pace up and in the end that took advantage in the
best way of Brave Inca's speed. It took us two or three years to get the
hang of Brave Inca. A.P. had him in two or three minutes.'

McCoy was adamant the horse deserved another crack at the
Champion Hurdle and the long campaign back to Cheltenham began
with a win at Punchestown the following autumn. There was a hiccup
at Fairyhouse in December when Brave Inca managed only third to

Solerina in the Hatton's Grace – but Murphy began to suspect his horse simply didn't like Fairyhouse. Back at two miles he beat Harchibald at Leopardstown over Christmas and returned to the Dublin track to win the AIG Irish Champion Hurdle from Macs Joy. Brave Inca was now favourite for Cheltenham and McCoy couldn't see him being beaten. Brave Inca might not be a silky-smooth operator but, like his jockey, he tended to get the job done. In fact it was just that attitude that proved vital.

On ground officially described as good to soft, Brave Inca started a 7-4 favourite, a price that looked more than a little spare when McCoy had to give reminders to the horse after just the fourth flight. In front, Hardy Eustace made the best of his way home towards what would be a third consecutive championship. But he couldn't shake off his biggest rival. Both horses were far from in love with the sticky going but as they swept down the hill it looked a straight fight between the pair. Beside Conor O'Dwyer's high position in the saddle, McCoy looked to be in trouble, working remorselessly to keep tabs. Characteristically, though, Brave Inca kept finding for the pressure and, approaching the last, eventually managed to get on top. It was then that Barry Geraghty delivered Macs Joy with a seemingly perfectly timed run. Against any other horse and jockey it would have been a dagger blow. But incredibly Brave Inca responded again. He passed the post a length ahead with his normally undemonstrative jockey punching the air.

'It's unbelievable how much belief A.P. had in the horse that day. He couldn't see him beat. It was frightening really but it made my job so much easier. He had every eventuality covered and knew to the ounce what he could get out of the horse,' Murphy remembers. 'I mean it as a compliment but normally Tony really is a horse's worst nightmare. But with Brave Inca the one time he ever had a hard race was in that Champion Hurdle. Tony understood quickly that the thing with the horse was to keep him happy and interested. He always said we couldn't force him to do anything, which for A.P. is some statement.' Murphy believes the jockey had Brave Inca sussed but it worked both ways. After a while Brave Inca knew what he could get away with. It might have looked like the two of them were in trouble but Murphy reckons there was a smile on both their faces. He concludes: 'Tony really is the best of the best, one of the greatest there's ever been. I don't remember the older jockeys but the records speak for themselves. Some jockeys get the last pound out of horses. He gets the last ounce.'

There have been some memorable McCoy rides in the big races. Edredon Bleu's triumph in the 2000 Queen Mother Champion Chase was the epitome of what two-mile chasing is about, all blood and guts dash allied to dead-eyed jumping and the resilience to tough it out right to the line. Best Mate never reached his top level around Kempton in the King George but in 2002 McCoy stood in for Jim Culloty and got the triple Gold Cup-winner home. The 1998 Aintree Hurdle is McCoy's own idea of his best ever ride as he persuaded Pridwell to give the performance of his life in beating Istabraq. But Pridwell was something of a dodgepot. With Brave Inca, McCoy was on board an equine version of himself.

That must have made it doubly hard to take when he couldn't ride the reigning champion as he defended his title in 2007. The McManus retainer meant he had to ride Straw Bear in the Champion Hurdle, but after being beaten on Brave Inca six weeks earlier in the AIG there had been mounting speculation that Ruby Walsh was set to ride the horse anyway. Walsh had successfully deputised on Brave Inca the previous Christmas and it had been hard to ignore how much better the horse had travelled in that race. As it happened, the new team had to settle for second behind Sublimity but the new arrangement only confirmed a trend. Whereas his dominance in Britain was once a given, McCoy's position as *the man* is now under serious pressure.

Walsh's streak of big race victories only emphasises McCoy's relative lack of success in the major pots in recent years. And it's those top prizes that dictate racing's always-shifting pecking order. The two men themselves are the friendliest of rivals and Walsh bows to no one in his admiration for his pal. 'I give A.P. plenty of stick and tell him he's getting old but his desire is as fierce as ever,' he told an interviewer. 'He's an iron man. You see the winners he's had. Even if he's riding a winner one in every three, that must mean over 7,500 rides. We all fall at least one in every eight. So McCoy must have had 900 falls in his career and yet he's the same as he's always been – phenomenal.'

Numerically, though, the records keeping tumbling. In February 2009 McCoy became the first jump jockey to ride three thousand winners. Appropriately, it came on a freezing cold Monday in driving rain at lowly Plumpton. Starting the afternoon two shy of a landmark that had captured the media's imagination for more than a week beforehand, he won a handicap hurdle on Hello Moscow. Then he looked all over a winner on the odds-on Miss Sarenne, only for the horse to take a horrible fall at the last. Equally appropriately, her rider wiped off the muck, walked the mare back to the unsaddling area and proceeded to reach his goal on her stable companion Restless d'Artaix.

'Someone said if I ride until I'm forty-four, five thousand might be on,' cracked the centre of attention. 'I don't think I still want to be riding then. But four thousand, I don't see why not.'

A month later came a remarkable success on Wichita Lineman at the Cheltenham festival which summed up McCoy's remorseless will-to-win better than most of the other three thousand winners to date. But if the big-race trend is to be reversed, there's little doubt which one in particular would be most appropriate. If the Champion Hurdle has been kind to McCoy, there is no doubt the glaring omission on his big race CV remains the Aintree Grand National. In fourteen attempts he has a trio of third placings and a catalogue of misfortune to show for his trouble. In 2001 he passed the stands convinced he was going to win on Blowing Wind. But that proved to be one of the most remarkable Nationals ever. All but two of the forty runners exited for one reason or another on the ultra-testing conditions, including Blowing Wind. As Red Marauder struggled to success a distance clear of Smarty, McCoy remounted to beat Walsh on the former winner Papillon in their own private duel. Blowing Wind ran third again the following year behind Bindaree.

However, his misfortune in 2001 pales in regard to Clan Royal's disastrous exit in 2005. The previous year's runner-up was clear of the opposition on the run down to Becher's for the second time. Angled wide to take the famous fence on the outside, Clan Royal's view was suddenly filled by a loose horse running along the fence on the take-off side. There was nowhere for McCoy to go and Clan Royal came to a stop in a matter of strides. Walsh proceeded to win on Hedgehunter. 'Whether Clan Royal could have beaten Hedgehunter I don't know. It would have been between the two of them,' McCoy said later. 'The thing is it is very hard to get on the right horse for a Grand National. It only comes once a year, there are forty of you, and thirty fences. That's why it's such a head wrecker. If I haven't won a Grand National, it's always going to be a failure in my career,' he admits. 'Anyone's who's been lucky enough to be very successful, in any sport, and doesn't win what is probably the biggest event in their sport, I would like to think they would accept they've failed.'

If such self-criticism sounds desperately harsh, then it's only because he judges himself by his own impossibly high standards. He has already stated he will be the first to know when he should retire from the game because he will be the first to realise when those standards are not being met. But there is no sign of that yet. As most jockeys get older, they start to relish what is jokingly referred to as a 'married man's pace'. McCoy is now married, to Galway-born Chanelle Burke, and has a baby daughter, Eve. Some of the greatest thrill-seekers of the past have been tamed by the introduction of children to their lives. McCoy, however, has insisted that fatherhood and family life make no difference to his focus out on the track. Proof of that wasn't long in coming. Just weeks after Eve's birth, her father took a crashing fall in January 2008 at Warwick, which resulted in two fractured vertebrae. It was a serious injury that threatened his participation at the Cheltenham festival. Less than two months later he was back in action.

'I would never soften,' he said at the time. 'I think I'm soft anyway off the racecourse. But on it I'm unbreakable. I don't feel the need to be protecting myself. I think every time I'm on a horse, no matter how hard I fall, I'm going to get up. You have to take risks in this sport. And there's no excitement if you don't.'

Over the years some of those risks have been enough to make even those in the stands wince. McCoy himself dismisses any concerns held by those around him. He insists he is living the dream of that stubborn schoolboy from Moneyglass, and it's true that those who find out early what they like and then discover they're actually good at it are blessed. McCoy also dismisses the sacrifices he makes. After all, he chooses to make them and in the overall context the consequences of freely entered activities are small cause for pity. No one knows that better than him. A persistent horror, he admits, is the idea that people might mistake his openness about wasting as some attempt at attention-seeking. He may look like death warmed up sometimes but it is his choice.

The fruits of all that effort and will to overcome are in the record books and in a palatial home near Wantage. Most National Hunt jockeys are not wealthy compared to their flat race brethren, but McCoy is no pauper. He's much too shrewd a customer to underestimate the importance of financial independence, but the competitive fire that has driven him to such a status still burns brightly enough to make one wonder how much of that fortune he would swap for an Aintree National. It's not hard to imagine the sum would be substantial.

Already there is enough done to guarantee a wealth of professional respect. If squeezing the last ounce out of his horses is a job requirement, then extracting the maximum from yourself is a much tougher task. Even by the most severe standards, McCoy has done that.

'Tony is as fine a young man as you will ever come across,' Jim Bolger said in 2009. As examinations go, that's an honours result.

Cheltenham Festival Winners

1996
Grand Annual Chase	Kibreet

1997
Arkle Trophy	Or Royal
Champion Hurdle	Make A Stand
Gold Cup	Mr Mulligan

1998

Arkle Trophy	Champleve
Cathcart Trophy	Cyfor Malta
Pertemps Hurdle Final	Unsinkable Boxer
Vincent O'Brien County Hurdle	Blowing Wind

1999

Supreme Novices Hurdle	Hors La Loi
Mildmay Of Flete Trophy	Majadou

2000

Queen Mother Champion Chase	Edredon Bleu

2002

Cathcart Trophy	Royal Auclair

2003

Weatherbys Champion Bumper	Liberman

2004

Arkle Trophy	Well Chief

2006

Champion Hurdle	Brave Inca
Jewson Novices Handicap Chase	Reveillez
Spa Novices Hurdle	Black Jack Ketchum

2007

Spa Novices Hurdle	Wichita Lineman

2008

SunAlliance Novice Chase	Albertas Run

2009

William Hill National Hunt Chase	Wichita Lineman

Other Major Winners include

1996

| Mumm Melling Chase | Viking Flagship |

1997

| Scottish Grand National | Belmont King |

1998

Topham Trophy	Cyfor Malta
Aintree Hurdle	Pridwell
Paddy Power Gold Cup	Cyfor Malta

2000

| Paddy Power Gold Cup | Lady Cricket |
| Topham Trophy | Northern Starlight |

2001

| Paddy Power Gold Cup | Shooting Light |

2002

Long Walk Hurdle	Deanos Beano
King George VI Chase	Best Mate
Tote Gold Trophy	Copeland

2004

Long Walk Hurdle	Baracouda
Betfair Bowl	Tiutchev
Maghull Novices Chase	Well Chief

2005

| Powers Gold Cup | Like-A-Butterfly |
| December Festival Hurdle | Brave Inca |

2006

AIG Irish Champion Hurdle	Brave Inca
Sefton Novices Hurdle	Black Jack Ketchum
Hatton's Grace Hurdle	Brave Inca

2007

Christmas Hurdle	Straw Bear
Betfair Bowl	Exotic Dancer
Irish Grand National	Butler's Cabin

11

JOHNNY MURTAGH

If persistence really is a measure of self-belief, then Johnny Murtagh should never have experienced a moment of doubt. But nothing is ever that simple. During his dizzyingly up and down thirty-nine years, Murtagh has had to exhibit remarkable perseverance while also facing up to vulnerabilities of the rawest and most brutal variety. Whether confronting the weight problems that have dogged his career, or the alcoholism that threatened to end it before it even began, he has had to battle himself to such an extent that even after experiencing the most intoxicating highs the sport can offer, terrible doubts still led him to consider ending his life in a haze of booze, sadness and self-doubt. That in 2009 he stands on top of the racing game as one of the world's great jockeys makes that persistence, if anything, even more remarkable.

At an age when most jump jockeys have retired, conventional wisdom has it that flat jockeys are just coming into their own. Aidan O'Brien believes that Murtagh is now at his peak, with enough experience to cope with, and indeed thrive on, the pressures of being No.1 jockey to the world's most powerful racing empire, but still hungry enough to be bold. Several rather obvious puns can be employed on the hunger thread about Murtagh, but throughout his life a lack of boldness has never been an issue. At its best it translates itself into a brio and zest for life that percolates into simple things. It's there in the quick, cocksure stride, a gait generally not unfamiliar to the residents of Navan, the town near which he was brought up. It's also there in the resolutely direct approach he brings to engaging with people. Anyone uncomfortable about conversing with someone whose eye-contact never wavers might be best avoiding him. It's also part of how he sees himself: direct, to the point and honest with a minimal threshold for bullshit or liberties.

However, that brio has also taken him to places that should have been anathema to a professional jockey. A champion apprentice in his teens, Murtagh followed the same ruinous path pursued by many other promising young riders down the years. The rewards he felt his due, combined with a social nature, left him vulnerable to others and his own instincts. Drinking to celebrate quickly developed into drinking to console and soon no excuse to stare into a bottle was required. With his wits in a tangle, the discipline required to ignore unsuitable food vanished into a binfull of take-away trays. The resultant guilt only fuelled a need to get away from painful reality. When he was just twenty-three years of age, one of the most coveted jobs in Irish racing, as stable jockey to John Oxx, the man who more than anyone else has moulded his career, was gone. Less than two years later, he won it back. Those who dismissed the callow youngster with the wondrous talent, but a tenuous relationship with discipline, had got their first lesson in how never to underestimate J.P. Murtagh.

Doubters have had more occasions since to wonder if he has blown it. In 2003, frazzled by the self-loathing that binge drinking can bring, and wrung out by years of wasting, Murtagh lost the Oxx gig once and for all. For many, the idea that he could finally end the daily torture of keeping his weight under control was a happy one. It would allow him the chance to sort out deeper and more personal issues without the often intolerable strain of trying to maintain a body weight at least two stone less than what would be normal and healthy. But that is not Murtagh's way. 'Perseverance distinguishes the strong soul from the weak,' wrote Thomas Carlyle, a lapsed Calvinist who might not be an obvious Murtagh ally, but whose belief in the merits of stickability are enthusiastically echoed by the jockey. Within a couple of years came a third Epsom Derby triumph and, most importantly, a peace of mind that has been hard-earned but which currently sees him with the most coveted job in racing at Ballydoyle.

> It's all about staying in the game, giving yourself a chance. That's an attitude I've had right from the start. I wanted to give it my best shot and if it wasn't good enough, then so be it. But I wanted to give myself the best chance to fulfil my potential. What I really didn't want was to be sitting in a bar at fifty, talking to the lads about if only I'd done this or that. I've always had faith in my ability, and being able to do the job. It was just a case of doing the right things. There have been plenty of times, even when things have been going good, that I wake up in the morning and wonder about why I'm doing all this. It isn't just the bad times when that happens. You know, asking is all this worth it? But I keep coming to the same conclusion that it is.

Justification for such iron self-belief is littered over the last two decades – none more so than since replacing the disgraced Kieren Fallon as No.1 at Ballydoyle. In 2008, his first season, came a remarkable twenty-one Group 1 winners. Just as important, though, was the sense of a major talent finally being allowed full expression in the best possible circumstances the sport can provide. And it surely has been no coincidence that it has occurred at a time when the man on board gives every sign of finally being at peace with himself. Sadly it wasn't always so.

In an explosive *Sunday Times* interview, Murtagh recounted a winter break spent in Dubai in 2002–03. The previous season he had won the Epsom Derby on High Chaparral. He was recognised as one of the leading jockeys in world racing but the acknowledgement brought little satisfaction. Instead, there was only the guilt of drinking again. In truth, he had never truly given up.

'I had stopped drinking but didn't have one year sober. I would stay off it for nine months, then have one night out, wake the next morning, and start again,' he recounted before pointing back to Dubai. 'That winter I was living on the tenth floor of an apartment block and looking out over the balcony thinking people would probably be better off without me.

That's how close I came to not getting back. I came home and I was like a time bomb and it was ticking. I was arguing with people, getting in trouble with the stewards, using people, and finally realising I had to change.'

It was then that that famous persistence really kicked in. Murtagh had got on the wrong side of some people. Perceived arrogance masked a lot of insecurity but it was easy to dismiss him sometimes as boorish and attention-seeking. Even now there are those in the game who simply don't like him. Happily, they are in a small minority but not a fraction as small as any begrudgers there might be who don't admire and respect the man for the way he has turned his life around. Now, instead of attitude, there is mostly only determination to do the job well and to enjoy the process. The result is an engaging openness that has stripped away any arrogance there might have been.

I speak from the heart and I speak the truth. My motive for that interview was that it might help someone reading it. It certainly wasn't ego. I said what I felt had to be said and if it helped, then great. It is part of the consistency I want to build up in my career and in my life. I've learned there is no point being brilliant one day and crap the next. Doing my best every day is what is important.

The demands of living up to those standards are intense. Every calorie and every piece of carbohydrate is part of a calculation aimed at getting him to the race four to five pounds under nine stone. It demands a routine that he dismisses as being part of the job, the way traffic is a chore for office-bound commuters. But there are no weekends and Bank Holiday breaks from the morning run and the daily sweat in the sauna. It is as much of a mental challenge as it is physical and it is little wonder that he sometimes wakes up wondering if it is all worth it. In the circumstances, clinging to the positives is vital and there has been no more positive development for jockeys in Ireland than the increase in the minimum weights in races there.

It has been a huge help and it's great that Ireland was the first to go that way. It means not having to do 8.7 to 8.9 all week. Being able to do 8.12 or 9 st from Monday to Friday gives the body a chance. There's a chance of some sort of life with the family. At weekends then you can get it down to 8.9 again for the big races but mentally it is a massive benefit. It means a little thing like going out for dinner on Sunday night and not having to worry about doing 8.10 the following day.

But there is never any escape from the struggle. The stresses of managing weight have come under increased scrutiny in recent years with a number of Turf Club sponsored studies into the effects of dehydration. Issues with bone density and the possibility of greater head injuries if the body is dehydrated mean there is now a greater appreciation of the long-term effects from the rigours of a jockey's life. Any concerns about Murtagh living for the moment and leaving tomorrow to fate are firmly put to bed, however. Desperately wanting to make the most of his ability doesn't mean he is about to damage his future.

I've got a great doctor and I get checked out at the start of every year. It's a thorough medical, to make sure I'm all right, get the right boxes ticked off. The bone density tests I've had tell me I've the bones of a twenty-year-old but there are other little things. I always go to a dentist before the season starts to get my teeth done. Just to make sure there's nothing wrong. It's a long hard season and I don't want to be in the middle of it and find out something is brewing.

It's that level of thoroughness that characterises his approach these days, little things that contribute to the total. That fits into the Ballydoyle philosophy perfectly. Vincent O'Brien established the world's most famous training establishment on a basis of attention to detail. Nothing was too small to be overlooked. It's a mantra that has continued under the reign of his son-in-law, John Magnier, with Aidan O'Brien at the helm. One man unsurprised at how Murtagh has thrived in the environment is his former boss. The jockey describes John Oxx as 'a great man that I can't speak more highly of. He has had a huge influence on me and my family.' Oxx in turn never expected anything else but that his former protégé would thrive at Ballydoyle.

'Confidence is something he has never lacked. He is very positive at all times and thinks about his races a lot. He is particularly good on the big days,' says Oxx. 'What's important is that his instincts are so good. He always has a plan and is able to communicate it well. It might not always come off but his record shows he gets it right more often than not. He is not a jockey you want to interfere with too much because his instincts are top class. As a trainer, it's probably best to leave him to it,' Oxx believes.

'He has been at the top level for a long time now. Since 2000, really, when he had thirteen Group 1s. I see no great change in his riding but he does have more ammunition now. I remember telling him that every jockey improves with time and he has improved throughout his thirties. What has helped is that he is probably more settled in himself now. He is definitely more relaxed and more mature.'

That assessment reinforces what has been a rare constant in Murtagh's life and that is a natural talent for riding racehorses. That it originally coincided with a physical stature which has allowed him to exploit it to the full, was as fortuitous as the discovery of that talent in the first place. The only horses that featured in the life of the builder's son were ponies that grazed in the fields around home at Bohermeen. Instead, Murtagh's sporting outlets were in football and boxing. Good enough at the latter to become an Irish schools' champion, it was at a fight that his mother was informed that her son was the right size to be a jockey.

She wrote to the RACE apprentice centre for application forms and got a two-week trial for her fifteen-year-old boy. He thought it would be a laugh if nothing else, but he found everything to do with horses easy. Even the big show-jumpers at the Army Equitation school on the Curragh did what he asked them to do. And he looked good on them, like he'd been riding all his life, a natural. Best of all for the instructors, there were no bad habits to knock out of him. J.P. Murtagh was a blank canvas.

It was also his good fortune that RACE assigned him to Oxx to finish his practical education. With a list of owners that included Sheikh Mohammed and the Aga Khan, it wasn't the usual route for a hungry apprentice on the make because opportunities to race-ride were bound to be limited. However, the Curragh trainer is renowned for an innate decency that makes Currabeg stables a good place to work. Any idea that the new boy might be overawed by working in a new and adult world quickly disappeared.

'He was always a sharp little fellah, always on the ball,' Oxx remembers. 'He didn't stand out straight away but as the year went on he started cantering away and you could see he rode quite well. From the first time he started riding fast work, though, you could see the potential.' At seventeen came a first winner, Chicago Style at Limerick, and a couple of years later there was an apprentice championship. So far, so normal for a talented apprentice. Except circumstances at the Oxx yard were far from normal in the early 1990s.

Ron Quinton, a veteran Australian rider, had never quite settled as No.1 jockey. His Aussie style didn't impress Irish punters and as Murtagh's profile increased, it was increasingly obvious that the former Sydney champion's days were numbered. In 1992 the changeover happened. Just seven years after first sitting on a racehorse, the ex-boxer was in possession of one of the best jobs in Ireland. And it looked on the outside as if he knew it only too well. Confidence turned to conceit and his drinking started to spiral out of control. Just a year after getting the job, he lost it. A party on a Thursday meant a serious sweat on a Friday – except he couldn't sweat. On Saturday Murtagh put up 3 lb overweight on a horse and got beaten a neck. Oxx was left with no choice. His owners were talking.

'He was quite young and he had this job thrust upon him. When we think back to being twenty-three, I don't think most of us can say we'd have done much better. A lot is expected of a young jockey,' Oxx says. 'It was a general lack of discipline, I suppose is the best way to describe it. He could still ride very well but he hadn't realised there is more to it than that.'

The first step to finding out was a six-week stay in Dublin's St Patrick's clinic. Initially it looked to have stalled any self-destructive behaviour to such an extent that he was ultimately able to get his job back. Oxx recalls: 'One man who played an important role in getting Johnny back was the Aga Khan's bloodstock manager at the time, Ghislain Drion. He had always been positive about Johnny and was willing to give him every chance. I think Monsieur Drion had more of a crucial influence than most people realise. It encouraged me, too, because I wouldn't have been able to have him back without Monsieur Drion or the Aga Khan being in agreement.'

Not unreasonably, then, Murtagh was on the Aga's filly Khaytada in the 1995 Irish 1,000 Guineas, which was a blow as Christy Roche powered clear on the stable companion Ridgewood Pearl. It was a temporary blip. Murtagh was back on board for the Coronation Stakes and the Prix Du Moulin which set the partnership up for the Breeders' Cup Mile at Belmont Park; 8 st 7 lb was a push for the jockey but his new father-in-law, the legendary Tipperary hurler Babs Keating, accompanied the Oxx team to New York and his motivation was important in making the weight. The race itself was comparatively straightforward, Ridgewood Pearl overcoming soft conditions to bring a spectacular career to a successful conclusion.

I was just after getting my job back and it just brought a great year to a perfect end. You need a special horse to win a Breeders' Cup and that's what she was. With most of them, if everything is right, they might squeak a Group 1. But it's the ones that can win three or four of them, they are the special ones. Ridgewood Pearl was like that. She was so straightforward, always worked well, always ate up, never a problem.

Murtagh wound up 1995 as champion jockey. He retained the title the following year and added to his Group 1 tally with another star Oxx filly, Timarida. Ebadiyla provided a first classic in 1997, while a third championship came his way in 1998. There were good times but problems with alcohol wouldn't go away and weight was a constant struggle. There was no getting away from the reality, though, that he was a man to reckon with on the big occasion. Another Irish Oaks on Winona and an Ascot Gold Cup on Enzeli only emphasised the point. But the best was yet to come.

The wonder of Sinndar is that we might not ever have seen the best of him. As a classic Aga Khan-bred horse, his two-year-old Group 1 success in the 1999 National Stakes was evidence of unlikely precocity. Nevertheless, there were Derby quotes as high as 25-1 available the following spring. Victory in the Derrinstown Derby Trial confirmed his claims for travelling to Epsom, but on the run up to the race others were more heralded. It proved to be a vintage Derby. Sinndar overhauled the following year's Arc hero Sakhee to win going away. In third was Beat Hollow and fourth was Best Of The Bests, both subsequently Group 1 winners. Murtagh was at his clinical best around Epsom's switchback test, a foretaste of his subsequent mastery of the unique track. At thirty, he had fulfilled the dream – winning the Derby and being champion jockey.

Sinndar completed the Epsom-Curragh double in runaway style before being put away for an autumn campaign. A warm up in the Prix Niel set him up for an Arc clash with Montjeu. It was a mouthwatering prospect but the expectation was better than the reality. Montjeu was past his imperious best and had no answer to the Irish three-year-old, who won easily. Murtagh returned draped in an Irish tricolour, having conquered European racing's peak. No horse since Alleged in 1977–78 had ever won back-to-back Prix de l'Arc de Triomphes but Sinndar looked made for the task. He provided a career high at Longchamp and looked to be still improving. However, the Aga Khan decided to retire his star colt, having been beaten just once, on his three-year-old debut by Bach, in eight career starts. His final official handicap mark was 132, and Murtagh felt that was something of an insult.

He was a great horse. The pity is he didn't race as a four-year-old, when you see what Sakhee did the following year [2001]. Winning the Derby is something everybody wants. It's what you dream of because of all that history. When you ride in it and you don't win, it's the only time you get the feeling 'Jesus, another year before I get a chance again'.

Sinndar's Arc was the culmination of a remarkable year and the day itself at Longchamp encapsulated how a new riding force had burst onto the international racing scene. As well as the Arc, Murtagh also recorded Group 1 victories on Namid in the Prix de l'Abbaye and Petrushka in the Prix de l'Opera. In December, Daliapour's win in Hong Kong brought the jockey's Group 1 total to thirteen. He could do no wrong.

Michael Stoute, forced into scrambling for replacement jockeys after Kieren Fallon's horrific accident at Royal Ascot, discovered the virtues of having a younger Irishman riding for him. Petrushka had earlier landed another Irish Oaks and Kalanisi hammered a further nail into Montjeu's declining star by out-pointing him in the Champion Stakes at Newmarket. Just a couple of weeks later the Aga Khan's colt came from the rear of the field to nail his Breeders' Cup Turf opposition on the line at Churchill Downs. An exultant Stoute marched back to the winner's circle exhorting his jockey: 'Milk it Murtagh – Milk it!'

> The Derby was my big promotion that year. If there was a spare jockey required, my name was suddenly in there. Winners make more winners and suddenly I was in the right place at the right time. But that's what I mean about staying in the game and giving yourself a chance.

In comparison, 2001 was an anticlimax, but it did provide an important link up with a young trainer rapidly on the rise. Aidan O'Brien ended the year with twenty-three Group 1 winners, including a Derby victory with Galileo. It was a display of overwhelming dominance and in the middle of it Murtagh secured an Irish 2,000 Guineas and a St James's Palace Stakes on Black Minnaloushe. It was a taste of things to come. Murtagh was becoming one of O'Brien's favourite substitutes to fill in on Mick Kinane's discards.

Kinane was suspended for the Guineas in 2002 and it was Jamie Spencer who subbed on the apparent Ballydoyle No.1 Hawk Wing. But it was Murtagh who won, carrying the colours of the Manchester United manager Sir Alex Ferguson, to a narrow success on Rock of Gibraltar. A month later it got even better. Kinane was back on Hawk Wing in the

Derby, leaving High Chaparral for his Irish colleague. Coming down the hill, High Chaparral was behind his stamina-suspect stable companion and Murtagh made an audaciously early move coming to Tattenham Corner. It was crucial. Hawk Wing folded inside the final furlong and Murtagh's mount resolutely kept going, just as his jockey calculated he would.

> High Chaparral had great stamina and he loved a battle. Maybe in hindsight that move won us the race, but he was a really good horse. If Sinndar and High Chaparral had faced each other it would have been like Ali versus Frazier. They would have killed each other. They were two great, great horses.

It was a period of huge professional achievement for Murtagh, but his personal demons were threatening to make it useless. 'I had some great times through those years, big winners and a lot of laughs, but there was always something missing, and the fact that I didn't know what it was made it worse,' he later recounted. It was time to face up seriously to his problems with alcohol. His father had successfully fought back from alcoholism and now the son faced up to his biggest struggle. With the support of his wife, Orla, Murtagh slowly started to feel better about himself and the connection between that and not drinking was obvious. Not drinking provided a priceless peace of mind. But it took time.

As always, there were exhibitions of brilliance in the saddle, such as in the 2003 Irish Derby victory on Alamshar. The Aga Khan also ran the favourite Dalakhani, an unbeaten Prix du Jockey Club winner, ridden by the latest riding sensation in France, Christophe Soumillon. The Belgian-born jockey is another who is rarely short on confidence, but on a first foray to the Curragh it proved misplaced. Scared of being boxed in by a bunch of Ballydoyle pacemakers, he had Dalakhani racing much too prominently and went for home too soon. Murtagh tracked him throughout and nailed him on the line.

But earlier in the season the Irishman had got it badly wrong in the Irish 1,000 Guineas on board the champion French filly Six Perfections.

Replacing Thierry Thulliez for his local knowledge, Murtagh rode a race that made Soumillon look like a Curragh veteran. Subsequent form proved Six Perfections was the best in the race if allowed to deliver her killer late thrust. With half the Curragh available to him on the outside, however, Murtagh chose to take an ambitious route up the rail. Mick Kinane sized up the situation in a second. On board Yesterday he kept his big rival trapped in a pocket until there wasn't enough ground left for Six Perfections to bridge the gap between the two. French trainer Pascal Bary's face in the parade ring afterwards was a picture of Gallic frustration. No more than his jockey's was. Never one not to make his feelings known on a subject, Murtagh's face is usually an accurate barometer of where he's at.

As Oxx says: 'He's someone who wears his heart on his sleeve. He is passionate about his work; in fact he is quite exuberant about it, so you can see these little changes to his mood. He doesn't let things roll off him, or take criticism lightly. He's not like Mick Kinane that way. Mick's mood never changes.'

Murtagh is taller than the man who is eleven years older than him but Kinane's shadow has been immense throughout his career. The downside to that is having such a competitor against him every day, but the considerable upside is the role Kinane has played in paving the way for Irish-based jockeys to have international careers. By the end of 2003, though, Murtagh's weight problems resulted in another split from Oxx, this time for good. Kinane split from Ballydoyle and filled the vacancy with the Curragh trainer, leaving Murtagh to recover and start the following season as a freelance. Jamie Spencer's short stay led to speculation in early 2005 that Murtagh was in line for the coveted position. It wasn't to be, as Kieren Fallon got the job. It hurt at the time but now Murtagh is fatalistic about the delay in moving to Ballydoyle.

A few years ago my chest would have been out if I'd got it. But I really appreciate it now. My ego is long gone now and what I want is to stay in the game and do my best. Maybe it wouldn't have been the right time before but everything fell into place.

Even as a freelance, Murtagh's international profile remained high. In 2004 he rode a lot in the UK and enjoyed Group 1 success on the top mare Soviet Song, who landed the Falmouth Stakes, the Sussex Stakes and the Matron Stakes. Not being with Ballydoyle even had an upside.

Fallon's link-up left the ride on Motivator open and Michael Bell didn't hesitate in turning to Murtagh for the highly strung but brilliant son of Montjeu. An Epsom warm up in the Dante at York was authoritative but hardly earth-shattering. There were also real concerns that his suspect temperament would let him down in the intense Derby atmosphere. But all those fears vanished with a brilliantly executed victory. It looked like a potential superstar had just arrived but Motivator's spell as racing's latest Pegasus incarnate was a short one. A drop back to ten furlongs in the Eclipse looked set to work well until Fallon secured his revenge on Oratorio. He was to do the same in the Irish Champion Stakes and Motivator had no answer to Fallon's mount, Hurricane Run, in the Arc. 'On the day he won the Derby, Motivator was very good, the way he travelled and quickened away. I don't like knocking him but he was a bit tricky. And I think the back problems that caught up with him might have started in the Eclipse,' Murtagh believes.

The jockey missed out on the Irish Champion run, however, after picking up a twenty-one-day ban for an outrageous incident at Leopardstown, when he punched Pat Smullen in the jaw just after the finishing post. The two men quickly made up afterwards and ended up laughing about it. But it was a reflection of the intensity of competition in Ireland and the standard of jockeyship needed at the very top level. It brings a pressure that Murtagh himself has described: 'There are times it can wreck your head that you will do something stupid. You don't want to let people down. I see apprentices coming through and they don't know what they're in for.' However, it's those personal standards that have also kept him at the forefront of international competition for the last decade, and there has even been time to test his mettle in the jumping game. During the winter of 2005–06 he linked up with his friend Michael Halford by riding for him over hurdles. It yielded winners but also a couple of agonising runner-up placings on

Golden Cross – including the World Hurdle at the Cheltenham festival when only just failing to overhaul My Way De Solzen.

Anyone who believed that was a sign of a return to the bad old days of fluctuating weight problems was quickly put right. The consistency that Murtagh has yearned for throughout his career started to shine through. Kieren Fallon's inability to ride in Britain allowed Murtagh in for a string of big race opportunities and he wasted little time making the most of them. Dylan Thomas won a King George while the filly Peeping Fawn went on a midsummer rampage in 2007 which took in the Irish Oaks, the Nassau Stakes and the Yorkshire Oaks. There was also a vintage effort in the Fillies Mile at Ascot when Murtagh rode his French rival Stephane Pasquier to sleep on board Listen.

The net impact was that when John Magnier & Co. eventually cut their ties with Fallon, there was little doubt who was destined to replace him. And there was little doubt he would accept. 'When you look at the people who've done it – Piggott, Eddery, Kinane, Spencer, Fallon – and realise you're in their company now, it's just a great feeling,' he said. There was some initial speculation that Murtagh might be a stop-gap measure until Fallon had served out his drugs ban. Such scepticism was fuelled by the terms of the deal which saw the new man signed for just a single year. But what a year it turned out to be.

Duke Of Marmalade kicked off 2008 with victory in the Prix Ganay at Longchamp but it is the three-year-old classics that are the holy grail at Ballydoyle and Murtagh instantly proved his ability to get it right when it counts. New Approach might have been the stand-out favourite for the 2,000 Guineas and looked all over the winner when kicking on over two furlongs out at Newmarket, but it was the relatively un-heralded Henrythenavigator who swept through to challenge and to get his head in front when it mattered. New Approach was fighting back but too late. Henry confirmed this outstanding piece of form in even more impressive style in the Irish Guineas at the Curragh. Then came two victories over his old rival, and future Breeders' Cup Classic winner Raven's Pass, in the St James's Palace and the Sussex Stakes. In stake terms, however, even Henry had to concede to Duke Of Marmalade, who won five Group 1s in a row to highlight a season that yielded twenty-three top-class victories to Ballydoyle and twenty-one to their new jockey.

During the summer the team looked all but unstoppable. Royal Ascot turned into a benefit, with Murtagh becoming leading jockey there for the third time in his career with six winners. They included Henry, the Duke and also Yeats, who landed a third Gold Cup in a row. Two other rides on the Saturday, Macarthur in the Hardwicke and Honolulu in the Queen Alexandria, might not have had the same prestige as their stable companions but they did highlight a jockey riding with supreme confidence. The drawback with such success is the attention it brings to almost every detail of that success. Haradasun's victory in the Queen Anne provoked grumbling in Britain about Ballydoyle's use of pacemakers. They became full-throated shouts of protest after the Duke's victory in the re-scheduled Juddmonte International at Newmarket.

Colm O'Donoghue on the O'Brien pacemaker, Red Rock Canyon, eased off the fence at the four furlong marker, allowing Murtagh through to win. Accusations of team tactics were immediately thrown about but the stewards on the day were satisfied no rules were broken. And it's quite possible that nothing else could have been done, except that Murtagh, in the full glow of victory, informed a reporter that he had told O'Donoghue beforehand to do what he did. When the quotes appeared the following day, the British Horseracing Authority had found an avenue into holding a disciplinary enquiry.

Murtagh, O'Donoghue and O'Brien were summoned to London. After a three-hour enquiry, both jockeys were found to have broken the rules of racing and were banned for a week each. O'Brien was fined £5,000 for not providing adequate instructions. The BHA repeatedly stressed the Irish team had broken the rules through 'ignorance rather than calculation' and there was 'no question of cheating'. For most observers, though, there were serious questions arising from the case for the BHA, a body that had managed to mangle its public image in relation to the previous year's race-fixing trial, and whose ability to pluck a public relations disaster from the jaws of normalcy appeared to remain strong.

There was a time when such an outcome would have had Murtagh simmering with rage. Behind the scenes at Ballydoyle there was plenty of resentment at a furore that was perceived to be media-driven. But in public, at least, a determinedly level-headed stance was presented to the world. 'You should know when you go to ride in any country that these are the rules here and that's what you're allowed and not allowed to do,' he said. It was impressively diplomatic and low key, just as the Coolmore supremo, John Magnier, would have appreciated. In hindsight, there was also a resonance to those words on the back of a trip to Australia for the Melbourne Cup.

The presence of Septimus and two other O'Brien-trained runners in the race that stops a nation was almost the only show in town on the run up to the Flemington showpiece. Local horsemen proclaiming that Septimus had it in him to beat the locals at his leisure only guaranteed more attention. Murtagh was also an attraction, having ridden the star Australian sprinter Choisir – 'he and Namid are the two best sprinters I've ridden' – to win twice at Royal Ascot in 2003. But it all went horribly wrong as O'Brien's plans to dominate the race from the front blew up in his face.

In a jurisdiction where pacemakers are not allowed, the stewards hauled the three jockeys in and then summoned O'Brien back from his hotel hours after the race. The enquiry represented a mammoth clash of racing cultures. The only stewards' enquiry into the race that would have happened in Europe was how the Bart Cummings-trained winner, Given, had improved its form so much in the short period since its previous race. There was also tension surrounding O'Brien's habit of starting sentences with 'Listen,' a simple verbal punctuation mark here, but a linguistic red rag to an Australian stewards' panel apparently determined to flex its power against some big-name Europeans. However, O'Brien eventually did get his way, the Aussies listened and the controversy over riding tactics extended only to some typically splenetic press coverage which poured scorn on any chance of the

Ballydoyle powerhouse ever coming to terms with the demands of Australian racing.

That's a view that fits into the 'hostage to fortune' category. If ever a racing outfit has had the financial clout to dominate wherever it wants, it is Coolmore-Ballydoyle. Just as important is the evidence of the last decade, which suggests that the personnel at the top of it rarely make the same mistake twice. Certainly in terms of their jockey arrangements, there now appears to be a stability that O'Brien, for one, had been yearning for. That it is being provided by a man who once seemed to be heading down a self-destructive route only emphasises Murtagh's achievement.

The trainer put it simply at the end of 2008: 'He has been an unbelievable asset and no words of mine could explain the difference he has made. He has so much natural ability as a horseman and a jockey and he is at that stage of his career where all the things have come together to make him the top class jockey he is. He did all the wild things when he was younger and he is not going back there.' Instead Murtagh's focus is remorselessly on the future and on continually improving himself as a jockey.

In 2009, success continued to flow, with both Fame And Glory and Mastercraftsman proving to be hugely valuable classic winners. There was also a historic four-in-a-row for Yeats in the Ascot Gold Cup, a comparatively sentimental victory in the greater Coolmore scheme of things where speed is more prized than stamina, but no less enjoyable for that.

> I love everything to do with Ballydoyle. From day one John Magnier has been completely straightforward, always asking what I'd like to do in any race. It's all so organised. Aidan is the boss and calls the shots. People say he has good horses but he makes them good. He is a genius with horses. Mine is a little job, just steering them in the right direction.

He's sticking to that view, too. After all, that's what persistent people do.

Classic Wins

1997
Irish Oaks   Ebadiyla

1998
Irish Oaks   Winona

2000
English Derby   Sinndar
Irish Derby   Sinndar
Irish Oaks   Petrushka

2001
Irish 2,000 Guineas   Black Minnaloushe

2002
English 2,000 Guineas   Rock Of Gibraltar
English Derby   High Chaparral

2003
Irish Derby   Alamshar

2005
English Derby   Motivator

2007
Irish Oaks   Peeping Fawn

2008
English 2,000 Guineas   Henrythenavigator
Irish 2,000 Guineas   Henrythenavigator
Irish Oaks   Moonstone
Prix Royal Oak   Yeats

2009

Irish 2,000 Guineas	Mastercraftsman
Irish 1,000 Guineas	Again
Irish Derby	Fame And Glory

Other Major Winners include

1993

National Stakes	Manntari

1995

Coronation Stakes	Ridgewood Pearl
Prix Du Moulin	Ridgewood Pearl
Breeders' Cup Mile	Ridgewood Pearl

1996

Bayerisches Zuchtrennen	Timarida
Yorkshire Oaks	Key Change
Irish Champion Stakes	Timarida

1998

Moyglare Stud Stakes	Ebadiya

1999

Ascot Gold Cup	Enzeli
National Stakes	Sinndar

2000

Yorkshire Oaks	Petrushka
Bayerisches Zuchtrennen	Greek Dance
Prix du l'Abbaye	Namid
Prix de l'Arc de Triomphe	Sinndar
Prix de l'Opera	Petrushka

English Champion Stakes	Kalanisi
Racing Post Trophy	Dilshaan
Breeders' Cup Turf	Kalanisi
Hong Kong Vase	Daliapour

2001

St James's Palace Stakes	Black Minnaloushe
Ascot Gold Cup	Royal Rebel
EP Taylor Stakes	Choc Ice

2002

Ascot Gold Cup	Royal Rebel
Prix du Cadran	Give Notice

2003

Golden Jubilee Stakes	Choisir
Kings Stand Stakes	Choisir
King George VI & Queen Elizabeth Stakes	Alamshar

2004

Matron Stakes	Soviet Song
July Cup	Frizzante
Sussex Stakes	Soviet Song
Falmouth Stakes	Soviet Song

2005

Falmouth Stakes	Soviet Song

2007

Tattersalls Gold Cup	Notnowcato
Golden Jubilee Stakes	Soldier's Tale
King George VI & Queen Elizabeth Stakes	Dylan Thomas
Falmouth Stakes	Simply Perfect
Nassau Stakes	Peeping Fawn

Yorkshire Oaks	Peeping Fawn
Prix Vermeille	Mrs Lindsay
EP Taylor Stakes	Mrs Lindsay

2008

Prix Ganay	Duke Of Marmalade
Tattersalls Gold Cup	Duke Of Marmalade
Coronation Cup	Soldier Of Fortune
St James's Palace Stakes	Henrythenavigator
Ascot Gold Cup	Yeats
Eclipse Stakes	Mount Nelson
King George VI & Queen Elizabeth Stakes	Duke Of Marmalade
Sussex Stakes	Henrythenavigator
Juddmonte International	Duke Of Marmalade
Phoenix Stakes	Mastercraftsman
Prix Morny	Bushranger
Middle Park Stakes	Bushranger
Criterium de Saint-Cloud	Fame And Glory

2009

St James's Palace Stakes	Mastercraftsman
Ascot Gold Cup	Yeats

12

RUBY WALSH

There are fundamentals to being a jockey, such as a deficit of weight and a surfeit of courage. For jump jockeys, in particular, the raw bravery required to do their job runs the line between gallant and plain off-the-wall crazy. So in a profession where guts are a fundamental, any edge usually comes from what's whirring between the ears. And no brain whirrs more powerfully than Ruby Walsh's.

Just as Cesc Fabregas teases his way around the football field or Brian O'Driscoll times a pass during a rugby match, there is a calculation to how Walsh rides a race that is impossible to ignore. The great Dutch footballer Johan Cruyff once explained the importance of sporting intelligence by pointing out that insight is often confused for speed – 'If I start my run earlier than the others, I appear to be faster.'

Other jockeys might start their runs earlier than Walsh but none time them better. Whether it's riding from the front, the back, inner midfield or outer, the thirty-year-old multiple champion has no equal when it comes to being in the right place at the right time. In a sport where victory can be achieved by the width of a horse's nose, even the tiniest percentage advantage counts, and nobody calculates that edge better. During a race it is impossible not to pick out Walsh's arched figure as a reference point for pace. At the finish, all that tightly coiled will-to-win blends into a horse with a neat ferocity. It is a blend that has seen him become a benchmark for the current crop of riders. There are plenty of veteran observers who believe he is the most complete jump jockey the sport has ever seen. Walsh has no weaknesses. Strong in a finish and naturally gifted over a fence, he is also a consummate stylist. But, most importantly of all, nobody has ever thought their way through a race better.

Examples of that edge paying off have been numerous and have come on some of the greatest horses of the last decade: none bigger than Kauto Star, who completed a childhood dream for his rider by winning the 2007 Cheltenham Gold Cup and becoming the first to regain the crown two years later. The latter was something of a coronation for a truly exceptional horse. But the first was as much a test of the jockey as the animal underneath him. Looking back at that race, it is impossible not to admire the skill required to preserve a then-suspect stayer's stamina around the testing track, but also the strength of mind needed to do it when it counted most. Passing the post, Walsh dissolved into an exultant fist-punching display of happiness and relief. During the race, however, a polar bear would have shivered at the cold execution of a minutely teased-out plan.

It's been the same after a pair of Grand National wins, also, and almost every other big race worthy of the description. In 2009 came a record seven winners at the Cheltenham festival. But, crucially, there are just as many examples from nondescript meetings throughout Ireland and Britain. Walsh's appetite for success isn't sated by the big stuff alone. It's why he is revered by punters as well as professionals. It doesn't matter if it is Cheltenham or Kilbeggan, Punchestown or Ludlow, he wants to win and the process of winning begins well away from the track. A jump-off-and-wing-it approach is not the Walsh way.

Most races are won mentally. It's about knowing when the pace is too strong or too easy, or finding the best ground or knowing who to follow. But it's also important for a jockey to know what he's up against. Jockeys have to know their opposition, especially jump jockeys. The last thing you want tearing down to the first fence is to be behind some horse whose trainer hasn't schooled it properly and ends up tearing through the back of it, bringing you down into the bargain. You don't want to be caught in the wrong place and that means watching a lot of races. You have to get to know how certain trainers do things. Looking in the formbook helps, but the guy doing the formbook can't put down everything he sees on a video. So you've got to put in the time. It's tiring coming towards the end of the season but you've got to do it.

Evidence of such a strong mind has been there from the beginning of his career. For one thing, the name Ruby, short for Rupert, also his grandfather's name, was not exactly guaranteed to allow him to blend into the schoolyard. Some sons can also feel in the shadow of their fathers, especially if following the same career path, and as a personality, Ted Walsh casts a shadow of Kilimanjaro-like proportions. A famously effective eleven-times champion amateur jockey, Walsh Senior's profile was raised immeasurably higher still by a television career that has turned him into one of the sport's most instantly recognisable figures. Because Ted Walsh is so popular among the general public for his blunt, outspoken views, the odds were heavily stacked against the youngster being defined in the racing world as anything other than his father's son. But that was to underestimate Ruby Walsh's own singular personality. The strength of it originated from all the family, but especially from his mother, Helen.

I would say I'm actually a bit more like my Mum than my Dad. We're different in some ways. I'd read a book, for instance, but my Dad never would. Mum, though, reads a lot. Dad has an unbelievable memory for facts and figures and he remembers everything about everyone. If he's in an argument, he throws stuff out so quick, whereas I'd be more like Mum. She would be more philosophical and takes more time about making a decision. If I'm given a question, I tease things out a bit like her. But Dad's best answer is always his first.

But what of the challenge of following in his father's footsteps?

I never found his television profile a problem. It was more the fact that he was 'Ted Walsh – champion jockey'. I was sixteen starting out and not really able to give one a real drive. So there was all that 'oh, he'll never be as good as his oul fellah'. But you get over that.

What was harder was the stuff about getting chances because of your name. Maybe the name was a help in getting some chances a bit quicker but it doesn't matter at all if you can't ride. Johnny Murtagh had no name starting out, David Casey had no name, Tony McCoy had no name. People can work things out very quick. If there's talent there, it will be seen. If you're not able to do it, no name in the world is going to help you.

Willie Mullins was a man able to identify with that. As the son of a legendary trainer in Paddy Mullins, he enjoyed a successful amateur career as a jockey before entering the training ranks in his own right. There was a period, though, when the two jobs overlapped, not exactly a recipe for a stress-free existence. It was in such a mood that he eyed the prospect of making the weight for Young Fenora in a bumper at Leopardstown in November 1995. Young Fenora was a challenging ride in the sense that all she needed was a pair of high heels to qualify as a total bitch. Mullins thought of a relaxing lunch and asked his wife Jackie if the young Walsh lad might ride instead. Watching the race, the two of them immediately realised they were witnessing something different. Young Fenora didn't run particularly kindly but she ran more kindly than ever before and kindly enough to win. In a vision of the future, her young jockey settled out the back before gradually making ground, all the while persuading his mount that this wasn't such a bad business after all. 'It was an exceptional ride,' Mullins still remembers.

Such an experience only added to the young amateur's certainty that racing was the life he wanted. A good student and versatile enough on the sports field to earn a trial at scrum half for the Leinster under-16 team, he completed his Leaving Cert but only because his parents insisted. He felt lucky – 'I was sitting in school watching lads fill out their college application forms and not knowing what they wanted. It would decide the rest of their lives. What an impossible decision' – and couldn't wait to get out.

Aged eighteen, he ended the 1997–98 season as champion amateur and again emulated his father with the same title the following year. It's one of the curiosities of the sport in Ireland that riding amateur is a full-time job, but it was obvious that the teenager was a future professional. No one realised that better than Mullins. The Champion Bumper at Cheltenham was already turning into a lucrative target for the trainer and in 1998 a prime contender was Alexander Banquet. The horse's prospects were enough to have the legendary Richard Dunwoody ringing up to ride him. It was hardly a call out of the blue. Dunwoody had ridden Florida Pearl to win the race the previous year. But Mullins stood by his amateur. 'Not everyone would have done it. I was just Mr R. Walsh. But he kept me on,' Walsh recalls. The trainer's faith was vindicated in memorable fashion and a close personal and professional friendship developed.

> Willie is a friend of mine as much as anything else. I could ring him up about more or less anything in terms of advice. At this stage [2009] we don't actually have to say that much to each other. He always says to ride with confidence and trust your instincts. And he always asks: 'What do you think?' There's a trust there. He might ask 'further?' about a horse's trip and I'll just nod.

What Mullins realised more quickly than most was the maturity in the young amateur who was soon to become a champion professional. It had nothing to do with his prematurely grey hair or the way he quietly went about keeping weight off his spare frame. But there was a calm and an ease with himself that was unusual in one so young. Throwing in an insatiable appetite for work, a desire to improve and a lifetime of soaking up his father's advice meant there was no question who the trainer regarded as his No.1.

Even as a child Walsh accompanied his father to the races and, by keeping his ears open, received an education in tactics and an appreciation of racing's subtleties that would prove invaluable. An inveterate talker anyway, Ted Walsh had an avid audience as his youngest boy walked every track in Ireland alongside him. Along the way, the future champion learned where not to go on heavy ground at Clonmel, where to make his move around Tramore's notoriously tight track and who not to follow in any kind of race. There were also examples of who to follow and, if possible, copy.

For any aspiring jockey in the 1990s, Richard Dunwoody was a hero. Walsh still talks excitedly about Dunwoody's poise in the saddle, the absolute determination to win, clothed in an artist's style. His own burgeoning career coincided with the end of Dunwoody's when the Co. Down-born jockey was effectively riding with only one arm – 'and he was still better than everyone else!' But there was also someone closer to home who was even more of an influence on him. Charlie Swan didn't have as tidy a seat as Dunwoody, but the importance of Swan's thinking was drummed into him by his father.

> Following Charlie around in a race was incredible. He just saw things that others didn't see. He'd be sneaking along not looking to be doing much but most of the time he'd get horses to produce more than they would for any other man. He didn't have Dunwoody's style and when you're a young lad all you see is the style. But tactically, Charlie was something else.

The admiration isn't a one-way street. Even in his pomp and riding Istabraq to a trio of Champion Hurdle wins, Swan couldn't help but be impressed by the youngster sitting near him in the weighroom. There was an intensity there and a curiosity that meant Walsh wasn't shy in asking questions. Swan's verdict now is simple.

'Ruby's the best we've ever seen, by a long shot. I think he's probably the best we will ever see,' he says. 'He has everything. He's a good judge of pace, he's got great hands, he's brave. It's all there.' Swan noticed Walsh's promise early. 'Even as a kid there was something about him. He was always a horseman but he has also worked hard at the game and has never stopped trying to improve himself. It's wonderful how he knows the opposition so well. When he rides for you, he knows everything there is to know about the horse without even sitting on him. He'll end up telling you stuff. He's a nice fellah as well but very focused. He can definitely call a spade a spade – like his Dad.'

Soon proof emerged that Walsh would be a serious threat to Swan. In his first season as a professional (1998–99), twenty-year-old Walsh was crowned champion jockey. It brought to an end Swan's unprecedented streak of nine championships. A new era looked to be dawning. However, jump racing doesn't allow such neat conclusions to be drawn. In October 1999, Ireland's new champion went to the Czech Republic to ride Risk Of Thunder in the famous Grand Pardubice race. Before the main event, however, he jumped on another Enda Bolger-trained horse, Shannon Fountain, in a cross-country event. Later he recalled: 'I was swinging along on the rail with two Czech riders right behind me. I was shaving the rail but then I saw the connections on two parts of rail coming up had not been closed. There was a gap and then the rail started again. I'd nowhere to go and we met the start of the rail straight on. I got a kick coming after me but it was the rail that broke my shin. I knew straightaway I was in trouble.'

It was five months before he was able to ride again. In his absence, another new champion was crowned. Barry Geraghty joined Walsh and Paul Carberry at the top of the racing tree in Ireland. A year before, Carberry had won the Aintree Grand National on Bobbyjo, who was trained by his father Tommy. Even for a young man in a hurry to make up for lost time, the chances of a similar victory just twelve months later seemed remote. But this was the beginning of an unprecedented level of success for Irish-trained horses around Liverpool. So the Walsh family went to Aintree in 2000 with a chance of winning. In the National a chance is all anyone can ask for: if only that could be got across to Papillon.

In many ways, Papillon wasn't a Ted Walsh type at all. The giant bay was owned by an American friend, Betty Moran, and possessed the good looks of a dressage animal. He also possessed more than a little talent, but despite having finished runner up to Bobbyjo in the 1998 Irish National, the popular perception was that Papillon couldn't be relied upon to burst a gut in pursuit of victory. A little bit soft was the consensus on the

Aintree build up: well handicapped but would he do it? The first three or four fences would tell a lot and for a young man having his first National ride it was an onerous responsibility trying to quell his own excitement while also attempting to cajole a temperamental partner into enjoying himself. But for the first time the wider racing world saw at first hand Walsh's famous big-race temperament.

Papillon decided to like Aintree's unique challenge. That was good news for Walsh, his family looking on in the stands and millions around Britain and Ireland. The big horse was the subject of a major public gamble that saw 33-1 morning odds dissolve into a 10-1 SP. With thirty fences just waiting to trip up any presumption, there was never going to be over-confidence once Papillon found his rhythm. But it was also impossible not to notice the ease with which he travelled throughout and the lightness of touch that encouraged him to tackle those fences with enthusiasm. Combined with that sprinkle of class he always possessed, it meant that only Mely Moss was a challenger over the last two fences. Up the long run in, it was an eyeball to eyeball struggle but, after giving him the kid glove treatment for four and a quarter miles, Papillon's jockey unleashed a resolutely demanding fist for the last two furlongs. The horse responded and the world was treated to a wide-eyed mixture of disbelief and happiness as horse and rider passed the post. Then there was unconfined joy as Walsh saw his younger brother Ted sprinting out to meet him. With his parents and two sisters, Jennifer and Katie, also there, it was a wonderful family moment. It would have taken a cold soul not to smile at their uncomplicated delight.

Not surprisingly, most attention centred on the winning trainer. Ted Walsh is one of those rare racing faces that are known outside the sport's natural fanbase alongside John McCririck and Frankie Dettori. An inclination towards calling a spade a shovel has a populist appeal that goes far beyond racing's sometimes narrow confines.

His son isn't as vocal and there is a reluctance to engage enthusiastically with the trappings of success. Fundamentally, he knows they are irrelevant to what really counts, which is passing the post in front. Here was one National-winning jockey who was never going to lose the run of himself. If Walsh is more reticent than his father, however, it doesn't mean he is shy in putting his view forward if he feels it is required. To use the stock phrase, he doesn't suffer fools gladly and he can be brusque with those he doesn't rate. At the same time the natural intelligence that so distinguishes his riding on the track can also make him interesting company off it. There might sometimes be as much fat on that staccato conversation as there is on himself, but there is an articulacy that he has clearly inherited.

The strength of the Walsh family unit was emphasised just sixteen days afterwards when Commanche Court completed a National double in the Irish version at Fairyhouse. Owned by businessman Dermot Desmond, the former Triumph Hurdle winner forged ten lengths clear of Foxchapel King to inject further oxygen into the 'Ted & Ruby' show. By the time Commanche Court brought the curtain down on a remarkable season by winning at Punchestown, there can't have been too many households in Ireland who weren't aware of the father and son team. Through it all they played the media game and did every interview, while never appearing to be more happy than when sharing the moments privately with their family. Less than a year later they came agonisingly close to what would have been the greatest win of them all.

Ted Walsh has always maintained that the Cheltenham Gold Cup is the Turf's greatest race and that belief has transmitted itself to his son. In Commanche Court they believed they had a horse capable of bringing off the dream result. On ratings, he had something to find with some of the opposition, but he loved quick ground and he was proven around Cheltenham. He was also battle-hardened, something Best Mate, the new steeplechase star in Britain, wasn't. Entering the straight, the Irish horse hit the front and briefly the perfect result looked on. But Commanche Court made a mistake at the second last and Best Mate made the most of a dream run up the inside. At the line there were less than two lengths between them, something that still provokes regret in Walsh.

Coming down the hill I should have kept Joe Tizzard [on the eventual third, See More Business] clung to the rail. But instead there was room for Best Mate to get through. And I know I hit the front too soon. Commanche never did much in front and he missed out the second last. I should have taken my time more getting there. Things might have been different if I'd done things different – or not. But we'll never know. When you finish second you always wonder about what you might have done different. I don't mind getting beaten if I've done things right. What I don't like is having a doubt in my head.

The memory would nag at him for some time. It would take five years to put things right. However, the association that would enable him to land that elusive Gold Cup had already been made. It took the Kildare jockey to a tiny Somerset village and a man whose focus on the business of winning is as intense as his own. Paul Nicholls has no racing background. Yet the Bristol-born son of a policeman has turned the hierarchy at the top of British jump racing on its head. Such an impact seemed unlikely after a nine-year career as a jockey that yielded 130 winners. Significantly that tally included several visits to the big time with back to back Hennessy wins on Broadheath and Playschool and an Irish Gold Cup success on Playschool as well. Eventually, battling weight became too much and he took out a trainer's licence in 1991. It took only eight years to scale the Cheltenham heights with a unique treble in 1999 that took in the Arkle Trophy (Flagship Uberalles), the Champion Chase (Call Equiname) and most famously of all the Gold Cup with See More Business.

Along the way some of the biggest names in the jockeys' room had ridden for Nicholls, including Mick Fitzgerald, Tony McCoy and Timmy Murphy. For various reasons, however, none of them worked out long term. Nicholls wanted a top-flight rider he could rely on. His landlord and principal owner Paul Barber is a long-time friend of Ted Walsh and it wasn't long before their gaze eventually settled on one man. It was a huge compliment and potentially also a huge headache.

As No.1 jockey to Willie Mullins, Walsh would need real diplomatic skills to keep both trainers happy on both sides of the Irish Sea. But there was one plus. More and more at the start of the decade, Ireland's major racing fixtures were taking place on a Sunday, leaving the traditional Saturday dates free for less than high class action. In the UK, the tradition of running prestige races on a Saturday is largely maintained, despite there being more Sunday racing. Clashes between Mullins and Nicholls' horses at the festivals were inevitable but Walsh resolved to make the situation work. An early Grade 1 victory on Fadalko in the 2001 Melling Chase at Aintree was a first major win for the Nicholls-Walsh association. There were hiccups with injury, especially a bad hip suffered at Listowel later that year, but gradually the wheels on a partnership that would dominate British racing began to turn more fluently.

It was definitely a headache. There were times I was almost afraid to ring Paul to say sorry I can't ride on a certain day. But I know him now and he knows me too. At this stage I can tell from his and Willie's voices when they really want me on one of theirs. With Paul there was a while when he would be asking 'why didn't you do this or do that in a race?' but he has a lot more faith in me and the things I do now. Before there were always instructions: now it's more 'what do you think?' I suppose with time he has developed more confidence in me and maybe more confidence in himself. But win, lose or draw, we know each is trying their hardest.

That effort started paying immediate dividends. Horses emerged from the Nicholls academy of the calibre of Azertyuiop, whose 2003 Arkle Trophy added to major victories that season for Strong Flow in the Hennessy and Ad Hoc in the Betfred Gold Cup. In Ireland, there were other significant wins that only encouraged Walsh to maintain the relentless tempo. Even then, however, there were those who doubted that he could cope with all the travelling that goes into keeping two major yards happy. But Walsh doesn't appear to mind the early starts and the well-worn trek to Dublin airport.

If I'm not going to the likes of Worcester or wherever, then I'll be riding out at Willie's or at Dad's. If travelling to England means getting up at 6 a.m. rather than 7 a.m. then so what? If I start thinking I'd rather be riding out than riding in races, then I should probably give it up. That's what I do. I ride races. There are places that wouldn't be the highlight of my year. You go to Folkestone for instance and it is always fucking freezing. But for me that's an hour and a half from Dublin to Gatwick and then down. If you live in the Cotswolds, you've got three or four hours behind a wheel just to get to Folkestone. The same if you're in Dorset or Somerset. People say 'why don't you move?' but home is home. It's the same for everyone. My family is here. That's home. OK Folkestone isn't a highlight – neither is Wexford. But you go to these places because that's how you get to the stuff you really want. The weekends from mid-October on are what I live for. Those Saturdays when the Hennessy or the Tingle Creek is on in England and the Sundays in Ireland like when the Royal Bond or the Drinmore are at Fairyhouse.

No matter what the quality of horse he ends up on, however, injuries are still an inevitable part of the job. A couple of fractured wrists, dislocations and fractures to his hips, cracked vertebrae and dislocations to both shoulders are painful evidence that Walsh is no different from any of his colleagues in that regard. Despite picking up another championship in the 2000–01 season, injuries did interfere with his pursuit of more titles until the 2004–05 season when he resumed his place at the top of the numbers pile in Ireland. But an injury-free run also meant a hot-streak in major prizes.

Silver Birch's Welsh National victory in December 2004 was relatively straightforward. But three months later the Irish National at Fairyhouse was a last-gasp affair. Numbersixvalverde's chance was enough for Walsh to do some serious sweating to make 10 st 1 lb, but Walsh needed all his strength to force the Martin Brassil-trained horse home by three quarters of a length. The runner up was Jack High, trained by a certain T.M. Walsh.

Best of all, however, came twelve days later. Only a select band of jockeys have won more than a single Aintree Grand National, but Hedgehunter proved himself to be among a select band of Aintree horses. A gallant effort in 2004 had ended with a last fence fall under David Casey but this time the giant stayer made no mistake. Ridden with more restraint by Walsh, Hedgehunter made light of an 11 st 10 lb burden to run out a fourteen-length winner over the Nicholls-trained runner up Royal Auclair. It fulfilled a lifetime's ambition for Willie Mullins and no one was happier than his jockey.

Hedgehunter in 2005 was very special. I'd been ten years with Willie at that stage and he's stood by me all that time. Even if I was coming back from injury, he still put me up on everything. At this stage the only ones who are still there from when I started are Willie, Jackie, Patrick, the housekeeper, the gardener and myself. The horse was brilliant that day. He won easy and made it easy for me.

It also meant that an unprecedented clean-sweep of the four major Grand Nationals of the season was very much on. Walsh had proved his Scottish National credentials already with a 2002 victory in the Ayr marathon on board Take Control. His success had been all about guts and resilience. But Cornish Rebel presented a more subtle challenge. Best Mate's half-brother had enough class to win a Grade 1 over hurdles but also exhibited a forte for quirkiness throughout his career that didn't make him a natural Grand National candidate. For much of the four miles and one furlong, though, Walsh massaged his mind into believing otherwise. A remarkable National story looked on for all the straight. Cornish Rebel even appeared to buy into the moment by overcoming the sort of interference at the second-last that presented him with a good excuse to chuck it in. Once over the last, there was only Joes Edge to beat. The huge crowd rose to acclaim a special achievement. Nicholls, who was watching on a big screen, started running for the winner's enclosure. But then Cornish Rebel's ears started to prick. Suddenly Joes Edge was back in front. They flashed past the post almost together but almost wasn't enough.

For once the paper-thin short-head verdict went against the history-seeking jockey.

Cheltenham's 2006 festival yielded another leading rider award but also frustration. Hedgehunter proved himself to be much more than a staying plodder by running second to War Of Attrition in the Gold Cup. Less than a month later only Walsh's old ally Numbersixvalverde foiled Hedgehunter's Grand National follow up bid by six lengths. But that paled to the forty minutes on the second day of Cheltenham when a pair of supposed hotpots failed to do what their odds suggested they should.

Kauto Star, a French-bred six-year-old, was having only his fifth start in Britain but, despite that inexperience, he started favourite for the Champion Chase. He made it only to the third fence before taking a crashing fall. Walsh's physical pain was bad enough but nothing compared to the sense of opportunity lost. Moscow Flyer was a shadow of his former self and it was left to the unconsidered 16-1 shot Newmill to win. It didn't get better in the very next race. Denman, a giant-framed Irish point to pointer, was unbeaten and a red hot favourite for the SunAlliance Hurdle. He jumped the last in front but was out-kicked up the hill by Nicanor. Jump racing is such an attritional game that talking about 'another day' doesn't really console anyone. But there were in fact so many better days to come.

The intuitive skill that has taken Nicholls to the peak of his profession told him that Kauto Star was worth a try at longer distances the following season. A canter around Aintree preceded the Betfair Cup at Haydock, the first leg of a series also taking in the King George and the Gold Cup that would result in a million-pound bonus by the sponsors if won by a single horse. Kauto Star was a revelation, oozing class and style before quickening clear up the run to make doubts about the three-mile trip appear ridiculous. Walsh spent most of the last half-furlong patting the horse's neck in an untypically premature celebration. His reaction was different because the horse felt in a different league. So much so that after winning at two and a half miles, then three, Nicholls felt no compunction in dropping Kauto Star back to two miles for the Tingle Creek. It was unorthodox but that didn't matter.

He beat the best two-milers around before stepping back to three miles again in the King George. A couple of bad jumping mistakes couldn't stop the Kauto express.

'He was such an amazing horse that season [2006-07],' admits Walsh. 'It was an unbelievable year. He did it all: two miles to three miles and three miles to two. Kauto Star's the best horse I'm ever likely to ride.'

Confirmation came on the day that matters most. A lot was against the favourite in the Gold Cup. Those who insist it is a stayers' race were adamant a horse with such speed couldn't last the trip. Kauto Star also had an annoying habit of carving a hole in the last fence in his races. But all that didn't matter. Maybe Kauto Star didn't have to be at his absolute best, but then neither did Desert Orchid when he won his Gold Cup. After his near-misses of the past, Walsh could have been forgiven for being nervous in the race he wanted most of all but his ride was a masterclass of patient calculation. Not for nothing were the pair cheered back to the winner's enclosure with an enthusiasm that Cheltenham's die-hard fans reserve for the true champions. Before slipping off the saddle, the winning jockey glanced up at the Channel 4 paddock commentary box where his father was working and clenched his fist in acknowledgement. If ever television has transmitted an image of pride it was Ted Walsh's teary response.

An almost perfect season ended with a perfect statistical kick. Between Ireland and Britain, Walsh ended up with the remarkable tally of 198 winners. However, the record books show a much rounder figure. Two disqualifications for horses failing drugs tests meant another pair of winners for the man who finished second to them. The magic two hundred was up, a feat repeated in 2007–08 with a pair of winners on the final day of the season at Sandown. The rate of success guaranteed a sixth jockeys' title in Ireland and acknowledgement in the UK that the long-time darling of the jumps scene there, Tony McCoy, had a worthy rival.

It's hard to imagine two such high-profile rivals enjoying the sort of friendship that Walsh and McCoy have. Roger Federer might crash in Rafael Nadal's house in Majorca some day, but not while their competition is so intense. And Tiger Woods is unlikely ever to want another pro golfer prowling around his gaff. But jump racing's best known jockeys are such good friends that Walsh famously stays in McCoy's house when in England. Their attitude is simple. Both would cut the nose off the other in order to win out on the track, but everything is forgotten once they're off it. Maybe other sports are too intrinsically selfish to allow such magnanimity between competitors, but racing is a sporting law unto itself. Squabbles may break out in the jockeys' room, and only the hopelessly dewy-eyed will believe that everyone likes each other. Underneath it all, though, is a camaraderie that maybe only those who have jumped out of a foxhole under fire will truly understand. When risk and pain are as much a part of your job as boredom and biscuits are for the rest of us, there isn't much point in petty back-biting.

In early 2008, however, anyone with even the remotest connection to racing possessed an opinion as to who would win the Gold Cup. Kauto Star versus Denman might not have been the Beatles and the Stones or Blur and Oasis, but in the way that music fans can view their idols as projections of how they see themselves, so it was with these two horses. Kauto, the reigning champion, brought a touch of class and speed that somehow seemed to fit his French background. Denman, on the other hand, had the massive frame and rampaging front-running style of a classic Irish point to pointer. They were clearly the two best steeple-chasers around and, freakily, they both lived next door to each other in Shepton Mallet.

At Christmas, Kauto Star won a second King George in a manner that suggested he was, if anything, improving. McCoy tried everything on Exotic Dancer to beat him but admitted afterwards: 'It's kind of tough coming to the fourth-last in a King George hearing someone behind you going "whoa-whoa".' A couple of days later Walsh and Denman landed the Lexus Chase at Leopardstown. He won but wasn't at his most impressive. His best form had come the previous month at Newbury with a pulverising performance under top weight in the Hennessy. It came in the middle of a five-week injury lay-off for Walsh, so Nicholls' No.2 rider,

Sam Thomas, was on board. On the run up to Cheltenham, Walsh had to make a choice, except was it any sort of choice really? As he asked himself, how do you 'turn your back on the best horse you've ever ridden'? The answer in hindsight was through a lack of information.

> It was a big one to get wrong and it basically came down to not being on Denman in the Hennessy. I didn't get that feel that a horse gives you at their peak. Instead, I looked at the form alone and the second horse in the Hennessy hadn't exactly shone a strong light on the race afterwards. So, purely on form there was a doubt. If I'd ridden Denman in that Hennessy, things could have been different. I might have ridden him in the Gold Cup instead. It just shows that studying form only gets you so far. I know it would have been hard to turn your back on the best horse you've ever ridden but at the end of the day this is a business too. There's no room for sentiment. I rode Denman to win the Lexus but I didn't test him – maybe I should have!

At the line in the Gold Cup the only real surprise was that Denman won by only seven lengths. Dominant throughout, the supposed No.2 with Thomas riding had Kauto Star struggling from a mile out. That he fought all the way to the line indicated what a champion he is. In turn, he only had a short head in hand of Neptune Collonges, who completed a Nicholls clean sweep. Walsh was understandably gutted. The race he loves most had taken another swipe at him. But he presented himself for the post-mortems as a total professional, and fluently explained his belief that the real Kauto Star hadn't shown up. It was hard to argue with. For a Tingle Creek winner to be off the bridle after two and a half miles was amazing. Walsh answered everything but the sting of defeat was still too raw to allow Channel 4's Derek Thompson to get away with asking if he'd like to have the choice again: 'I've been asked some stupid questions, Derek, but that is the most stupid.'

A year later and it was a very different story. In fact, only the neck that separated Celestial Halo from Punjabi at the end of the Champion Hurdle prevented a clean-sweep of Cheltenham's four championship highlights. As it was, a final tally of seven victories included Kauto Star's second Gold Cup, back to back wins in the Champion Chase for Master Minded and a wonderfully subtle success for Big Buck's in the World Hurdle. Throw in three winners for Mullins, and Cheltenham 2009 revolved around only one man. On a racecourse where, only four months earlier, Walsh had suffered a fall bad enough to force the removal of his spleen – he was back riding in less than four weeks – had come a run of success that has propelled him to a level of public visibility few within racing ever get to know. But it is unlikely to ever impact on the man himself.

Walsh is famously focused on his career but there is also a perspective to his life that allows him a peep outside the sport sometimes. He remains a general sports fan and has been known to follow the Ireland rugby team as well as the Munster and Leinster provincial sides. The Irish out-half Ronan O'Gara is a friend. He is also a football supporter, especially Manchester United, and isn't slow in expressing his opinions about a wide range of subjects. Married to Gillian, he is close to his family with his older sister Jennifer still acting as his agent. With so many hangers-on in the sport only too eager to befriend any jockey, never mind one at the top of his profession, it is a major plus to know there is a small band of people behind him whom he can completely trust.

But it's hard to see such an individual having his head turned by fly-by-nights anyway. His ease of expression is matched by a clarity of thought. His great childhood idol Richard Dunwoody remains an enigmatic figure, travelling the world looking for new excitement to replace the high he got in a sport he wasn't ready to leave. Those ventures have included a marathon trek to the South Pole where the ex-champion lost the sort of weight that would have been scary during his riding days.

Dunwoody's an amazing man and he was an amazing rider. Since I've started riding in England more, I'm even more amazed. Some of the stories about him are incredible. His autobiography was called *Obsessed* and he really was. He ate, slept and drank racing. But I don't know if he really enjoyed it. He wins a Cheltenham Gold Cup and straight away all he's thinking about is the Grand Annual. I mean, you can't get any better than the Gold Cup. You need to enjoy it while it's there. I always wanted to ride like Dunwoody. There was all that style and poise, even the angle of his head when he was riding. But I never wanted to be like him as a man.

Certitude is a lonely commodity in jump racing but it is hard to see Walsh eventually leaving the sport and missing it the way Dunwoody has. For one thing, he has already achieved more than most as a professional. Another reason is that, unlike McCoy, there's a strong chance he will eventually follow his father and grandfather down the training route. A student of racing's history, as well as its current form, the idea of training at the highest level appeals to him. But making long-term plans is not his way – 'I can't understand people who make five-year plans. They baffle me' – and he is determined to make the most of his riding career.

Happily his weight has settled down to such a level that he made 9 st 13 lb for a race in France in 2008. Such a mark seemed impossible as an amateur when he struggled to do 10 st 4 lb, but he puts it down to his increased riding commitments in Britain, with five or six mounts a day. With the amount of travelling that entails, there are a lot of demands on him. There are of course quite substantial paybacks. But there is no one more demanding of him than himself.

With his tally of Grand Nationals, Gold Cups, Champion Chases and almost every big race worthy of the name, there is very little left for Walsh to achieve. He is already assured of a place in racing history. But the drive that propelled him to the summit of his career doesn't just switch off. The one major omission on his CV is a Champion Hurdle. Nicholls tends to concentrate on future chasers rather than specialists over the smaller obstacles, while Mullins has had a number of hopefuls that never quite got to that level.

Along with Celestial Halo, Brave Inca's heroic attempt to retain his title in 2007 is the closest that Walsh has come to date. It meant taking the place of McCoy but sentiment was never going to be a factor. And for so long the horse looked like coming through. Brave Inca engaged in a sustained battle with Hardy Eustace from the front and made his major rival crack. But if it looked like job done, that reckoned without the quick early pace that left Brave Inca exposed to the hold-up horse Sublimity, who swept past. Be it Grade 1 or low grade handicap, however, it's the process of getting on the best horse that continues to fascinate Walsh. That at least partly explains how he reached the mark of one thousand winners in Ireland in May 2008 with Stylish Article at Sligo.

Definitely the hardest part of this job is getting on the right horse. If Willie or Paul or Dad don't want me, then I might have three or four offers to ride in a race and it's important that I stay on top of the form. If I'm on the worst of the three, I've no chance. There are far better judges of form in the weighroom. Some of the lads even have a good knowledge of the flat stuff which I wouldn't have a clue about. I could talk to Jennifer about some flat horse with decent form figures and she'll be the one to tell me 'nah'. Ideally I need to see a race to know what's going on but I do have my own opinion on form as well. There are certain things you pick up, like from June on, through the summer, a nineties-rated horse can win a maiden hurdle in Ireland. But once you get into winter, you need something a stone better. Any horse placed during the winter will win a summer race. There's an undoubted difference between the two.

It's that sort of calculation that makes a crucial difference. Walsh might have everything else needed to be regarded as one of the greatest jockeys ever seen over jumps but there's probably nothing more important than the ability to think his way through a race. And that's a gift any sports fan can admire.

Cheltenham Festival Winners

1998
Weatherbys Champion Bumper   Alexander Banquet

2002
Mildmay Of Flete   Blowing Wind

2003

| Arkle Trophy | Azertyuiop |

2004

Queen Mother Champion Chase	Azertyuiop
Grand Annual	St Pirran
Vincent O'Brien County Hurdle	Sporazene

2005

| *Daily Telegraph* Festival Trophy Chase | Thisthatandtother |
| Weatherbys Champion Bumper | Missed That |

2006

Anglo Irish Bank Supreme Novices Hurdle	Noland
William Hill Trophy	Dun Doire
Vincent O'Brien County Hurdle	Desert Quest

2007

SunAlliance Novice Chase	Denman
Ryanair Trophy	Taranis
Gold Cup	Kauto Star

2008

Queen Mother Champion Chase	Master Minded
Ballymore Properties Novice Hurdle	Fiveforthree
Triumph Hurdle	Celestial Halo

2009

David Nicholson Mares Hurdle	Quevega
Ballymore Properties Novice Hurdle	Mikael D'Haguenet
RSA Chase	Cooldine
Queen Mother Champion Chase	Master Minded
World Hurdle	Big Buck's
Vincent O'Brien County Hurdle	American Trilogy
Gold Cup	Kauto Star

Other Major Winners include

1999

Heineken Gold Cup	Imperial Call

2000

Aintree Grand National	Papillon
Powers Irish Grand National	Commanche Court
Heineken Gold Cup	Commanche Court

2001

Melling Chase	Fadalko

2002

Tingle Creek Chase	Cenkos

2003

Maghull Novice Chase	Le Roi Miguel
Aintree Hurdle	Sacundai
Hennessy Cognac Gold Cup	Strong Flow

2004

Welsh Grand National	Strong Flow

2005

Irish Grand National	Numbersixvalverde
Aintree Grand National	Hedgehunter

2006

King George VI Chase	Kauto Star
Betfair Cup	Kauto Star
Tingle Creek Chase	Kauto Star

2007

King George VI Chase	Kauto Star

Betfair Cup	Kauto Star
Lexus Chase	Denman
Guinness Gold Cup	Neptune Collonges

2008

Guinness Gold Cup	Neptune Collonges
Kerrygold Champion Chase	Twist Magic
King George VI Chase	Kauto Star

2009

Hennessy Gold Cup	Neptune Collonges

INDEX